THE SECRET DOME

THE SECRET DOME

ANTI-AIRCRAFT GUNNERY TRAINING IN THE SECOND WORLD WAR

EWAN WARD-THOMAS

Pen & Sword
MILITARY
AN IMPRINT OF PEN & SWORD BOOKS LTD.
YORKSHIRE – PHILADELPHIA

First published in Great Britain in 2025 by
Pen & Sword Military
An imprint of
Pen & Sword Books Ltd
Yorkshire - Philadelphia

ISBN 978 1 52678 573 2

A CIP catalogue record for this book is available from the British Library.

Typeset in INDIA by IMPEC eSolutions
Printed and bound in the England by CPI Group (UK) Ltd, Croydon, CRO 4YY

The Publisher's authorised representative in the EU for product safety is Authorised Rep Compliance Ltd., Ground Floor, 71 Lower Baggot Street, Dublin D02 P593, Ireland.
www.arccompliance.com

For a complete list of Pen & Sword titles please contact:

PEN & SWORD BOOKS LIMITED
George House, Units 12 & 13, Beevor Street, Off Pontefract Road,
Barnsley, S71 1HN, UK
E-mail: enquiries@pen-and-sword.co.uk
Website: www.pen-and-sword.co.uk

or

PEN AND SWORD BOOKS
1950 Lawrence Rd, Havertown, PA 19083, USA
E-mail: Uspen-and-sword@casematepublishers.com
Website: www.penandswordbooks.com

MIX
Paper | Supporting responsible forestry
FSC® C013604

To my daughters Gracie and Theadora Ward-Thomas, and my parents Michael and Evelyn

Contents

PART IV: Post War

Acknowledgements

This story would not have been told without generous help and advice from Frank Phillipson and Patrick Allen. Frank continues to share his personal experience and detailed research into the history of the Dome Trainer over the last forty-five years. He worked as a Design Draughtsman with RFD Co. Ltd./ GQ Defence Equipment Ltd between 1975 and 1986 and was involved in the post-war evolution of the Dome Trainer structures and equipment. Frank also worked on the new design of 17m diameter Dome structure for the ADT3 Rapier Missile System, with a prototype Dome built at Godalming. The contract with the British government was for five ADT3 Domes at Larkhill (Royal Artillery), West Raynham (RAF Regiment), Lossiemouth (RAF Regiment) and two more in Germany. Frank designed a 3D gimbal rig to photograph aircraft models in all attitudes required for the stop-frame process to make the films used in the ADT3.

The preservation and restoration of the Dome Trainer and memorial to the aircrew (see Plate 31) at RAF Langham airfield in Norfolk is thanks to the untiring dedication and perseverance of Patrick Allen. His commitment ensured the Langham Dome (see plates 23, 24, 25 & 26) and museum continues to serve the enjoyment and education of current and future generations.

My thanks to Stephen Walton and the staff at the Imperial War Museum who extracted the unique digital story within Henry's private journal and helped with both the RAF Langham Dome preservation and the BBC documentary in 2015. Errors or omissions are solely my responsibility.

Many thanks to the very patient and guiding hands of Heather Williams and the team at Pen & Sword for helping me to complete this book.

As is traditional, I am in awe of the patience of my wife Cordelia to allow me uncounted hours spent in the company of my grandfather, Lieutenant Commander Henry Christian Stephens, Royal Navy. When Henry died, my grandmother destroyed all his private correspondence, apart from the Dome Trainer journal. This is his story.

Ewan Ward-Thomas
London
March 2025

Context to the Dome Trainer Story

> *In 1942 we lost more than six and a half million tons of shipping by submarine attack, which nearly brought us to ruin. If on top of this the air attacks had continued the heavy scale of the early part of 1941, I am of the opinion that we should have been completely ruined. At the end of February 1941, the then 1st Sea Lord, Admiral of the Fleet Sir Dudley Pound, rang me up at Winchester on the telephone and asked if I would come and help. Of course, I would – so he sent his car for me. I had an office at Admiralty and got going at once to teach the Merchant Navy what I called 'Pheasant Shooting at Sea' . . . I realised at once that Stephens had in effect thrown us a lifebuoy in our time of greatest distress . . . The 'horror of the Blitz' attacks at sea had been dispelled by Stephens. The value of the shipping and cargoes saved by the improved standard of shooting resulting from the training which the Merchant Navy gunners, and the Navy and Army gunners on board the ships received in the Dome Trainer was immense. I should say that this value was in the order of £350,000,000.*
>
> **Admiral Sir Fredric Dreyer GBE, KCB, Royal Navy.**
> **Inspector of Merchant Navy Gunnery (1941–1945)**

After Royal Navy service in the First World War and working as a civilian photographer in 1939, everything changed for my grandfather, Lieutenant Commander Henry Christian Stephens (Royal Navy [RN] and Royal Naval Volunteer Reserve [RNVR]) (see Plate 1). The effectiveness of new airborne attacks and the terror generated by the Stuka dive bombers during the Spanish Civil war in 1937 were demonstrated to Henry and the British public by cinema newsreels from Pathé News. Henry realised that his old Navy shipmates could not defend ships against these new weapons of the air. He was soon proved correct.

At the outbreak of war in 1939, British armed forces were woefully trained and equipped to defend against air attacks, either on land or at sea. German pilots honed their skills with the latest equipment during the Spanish Civil War in 1939, in anticipation of a wider conflict. Whilst basic radar could track incoming aircraft, there were very limited skills or experience of defence on the ground to preserve Britain against this new threat.

We are surrounded by modern computer technology in a digital age, often without reflection or understanding of the previous military development and inspiration that created inventions such as the Dome Trainer, saving thousands of lives. The entertainment industry is strewn with awe-inspiring special effects and simulation decoys originally invented under pressure of combat necessity. Their creators fade without celebration or recognition.

After the First World War, Henry Stephens left the Royal Navy for civilian life. By September 1939 he was registered as a photographer for the *Daily Mail*. Against the background of ineffective anti-aircraft defence against new fighters and bombers, and the 1940 evacuation of Dunkirk, Henry designed and proposed to his old service contacts in the Royal Navy a revolutionary design for gunner training that he named the 'Dome Trainer'. Henry continued a family tradition of inventions and innovation, both in industry and politics.

The British government recognised how civilian and military discoveries often helped to win battles, and rewarded certified inventors according to the war-winning value of their contributions. The first Royal Commission on Awards to Inventors (the Tomlin Commission) was established in March 1919 to consider and reward all inventions used by the Government during the First World War, and it returned to judge contributions in the Second.

The first day of the second Royal Commission on Awards to Inventors hearing into Henry's invention was 5 April 1948. Remaining on the Reserve list at the end of the war in 1945, Lieutenant Commander Henry Christian Stephens once again dressed in a dark blue 'Wavy Navy' jacket. Reserve Officers were known as such due to the wavy lines of gold braid on the cuffs of their jackets, as opposed to straight gold braid for Regular serving officers. A double gold wave braid on his service jacket and greatcoat shoulder boards confirmed Henry's rank. Leaving his London flat at Carlisle Place with a swift goodbye to his wife Elizabeth and young daughter Evelyn, Henry walked past a bomb-damaged Buckingham Palace, across Trafalgar Square and up the Strand. He was due to meet Admiral Dreyer, General Pile, other Royal Navy officers and his defence counsel at 9 o'clock. The Royal Navy had trained Henry to be early.

Henry Stephens joined the Royal Navy aged fourteen and served from 1911 to 1919, including as a midshipman at the Battle of Jutland in 1916, on the destroyer HMS *Milbrook*. Henry fully appreciated, therefore, the new challenge of defending a ship from the threat of sophisticated and deadly airborne attack. As a photographer, he designed the first sophisticated anti-aircraft gunnery training simulation technology he called a 'Dome Trainer'. In 1940 he revealed his invention to a colleague who remained in the Navy. Captain Phelips immediately advised Henry to re-enlist in the Royal Navy Reserve, specifically to develop the Dome Trainer.

This first design evolved into anti-aircraft gunnery training equipment for the Royal Navy, the Army and the Royal Air Force. Over 300 Domes for training naval and merchant navy crews, as well as soldiers and airmen, were exported worldwide, including to Canada (see plates 13 & 17) and the United States. These became a standard training method for merchant seamen against aircraft attacks on Atlantic convoys. During the

Second World War at least 500,000 gunners across Dominions and Empire countries as well as 'Free' forces of men and women from occupied countries, were trained in Domes (see Plate 19). Appendix F illustrates part of *The Gunnery Pocket Book (Royal Navy 1945)*, which explains the complexity and sophistication of naval gunnery in 1945.

Dome Trainers and the projection equipment within them in 1941 represented a cutting-edge invention. The sole purpose was to simulate for the trainees the confusion and noise of an air attack at sea or on land whilst attempting to aim and fire at enemy aircraft. The American secret 'Pinball' project in 1942 to fire live glass rounds at other aircraft in flight was a similar innovation, together with the U-boat destruction strategies created by WATU (Western Approaches Tactical Unit) in Liverpool from 1942.

Modern augmented reality blends a virtual, or pretend, reality and real life. The Dome Trainer was doing exactly this in 1941, long before digital computers. From such basic beginnings the Dome Trainer and other similar systems would develop into modern multi-screen projection for military computer simulation training, as well as entertainment services such as IMAX cinema. Initially adopted and built for the Royal Navy in 1941, a 'Dome Trainer' is now a standard description for similar battlefield simulation training structures.

The purpose of the second Royal Commission on Awards to Inventors was to recognise members of the public and the armed services who had valid copyright ownership of inventions and processes created during the Second World War from 1939 to 1945. Recognition was granted if proof existed that an existing copyrighted invention, design or process had been successfully and uniquely adapted to serve a useful wartime purpose. Some inventions are already famous, e.g., Frank Whittle's jet engine, time pencil fuses, tank flails (for mine clearance) and the 'Mulberry' floating harbours for D-Day. The inventor of an unpatented device was not entitled to any payment but relied on the recommendation of the Commission. Evidence was heard in public by barristers working for the Crown and barristers working for the claimants, with cross-examination by counsel for the Crown.

The summons from Lord Justice Cohen for April 1948 requested evidence from Henry as the inventor of the Dome Trainer. Henry's evidence as a private journal is lodged with the Imperial War Museum and represents a unique and detailed chronicle of the development of secret warfare technology, alongside Henry's personal dedication and perseverance (see Plate 4).

There are very few surviving Dome Trainer structures in Britain. The single example of a preserved Dome simulator and museum is at the former RAF Langham Airfield in Norfolk, restored in 2015 (see plates 23, 24, 25 & 26). This Dome demonstrates the concepts of Henry's invention and serves as a memorial to all the international service personnel who served at RAF Langham in the Second World War. In 2015 the BBC and Eye Films (Norfolk) broadcast a documentary about the Dome Trainer and Langham, narrated by Stephen Fry.

To appreciate the role Henry played in developing part of British and international defensive and offensive equipment in the Second World War, it is critical to understand the complex and colourful jigsaw of contemporaneous aspects which formed the defence of Britain at sea, on land and in the air. The work of Professor Reginald Jones, a British physicist and scientific military intelligence expert who played an important role in the wider defence of Britain, helps place the Dome Trainer in its correct historical context.

PART I

Family

Chapter 1

Life in the Royal Navy, 1918

Lieutenant Commander Stephens suffered from conflicting claims to his unique invention which had to be settled in a court of law. In defence of his claim as inventor, Henry was instructed to appear before the Royal Commission on Awards to Inventors (known as the Cohen Commission after the Chairman Lord Justice Cohen).

At 8.30 am on 5 April 1948, Lieutenant Commander Henry Stephens ordered tea in the Lyons shop at the corner of the Strand. Admiral Frederic Dreyer and General Sir Frederick Pile arrived at 08.45 and all three waited for 9 o'clock. Both men were supporting Henry in his claim. General Pile was responsible for British defences against aerial attack as General Officer Commanding-in-Chief of Anti-Aircraft Command from 1939 to 1945. Ironically, his youngest brother Cyril was killed in action with the Royal Flying Corps in 1917.

Kilburn and Strode, patent agents, were instructed by Henry to present his claim. Mr Pat Graham acted as Senior Counsel, supported by Mr Everington as a Junior. Henry could tell Dreyer and Pile he had finally completed the scale wooden carving of an eighteenth-century ship of the line, fully rigged, with the help of his stepson Anthony Chignell. Carving and building the ship had kept his mind occupied during the wait before the Commission.

Henry Stephens, Admiral Dreyer and General Pile were always early, reflecting their common experience of military service. Having joined the Royal Navy in 1911, Henry remained a stickler for punctuality. Max Arthur, compiling *Lost Voices* for the Royal Navy, explains a similar formative experience in 1915 for Frank Layard, joining the Navy in 1915. His was a typical Navy training on joining HMS *Indomitable* at Rosyth in September 1915:

> If sent on a message you could stand still only long enough to say 'Aye, Aye, Sir' and then you had to fly, and never should you be caught walking up or down a ladder; it must always be taken at a run.

From time immemorial, the services represented a career path for young men like Henry Stephens, especially when coming from a fatherless family of eight children recorded in the 1901 census, with a mother who died in 1902. After he left school, the British census of 1911 marked Henry, aged fourteen, as a 'cadet-pupil' aboard HMS *Worcester*, a Royal Navy training ship off Greenhithe, Kent. The Stephens family were subject to the traditional financial rules of the Royal Navy. As midshipmen, young men were still in training, and families, even in wartime, paid the Admiralty £50 a year to supplement the meagre pay of one shilling and ninepence per day. This fee was abolished after the Battle of Jutland in 1916, when the parent of a young midshipman who was killed in the battle received a reminder of the £50 due. Henry gained his seniority on 7 August 1913. Once qualified as a midshipman, Henry came under the Navy rules of RV.02. On 12 September 1913 he joined HMS *Hibernia*, a pre-dreadnought battleship launched in June 1905.

In the decades up to 1914, Britain and Germany were engaged in a fierce worldwide naval arms race to defend their foreign colonies supplied by merchant shipping routes across the world. The strength of the British Empire relied on the 'two-power standard policy', whereby the Royal Navy's assets and men were kept at a level equal to the strength of the next two strongest foreign fleets added together.

A month after the assassination of Archduke Franz Ferdinand and his wife Sophie in Serbia on 28 July 1914, the Austro-Hungarian government declared war on Serbia. What should have historically remained a local skirmish then exploded into the first global war. By 6 August, triggered by secret defensive alliances and years of empire-building tension and competition for military superiority, Germany, Russia, France, Britain and Austria were all fighting. Japan joined the war on 23 August, and the United States in April 1917. Over the next four years, twenty-one nations fought in the First World War.

The Royal Navy consumed men in ever greater numbers to defend the oceans that controlled a wartime empire around the world. Henry was posted to HMS *Milbrook* on 24 February 1916 and served until 3 October 1916. She was an Admiralty "M-Class" destroyer newly launched in October 1915 as one of 103 destroyers built for the Royal Navy during the First World War. From 1914 it was standard practice to place young men directly into danger before fully completing their training. Winston Churchill, First Lord of the Admiralty, told the House of Commons in 1914:

> The decision to send the naval cadets from Dartmouth to sea in time of war was arrived at a considerable time ago. It was felt that young officers of their age would be of great use on board His Majesty's ships, and that they would learn incomparably more of their profession in war than any educational establishment on shore could teach them.

Aged twelve, Archibald Dickson's experience illustrates a typical experience of service on joining the Royal Naval College at Osborne on the Isle of Wight, an essential step towards becoming a naval officer. Aged fourteen he moved up to the Royal Naval College,

Dartmouth, before being commissioned, at the age of sixteen, as a midshipman. By May 1916 Midshipman Dickson and his elder brother Robert were serving on ships in the Firth of Forth and at Scapa Flow in Orkney. The British Grand Fleet moved to the Scapa Flow anchorage to dominate the North Sea and Atlantic against the threat of German naval forces and to block shipping to Germany.

Henry Stephens witnessed significant change across the Navy from 1914 to 1939, especially in the defence of ships away from land bases. Basic dirigible airships and spotter aircraft were deployed by the Navy in small numbers in the First World War. Henry would have no idea that his future inventions would be instrumental in the defence of both naval and civilian shipping as well as the other armed forces and civilians in the Second World War.

Both Dickson brothers and Henry Stephens fought in the major sea battle of the First World War, off Jutland, Denmark. The engagement lasted from the evening of 31 May to last light on 1 June 1916. The Battle of Jutland, known to the Germans as the Battle of the Skagerrak, involved a total of 100,000 men aboard 250 ships over 72 hours.

Both sides suffered from confusion, poor communication, total darkness at night and very limited daylight visibility. Bad weather grounded the German Zeppelin airships, and a Short 184 seaplane was the first aircraft to take part in the battle. Launched from HMS *Engadine*, the seaplane flew a 50-minute mission scouting ahead of Admiral Beatty's battle-cruisers. Pilot Frederick Rutland took the Short (top speed of 88mph) to within one and a half miles of the German Fleet at an altitude of just 1,000ft, while observer George Trewin radioed the number of enemy ships sighted and their location. Rutland was awarded the Distinguished Service Cross, labelled 'Rutland of Jutland' by the press and singled out in Beatty's dispatch on the battle.

Death was sudden and on a huge scale, with battle-cruisers losing almost all crew when ships' magazines blew up. This was due to the design of the battle-cruisers built with thinner armour to permit a faster speed. This was compounded by operational errors. To achieve a faster rate of fire, critical safety rules were ignored. Anti-flash doors were kept open, and large numbers of cordite charges were stacked in gun turrets for faster loading.

During the opening phase of the battle-cruiser action on 31 May, known as the 'Run to the South', at 4.00 pm Vice-Admiral Sir David Beatty's flagship HMS *Lion* was hit by a German shell from the battle cruiser SMS *Lützow* which destroyed *Lion*'s 'Q' turret. The ship was only saved from complete destruction by the severely wounded Major Francis Harvey flooding the magazine, winning a posthumous Victoria Cross.

At 4.06 pm, the battle-cruiser HMS *Indefatigable* was hit on her thin deck armour near the rear turret by 11-inch shells from the German battle-cruiser SMS *Von der Tann*. The ammunition magazine below the turret exploded, blowing off the rear of the ship. Three minutes later, after more direct hits on the forecastle and forward turret, the magazines below these also exploded, destroying the ship. Only three of the 1,019 officers and men survived. Mount Indefatigable in Canada was named after the battle-cruiser in 1917.

At 4.26 pm the crew of HMS *Queen Mary* were obliterated by German shells. The first shot penetrated the thin armour of the forward gun turrets, instantly causing the forward ship's magazines to explode. A second shell fell into the rear 'Q' turret. With flash doors left open to facilitate faster shooting, the magazine below exploded., and 1,266 men vanished, including Midshipman Archibald Dickson. There were eighteen survivors.

At 6.15 pm the German light cruiser SMS *Wiesbaden* and the rest of the German II Scouting Group encountered the light cruiser HMS *Chester*, scoring several hits. As the two navies disengaged, Rear-Admiral Horace Hood's flagship, the battle-cruiser HMS *Invincible*, scored a hit on SMS *Wiesbaden*'s engine room that disabled her. The German ship sank at 2.30 am. Only one crew member survived from 598 officers and men.

The German pre-dreadnought battleship SMS *Pommern* engaged the British battle-cruisers commanded by Beatty. She was one of a class nicknamed 'five-minute ships' by the Germans due to the time they were expected to survive if confronted by a British dreadnought. SMS *Pommern* was hit once by a 12-inch shell from the battle-cruiser HMS *Indomitable*. During the confused night actions in the early hours of 1 June she was struck by torpedoes from the British destroyer HMS *Onslaught*. This impact exploded the 6.7-inch gun magazine, splitting the ship in two and causing her to sink in 20 minutes. There were no survivors from a crew of 839.

At 6.35 pm there was a sudden British casualty in the form of HMS *Invincible*. She was lead ship of a class of battle-cruisers built for the Royal Navy up to 1910, and the flagship of the 3rd Battle-Cruiser Squadron in 1916. A thick sea mist cleared and HMS *Invincible* abruptly appeared as a clear target before the German battleships SMS *Lützow* and SMS *Derfflinger*. The German ships fired three salvoes each at HMS *Invincible* and she exploded and sank in 90 seconds. At least one 12-inch shell penetrated the front of 'Q' turret and detonated the magazines. The ship immediately blew in half, and 1,026 officers and men were killed, including Rear-Admiral Hood. There were six survivors.

With twelve other Flotillas as part of the Eleventh Destroyer Flotilla, HMS *Milbrook* (and my grandfather, Midshipman Stephens) acted as alarm screens at Jutland five miles behind the principal Royal Navy battleships. Due to intercepted messages, the Germans knew that this screen stood between them and home ports. The final stage of the battle from 10.00 pm in total darkness was marked by multiple 'shoot and disengage' clashes between the British destroyer screens, British battleships and their German counterparts. The Fourth Flotilla lost 70 per cent of its ships before the Germans broke through and returned home, to remain in port for the duration of hostilities. Max Arthur described the further experiences of Frank Lanyard as a midshipman, similar in duties to Henry Stephens:

> Our life as junior midshipmen in the *Indomitable* was hard but by no means as tough as in some other gun rooms at the time. It was traditional that 'Young Gentlemen' must be taught that forgetfulness, carelessness and slackness could not be tolerated. A gunroom punishment book was kept and during our twelve months as junior midshipmen the records of beatings varied between the six of us. At sea we were in three watches acting as lookouts in the foretop by day and as assistant 4-inch gun and searchlight control officers by night. We also had bridge duties, and at least twice a night had to fetch cocoa for the officers on watch who were standing on the exposed bridge for the entire period. At the end of the watch, it was our job to go below and wake the relief officers. No relief crew could ever be late, but also God help you if you broke the 'calling' rules. Never, ever could you shake or touch an officer or raise your voice to him. You had to switch on the light, call him by name, tell him the time and the weather, and repeat this until he was awake, and you saw him get out of his bunk.

Frank continued his description of the life of a midshipman:

> Our gun room contained three commissioned officers: the senior Sub-Lieutenant who was mess President; another Sub and a one-stripe Assistant Paymaster. There were also nine Senior Midshipmen and an Assistant Clerk who ranked as a junior midshipman like us. The Senior Midshipmen were called 'snotties' as they traditionally wiped their noses on sleeves until the Navy placed three buttons on the jacket cuffs. We were called 'wonks' or sometimes 'warts'. We took it in turns to be duty 'wonk', and this was the day when you had to be particularly alert to avoid trouble. The duties included waking the Sub-Lieutenant, running his bath and seeing that he got up, being always available in the mess to run messages; ready to jump up and light the Sub's cigarette, never forgetting to carry a box of matches and in fact, acting as a general dogsbody.
>
> If at any time the Sub shouted 'Breadcrumbs!', the junior midshipmen had to stuff their fingers in their ears and shut their eyes. Something that was going to be said that was not fit for the ears of the young gentlemen. If, on hearing the shout 'Negative Breadcrumbs', you looked up, this revealed that you had not stopped your ears properly. You received a bang on the head.

After Jutland the British retained control of the North Sea and continued to cut off Germany's trade routes. The worldwide blockade of German sea trade from 1914 contributed to their eventual surrender in 1918, after Germans had starved during the 'Turnip Winter'. The Kaiser was forced to abdicate, replaced by the Weimar Republic, and Henry Stephens returned to civilian life in 1918.

Chapter 2

The Stephens Family, 1896–1918

The principal Henry Stephens (sometimes confusing, as he was the third of that name) in the story was my maternal grandfather, born on 19 December 1896 into an established British industrial and politically active family. This historic year was marked by the Austrian Wilhelm Röntgen discovering X-Ray radiation and Bridget Driscoll recorded as the first motoring casualty, killed by a Benz car at Crystal Palace.

My ancestor Joseph Stephens was born in 1770, died on 20 February 1820 in Redbourn, Hertfordshire, at the age of fifty, and was buried in Redbourn. He married Catherine Farey, aged twenty-nine, in Holborn on 24 July 1792. The first Henry Stephens in the story was born on 11 June 1797, when Joseph was twenty-seven and Catherine was thirty-four. Siblings included John, Joshia, Ellen, Frances (Mrs Liley) and Catherine (Mrs Carter). In 1801 Joseph and Catherine moved from Holborn in London to take over as landlords of the Bull Inn at Redbourn, Hertfordshire. The Inn was very successful, traffic at the time being recorded as sixty northbound coaches every 24 hours via nearby St Albans.

The first Henry Stephens started a medical career on the bottom rung of the ladder aged fifteen, signed by Joseph as an apprentice to John Wakefield and Benjamin Sommers, based in Studham, Berkshire. The contract stated that Henry was ready to 'learn their art' as surgeon and apothecary, including the use and manufacture of chemicals used in written records. Henry's daughter Martha later described how the apprentices were given donkeys to transport bottles of medicine and parcels to patients.

The senior medical ranks in early nineteenth century England were either physicians, surgeons or apothecaries. Physicians earned a degree from Oxford or Cambridge and were called 'Doctor'. They wrote prescriptions but did not operate or train apprentices. A surgeon signed up as an apprentice over six years, with formal education at a private medical or anatomy school and some years in hospital wards. Their licences were granted by the Royal College of Surgeons.

Apothecaries also spent six years as apprentices to a medical practitioner before being licensed by the Society of Apothecaries. They made and prescribed medicines but did not operate. As part of a typical hospital, their realm at St Thomas's Hospital was next to the female operating theatre. In the Herb Garret, as the chief medical chemist, the Apothecary created, sold and dispensed prescriptions for surgical cases, dispensing medicines to patients if a physician was absent.

Four years later, in 1815, Henry enrolled as a medical student in London at Guy's and St Thomas's Hospital. As always in war, which had culminated that year in the defeat of Napoleon at Waterloo on 18 June, medical knowledge was advancing. At the time, replacement teeth were traditionally made of ivory taken from hippopotamuses, walruses or elephants. A longer-lasting solution was found to be carving an ivory base and adding human teeth. With over 50,000 soldiers killed at Waterloo, mostly healthy young men, 'Waterloo teeth' were sold, many scavenged from dead soldiers. Since their owners had mostly been too poor to afford sugar, specimens were in far better shape than the teeth of richer clients.

In 1884, as surgeon at St Thomas's hospital until 1863, John Flint described his working area:

> Behind a second partition stood the pupils, packed like herrings in a barrel, but not so quiet, as those behind were continually pressing on those before, crying 'heads, heads' to those about the table whose heads interfered with the sightseers. The confusion and crushing were always indeed very great, especially when any operation of importance was to be performed. I have often known even the floor so crowded that the surgeon could not operate till it had been partially cleared.

Many patients died of infections, with only 30 per cent surviving. The frock coats worn by surgeons during operations were, according to a contemporary, 'stiff and stinking with pus and blood', before the surgeon wiped his hands on them, ready for the next day. The patients on the operating table would have been fully awake and staring at the surgeon. They were given a wooden block to bite on, keeping the tongue intact and muffling their screams. There was no anaesthetic, as chloroform was not available until discovered in 1846 by Scottish gynaecological surgeon Sir James Young Simpson.

Training at the twinned London hospitals of Guy's and St Thomas's, Henry shared a house with three other medical students, Mr Kentish, George Wilson Mackreth and John Keats, the famous poet. Martha Stephens' diary notes that in 1816 her father helped Keats compose the line, 'A thing of beauty is a joy forever'. Poet Laureate Sir Andrew Motion unveiled a blue plaque (see Plate 3) in 2002 at 28 St Thomas Street, Southwark, commemorating Keats and Stephens as medical students at Guy's and St Thomas' Hospital from 1815, the year of Waterloo.

Henry and all the medical students would have been very familiar with the stairs to the roof space of St Thomas's Church. Next to the female operating theatre was the Herb Garret. Here, with a laboratory and dispensary, the Apothecary created and sold prescriptions such as a common cure for venereal disease, Richard Mead's 'Snail Water'. Mead was appointed to the staff in 1703, publishing his recipes in the *Pharmacopoeia Pauperum* directory of medical treatments in 1718:

> Take Garden snails, cleansed and bruised, 6 gallons. Earthworms washed and bruised, three gallons. Add common wormwood, ground ivy, carduus, each one and half pound of penniroyal, juniper berries, fennel seeds, aniseeds, each a half pound, cloves and cubebes bruised, each three ounces, spirit of wine and spring water, each of 8 gallons. Digest them for the space of 24 hours, and then draw it off to use.

The hospital accounts include two yards of canvas for a snail bag for the Apothecary on 18 July 1713. Additional records show an autopsy on John Shorter, who died from the effects of chloroform administered during an operation to remove an ingrowing toenail!

The slate board at the rear of the Operating Theatre illustrated the diary for the day as recorded in the *Lancet* for November 1823:

> November 25. At half-past one o'clock this day, the following clinical remarks were delivered by Mr Traver, in the female operating theatre, in reference more particularly to the case of compound fracture.

Henry and the others enrolled for twelve months as medical students at Guy's Hospital in October 1815. This involved paying in advance for lectures, buying a set of basic surgical instruments and renting lodgings. Henry and Keats typically signed up to attend a course on 'Anatomy and the Operations of Surgery' delivered jointly by Astley Cooper and Henry Cline. In March 1816 Keats was promoted to act as 'dresser' to the surgeon William Lucas for the next twelve months, taking the front two rows in the operating theatre and handing instruments to a surgeon.

However, all medical lecturing faced opposition from the church, since the cutting up of bodies was banned by religious authorities. Heavy rain and burst river banks were often an opportunity to claim exposed human remains for study, rather than obtaining them by breaking the law. Surgeons also purchased newly-buried corpses from 'body-snatchers', who then carefully reconstructed the empty graves. Body clamps were soon installed around the necks of the dead to deter thieves from dragging bodies from their caskets. In the mid-eighteenth century a fresh body sold for one guinea, increasing to thirty guineas by 1805. Children were known as 'smalls' and priced by the inch.

The insatiable demand for bodies for new paying students raised the importance of surgery, supported by the detailed drawings of rising star John Hunter's work and his massive collection of both exotic animal and human specimens. Scottish-trained, his elder brother William opened the first anatomy school in Covent Garden in 1748. Aged twenty, John was entrusted with gathering essential teaching material, a regular supply of fresh bodies dug up from paupers' graves. He recorded the dissection of more than 3,000 bodies, all carefully drawn and preserved as teaching aids.

As a practitioner, John paid for live teeth from pauper children to be transplanted into rich patients, the two sat beside each other for speed of operation. Following his wishes, when he died in 1793 his body was immediately dissected by his medical students. The Hunter collection in London was purchased by the British government in 1799 and gifted to the Royal College of Surgeons.

Another Scot, Robert Liston, qualified as a surgeon at the Royal Infirmary of Edinburgh in 1818. He quickly built a reputation as a fast and highly skilled surgeon. Appointed as the first Professor of Clinical Surgery at University College Hospital in London in 1835, he championed ether and demonstrated a first public operation in Europe with an anaesthetic on 21 December 1846.

Contemporaries labelled Liston the 'fastest knife in the West End'. He once removed a leg in under three minutes, but this operation caused three deaths. The patient died from infection; Liston's assistant lost all his fingers and died of gangrene; and a spectator's coat was cut by a bloody blade and he died of a heart attack. In another fast Liston surgery, a patient lost both his leg and his testicles in under two and a half minutes. A famous operation by Lister took four minutes to remove a 45lb scrotal tumour carried in a wheelbarrow by the patient to the operating table. Modern medical novelist Richard Gordon described Lister in 1993:

> He was six foot two and operated in a bottle-green coat with wellington boots. He sprung across the blood-stained boards upon his swooning, sweating, strapped-down patient like a duellist, calling, 'Time me gentlemen, time me!' to students craning with pocket watches from the iron-railing galleries. Everyone swore that the first flash of his knife was followed so swiftly by the rasp of saw on bone that sight and sound seemed simultaneous. To free both hands, he would clasp the bloody knife between his teeth.

In September 1829, at Trinity Church, Marylebone, Henry Stephens married Hannah Woodbridge. In the 1830s Stephens trained himself as an expert in cholera. Frustrated by the poor quality of the writing materials available for his own work and for his medical records, and using his medical skills as a chemist, Henry experimented with chemicals and ink-making at 54 Stamford Street. The site is now the Fountain & Ink bar, decorated with a Stephens Ink theme.

In 1832 Doctor Stephens created an indelible blue-black writing fluid with the help of 'chemical colour and ink maker' Ebenezer Nash of nearby Duke Street. He took out patents for Stephens' inks, pens and inkstands in 1837 and formed the Stephens' Ink company, a worldwide brand with an inkblot image that would sell for over 130 years. The ink was sold in pots made by Doulton in Lambeth.

After the death of their infant daughter Harriet in 1831 of cholera, and Hannah of consumption in 1832, Doctor Stephens married Anne Reilly, a 26-year-old spinster from

Holborn at St Andrew's church, Holborn. After a honeymoon in Brussels, Henry and Anne moved to 71 York Road, Lambeth. They had seven children. Their first was an infant called Arthur, Henry Charles (later known as 'Inky') in 1841, followed by Martha in 1843, Catherine (Kitty) in 1846, Harold in 1848, Ellen in 1853, and my maternal grandfather Julian in 1855. To accommodate their growing family, and as a result of financial success, Doctor Henry and Anne moved to Finchley, North London in 1846. Henry bought and renovated Grove House, in Ballards Lane. The outbuildings of Grove House were used as a laboratory for research and the manufacture of ink and wood stains. In 1851 the Great Exhibition in London's Hyde Park promoted Stephens' indelible 'blue-black writing fluid', and other inks received favourable press reviews.

Dr Henry died suddenly on 15 September 1864 at Farringdon Railway Station. The Stephens Ink business was taken over by his eldest son Henry Charles.

The second Henry (Charles) Stephens (known to posterity as 'Inky') (see Plate 5) therefore enters the story at the lying-in hospital at York Road in Lambeth on 2 February 1841, the second child of Doctor Henry and his wife Anne. In 1852 Henry Charles, aged eleven, returned from Paris to attend University College School in Gower Street for five years. Aged sixteen, he joined the School of Mines in Kensington to study chemistry and science whilst apprenticed to his father to learn the ink business. His father was a friend of scientist Michael Faraday, and both attended his lectures at the Royal Institution in London. In 1864, aged twenty-three, he took over Stephens Ink after the sudden death of Doctor Stephens.

Ink was difficult to make, and expensive. Although the recipe changed over the years, from Elizabethan times the staple of iron gall ink was made from claret, oak galls, ferrous iron sulphate and gum, fermented for several days before being boiled off. Ink used for quills made from heated bird's feathers was not suitable for the newly manufactured steel nibs. Henry therefore described his new product as 'a carbonaceous black writing fluid'. There are four types of ink in production today: aqueous, liquid, paste, and powder, which many school students acting as 'ink monitor' will remember mixing with water to fill classroom inkwells. Ink depends on the two compounds of colourants and binders.

Solvents may be organic or aqueous, with pigments more used than a dye; they are colour-fast, expensive, less colour-consistent and offering a narrower colour range than dyes, whereas dyes are stronger than pigments and have more colour density. When dyes dissolve into liquids they soak into paper, so are less efficient. Modern paper is made from cellulose as a wood-sourced material that is naturally charged, aiding ink retention.

Doctor Stephens transformed a previously difficult product into a domestic staple, fuelling the rise of letter-writing by the masses, and hence indirectly launching the entire postage industry. The new Penny Post in 1840 helped to build demand for effective writing materials. A letter took three weeks to reach New York and three weeks to return, before the telegraph was invented.

The first Stephens' patents for inks, pens and inkstands were granted on 28 March 1837. An advertisement in 1838 from Robson's London Directory informed 'the writing public' of the new Stephens patent writing fluids in carbonaceous black, dark blue, light blue and brilliant red, including a warning about infringing patents. Stephens ink was sold in bottles at six pence, one shilling and three shillings.

In 1867 Henry Charles, noted as 'Chemist', won a Silver Medal for Writing Inks at the Exposition Universelle at the Champ de Mars in Paris, followed by eight Gold Medals and eleven Silver Medals at international exhibitions held in Le Havre, Lyons, Vienna, Philadelphia, Paris, Boston (USA), Sydney, Melbourne, Christchurch, Amsterdam, Calcutta and Antwerp. The iconic 'inkblot' trademark was recognised around the world and selected by the fatal Terra Nova exploration to the South Pole with Captain Robert Scott in 1910. Sir Douglas Mawson selected Stephens products to record his Australasian Antarctic Expedition in 1911.

Following the 1918 Armistice, the First World War formally ended on 28 June 1919, and the Treaty of Versailles was signed with Stephens' indelible blue-black ink.

Henry had become involved, in support of his daughter, in the attempted kidnapping of his grandchildren. The *Tamworth Herald* on Saturday, 30 July 1898 reported:

> An extraordinary Kidnapping Case. An extraordinary case of kidnapping two children as reported from Hythe. The children kidnapped are two little boys, sons of Mr. Lewis Edmunds, Q.C., aged five and seven respectively. For some time past the children have been at a school in Folkestone, but a few days ago, owing to the fact the holidays were at hand, the father decided to have them removed to Hythe, in charge of a young lady who had previously acted as their governess. It appears that the father had some idea that an attempt would be made to seize the children, for towards the end of last week he accompanied them and their governess to Hythe, and remained there till Sunday or Monday, when he returned to London.
>
> He gave the governess his written authority to take charge of the children, this authority being dated 21st July. The children were carefully guarded by the governess and kept in the house as much as possible. On Tuesday, however, not wishing them to be too much confined to the house she allowed them to play on the lawn in front.
>
> They had not been there very long before the children were kidnapped and an extraordinary scene occurred. The governess believes some of the kidnapping party concealed themselves behind a wall as they rushed in and took her completely by surprise. Seeing that a rush was being made for the children, the governess screamed, and, in a few seconds, a wild struggle was taking place on the lawn. The screams of the governess attracted the attention of several of the neighbours and people in the house. She states that the first persons she saw

> run at the gate were the children's mother and her father, Mr Henry Charles Stephens, M.P. The governess who had clung to the younger child is said to have been attacked by the M.P. grandfather who held her by the throat and is alleged to almost throttled her.
>
> The capture of the second child quickly followed, and the carriage is reported to have been driven away at once in the direction of Folkestone. At Hythe on Thursday on the application of Mr Blaxland, solicitor to Miss Ford a summons for assault was granted against Mr Stephens, M.P. and a warrant was refused. The hearing will take place August 8.

Henry Charles was barred from contact with his grandchildren and he moved to Wiltshire. Aside from the family business and politics, he was a trained chemist and a local benefactor and philanthropist with a significant interest in agriculture and water management. In 1884 he purchased Cholderton Lodge and 823 acres of farmland to establish his estate, founding the Cholderton and District Water Company in 1904. Several of the Stephens family are buried in a private vault at the small Cholderton church.

Henry Charles left Avenue House to the Urban District Council of Finchley at his death on 8 July 1918, aged seventy-seven. His will stated that the house and grounds be granted on 'the condition that the same shall be open for the use and enjoyment always of the public under which reasonable regulations as may be made'. Now a charity, Avenue House was renamed Stephens House and Gardens in 2014.

In Britain, the statutory legal records of 'hatching, matching and dispatching' (births, marriages and deaths) are kept by a qualified Registrar using controlled-circulation ink. Registrars' ink cannot be rubbed out or washed off and must not fade with time. All births, marriages and deaths in Britain are required to be recorded in Stephens' indelible Registrar Ink. The birth of Gracie and Theadora Ward-Thomas (five generations after Inky) were recorded by the author with Stephens' ink in 1999 and 2001. The bottle label read: 'Stephens' Blue Black Record Ink (Registrar's Ink). An indestructible ink for permanent records.'

My great-grandfather Julian, a brother of 'Inky' Stephens, was born in January 1855 at the family home, Grove House, Church End in Finchley. Julian married Minna Mary Pélissier on 7 December 1881 in Finchley and they had nine children over fourteen years. The baptismal record of my grandfather Henry on 6 April 1897 notes Julian as a 'Colonial Merchant'.

Chapter 3

Henry Christian Stephens, Royal Navy, 1896–1953

My grandfather Henry Christian was the third and principal Henry of the family story. Born on 19 December 1896 at the family home, Grove House, Church End, Finchley, and baptised on 6 April 1897, Henry was three when his father Julian died in 1899, followed by his mother Minna Mary in 1902.

Before she married Henry in October 1920, my grandmother, Elizabeth Pauline (née Sharkey, also known as Lilly) had been married before. Born in Dublin in 1885, she is recorded with her mother in the 1901 census of the O'Gorman family, headed by Frederick (aged twenty-eight) and Bridget (aged thirty) at 41 Georges Avenue, Blackrock, Dublin. Elizabeth is noted as aged sixteen, a Roman Catholic and a scholar who could read and write. On 10 January 1902 Dermott O'Gorman (see Plate 28) was born at the same address, and he is recorded as a beneficiary under probate when my grandfather died in 1953.

Aged twenty-three, Elizabeth and her first husband William Green had a daughter on 19 July 1908, baptised as Phyllis Una Green in Dublin on 24 July 1908. A passenger list to Fremantle, Australia in 1930 records Phyllis as a typist aged twenty-three. Aged twenty-four, Phyllis married Thomas Hugh Chignell on 19 December 1932. Their son Michael Chignell was born on 7 July 1934 at Fareham, Hampshire, followed by his brother Anthony on 14 April 1939. The 1939 Register of Civilians records Thomas Chignell (dental surgeon) and Mrs Phyliss Chignell (unpaid domestic duties), with Anthony at school. Michael Chignell married Susan Morton in July 1970 in Winchester, and Anthony Chignell married Philippa Brayne-Nicholls in April 1962.

There is no available record of Elizabeth divorcing William Green, so it is assumed she was a widow. Leaving the Navy as a Sub-lieutenant in 1918, my grandfather Henry married Elizabeth Pauline in October 1920. He tried various careers, including sailing as a 'planter' to Bombay in 1928 on the P&O liner RMS *Mooltan* with Elizabeth listed as 'home duties', accompanied by their daughter, Evelyn Bridget Patricia, aged two. She was my mother.

On 19 December 1939 the Register of Civilians recorded Mr and Mrs Stephens living in Flat 3, 90 Charing Cross Road. Henry was registered as a press photographer (Royal Navy) at the *Daily Mail* under the Ministry of Supply. His wife Elizabeth was registered as an unpaid domestic.

On 14 December 1954 *The Times* reported: 'The engagement is announced between Michael Ward, the only son of the late Richard Ward-Thomas, and of Mrs Bowles, of 16, Duchess of Bedford House, Duchess of Bedford Walk, W8, and Evelyn Bridget Patricia, only daughter of the late Henry Christian Stephens and of Mrs Stephens of 31 Carlisle Mansions, Carlisle Place, S.W. 1' (see plates 28 & 29).

My mother married Michael Ward-Thomas in 1955 in Marylebone, and they had six children. Michael was born on 6 May 1926. Educated at Eton, after a short service in the Royal Navy he became a successful minerals and diamond trader at Selection Trust in Coleman Avenue. The firm was established in 1913 by the Americans Chester Beatty and Herbert Hoover (who became the thirty-first President of the United States in 1929).

My paternal grandfather Richard (Dick) Ward-Thomas was born on 11 December 1898. Also educated at Eton, Dick served as a Lieutenant in the Royal Field Artillery (RFA) during the First World War. He married Margery Edith Lily Madge on 21 November 1963 at St Paul's, Knightsbridge. With my father their only son, they divorced, and Margery married Michael Bowles. Dick died in August 1954 and Margery in 1980. My paternal great-grandfather was Ernest Ward-Thomas, born on 13 August 1860. Educated at Harrow, he was a wool broker in Hunsdon Bury, Hertfordshire. He married Mary Constance Christian on 1 June 1893 at St Stephen's Church, Cheltenham. Born on 17 November 1868, Mary was the second daughter of Admiral Henry Christian MVO, of Cheltenham. Ernst died in 1940, aged eighty. Mary died in 1952, aged eighty-four.

My maternal grandfather Henry Stephens died on 5 June 1953, in London, aged 56. My maternal grandmother Elizabeth Pauline died on 29 August 1968, in Cambridge, aged eighty-four. After a successful career in mining and business, followed by several years as National Hunt owner, my father died in October 2004. My mother ended her working life in 1994 as a best-selling historical novelist under the nom de plume of Evelyn Anthony, having been appointed the first female High Sheriff of Essex. She died in September 2018, aged ninety-two.

PART II

War

Chapter 4

Anti-aircraft Defences in the Second World War

To place the invention of the Dome Trainer in context, from 1918 to 1939 the British experience of defence against aircraft attack and of actual combat was only based on observation of overseas conflicts.

Banned by the Treaty of Versailles in 1919 but quietly rearmed by Hitler, the fledgling German air force saw action in the Spanish Civil War prior to the outbreak of war in 1939. The Nazi regime provided volunteers and 600 aircraft to the Nationalists in Madrid, taking full advantage of the opportunity to train their own forces, something previously denied them. Volunteers from countries including Britain joined the Republicans, who were also given support by Mexico and the Soviet Union. With fresh memories of the slaughter of 1914–18, Britain, the USA and France followed a policy of non-intervention, watching from the sidelines.

Aircraft emerged as the crucial new weapons. Making a combat debut in 1937 with the Luftwaffe's Condor Legion during the Spanish War, the Junkers Ju 87 or Stuka (from *Sturzkampfflugzeug*, 'dive fighter aircraft') was a dive-bombing ground-attack plane, easily recognizable by its inverted gull wings and fixed spread undercarriage. The Junkers 87 was also a psychological weapon with wailing sirens called *Jericho-Trompeten* (trumpets) on the legs which increased to screaming volume in vertical dives. The Stuka was joined by the German Heinkel He111, the Dornier Do 17 and the Messerschmitt Bf 109 fighter.

The Condor Legion was composed of volunteers from the Luftwaffe and Army, and the conflict provided invaluable combat experience and a testing ground for new technology and tactics. This was the initial development of the new *Blitzkrieg* or 'lightning war' strategy by Germany that proved so dominant during the initial stages of the Second World War. By co-ordinating air and land forces, a very concentrated offensive could strike a swift, heavy and focused blow on an enemy using mobile forces, including tanks and close air support.

At the outbreak of the Second World War in 1939, all governments now appreciated that extremely fast and very manoeuvrable low-flying enemy aircraft attacking soldiers, airfields and ships represented a far more significant threat than at first estimated by observation of the limited conflict in Spain. Effective defensive weapons against such attacks were almost non-existent, limited to Light Anti-Aircraft (LAA) guns. These ranged from small .303 or 7.7 rifle calibre machine guns fired by a single gunner, up to the new 40mm Swedish Bofors anti-aircraft gun crewed by up to five men.

Effective range to engage low flying aircraft was 1,200ft for small weapons and up to 12,000ft for the Bofors. In the rush to mobilise, training for the significantly increasing number of anti-aircraft gunners across all services was minimal. Retreat and successful evacuation under fire from Dunkirk in 1940 forced the British to abandon equipment in France. A tally of available Light Anti-Aircraft guns available in Britain in July 1940 after Dunkirk revealed that there were just 517. A pre-war plan for the provision of LAA guns had estimated that 4,410 should be available by this date.

Overseas fighting forces of the Navy and Army were a priority for LAA equipment, carefully balanced against the real fear of invasion across the Channel. First World War-vintage 'Lewis' machine guns and other obsolete weapons were pressed into use. With any new guns deployed only for combat, there was a lack of equipment to train new defensive anti-aircraft (A.A.) gunners. For training, simplified replica versions were produced with just the functional parts, either a single machine gun without a barrel or a larger weapon for the two-man operators of the 40mm Bofors. It was not until the mid-war period that British forces were supplied with adequate modern weapons. All over the world, in Europe, the Middle East, Russia, Africa and Asia-Pacific, all services needed scarce LAA equipment. Trained and experienced anti-aircraft (A.A.) gunners were rare.

Against such a background of ineffective ship or ground defence against new fighters and bombers, and the evacuation of Dunkirk, Henry designed and proposed to his old service contacts in the Royal Navy a revolutionary design for A.A. gunnery training. His invention was officially called the 'Dome Teacher' but it soon became known as the 'Dome Trainer', and this name was officially adopted toward the end of the Second World War.

The Luftwaffe began 1940 in Norway with numerous successful air attacks by the new dive-bombers against the Royal Navy, who threatened German naval and coastal operations. Ordered to bombard Stavanger airfield during the Nazi invasion of Norway, the British heavy cruiser HMS *Suffolk* was attacked on 17 April by Junkers 87 Stukas. Her stern was virtually destroyed, but she limped back to Scapa Flow with 33 dead and 38 wounded. Her sister ships HMS *Curacoa* and HMS *Curlew* were subjected to lengthy attacks. An indication of the experience of the crew was a report by one of the seamen: 'They threatened to take our masthead with them in every screaming nerve-wracking dive.'

The Navy sloop HMS *Black Swan* had a narrow escape. On 27 April, a bomb crashed through her quarterdeck, the wardroom, a water tank and the 4-inch ammunition magazine, before exiting the ship and exploding in the sea. A further indication of lack of training was that the *Black Swan* fired 1,000 rounds but failed to hit a Stuka. The lack of effective defence resulted in the loss of the sloop HMS *Bittern* on 30 April to a squadron of Junkers Ju 87 dive-bombers. Her air defences were six 4-inch A.A. guns and four 0.5-inch A.A. machine guns that proved ineffective. The C-class light cruiser HMS *Cairo* was damaged by German aircraft off Narvik on 28 May 1940 and was out of action for two months. The French destroyer *Bison* was sunk by a bomb exploding in a forward magazine.

The Tribal-class destroyer HMS *Afridi* was attacked by dive-bombers from both port and starboard in an 'anvil' technique on 3 May during the evacuation of Namsos in Norway. Her forward magazine was hit, killing 108 of the crew. Completed in 1938, the new ship was protected from aircraft attack by a single quadruple mount for a 40mm two-pounder Mk II 'pom-pom' gun and two quadruple mounts for 12.7mm Mark III machine gun. Smaller trawlers should have been difficult targets, but a Junkers Ju 87 sank *Jardine* and *Warwickshire* on 30 April, and the Polish troopship *Chrobry* was destroyed on 15 May.

German *Blitzkrieg* warfare swept across Poland to the east and Denmark, Holland, Belgium and France to the west. Key to this new strategy was pinpoint attacks from the air on defending forces as well cities and military bases. Once France fell the Luftwaffe turned their attention to Britain. In a prelude to a possible invasion, and to defeat the RAF, they initially carried out attacks on south and east coast shipping, hoping to entice British fighters to come out. In a further attempt to crush the RAF the Luftwaffe commenced attacks on RAF fighter airfields and aircraft production as well as engaging in dogfights in the air

After an RAF raid on Berlin the Luftwaffe changed tactics. On 7 September 1940 their attacks switched to London. Aerial bombardment of the capital and other British cites until May 1941 became known as the 'Blitz'. Air raid defences against the Blitz involved heavy A.A. weapons, whereas the Dome Trainer did not come into service until after the Blitz had ended, training gunners with light A.A. weapons to defend RAF airfields and aircraft factories from low-level attacks.

During the inter-war years Germany also secretly evolved a new submarine tactic to counter the convoy system. This was the 'wolf pack', whereby submarines would attack convoys in groups, exploiting gaps in convoy defence. In contrast, the British neglected to study submarine tactics after 1918, with an assumption that U-Boats would operate as they had during the First World War. Resources and skills were therefore urgently needed to defend both Royal Navy and Merchant Navy shipping from submarine warfare. This was reflected in the single-minded effort of Gilbert Roberts, Royal Navy.

As Henry's new shipmate, Gilbert was posted to the pre-dreadnought battleship HMS *Hibernia*. In command of the F-class destroyer HMS *Fearless* in 1937, Roberts patrolled the Spanish coast (during the Civil War) but was retired from active duty with tuberculosis in October 1938. However, from 1935 to 1937 Roberts also studied war games at the Portsmouth Tactical School, ironically placed near the squash courts building where the first prototype of the Dome Trainer was erected. Roberts was recalled to active duty in Liverpool to develop both defensive and offensive strategies against U-Boats which were decimating convoys and destroying essential supplies for Britain's war effort.

In response to catastrophic convoy losses, the Royal Navy had to develop new methods. In *A Game of Birds and Wolve*s, Simon Parkin describes the secret tactical unit created by the Royal Navy to defeat the German submarine threat. In January 1942, Captain Roberts created WATU (the Western Approaches Tactical Unit) within the convoy plotting facility in Liverpool, alongside another Dome Trainer for Atlantic convoy gunners.

Ironically, emergency electricity for WATU was generated by a reliable diesel engine from a U-Boat captured in the First World War. The unit designed a chessboard badge inscribed with 'Checkmate'. Both offensive and defensive war game examples include tactics called 'Raspberry' and 'Pineapple', immediately relayed to warships at sea tasked with destroying German submarines whilst merchant convoys were under attack. This new war game concept was ridiculed by senior Navy officers until the 'Beta Search' tactic was proven to Admiral Sir Max Kennedy Horton, a decorated First World War submarine commander, appointed as the Admiral responsible for defending convoys in the Atlantic. Five times, Horton took the role of a U-Boat submarine commander. Each time, Admiral Horton was sunk by escorts commanded by Miss Janet Okell, aged twenty. A member of the Women's Royal Naval Service, Okell had never been to sea and was not an officer. 'Raspberry' was named by Wren Jean Laidlaw as a snub to Adolf Hitler. The new aggressive predictive tactics resulted in dramatic losses of U-Boats and crews. From such basic beginnings was born the sophistication of strategy games deployed across modern computers and the 'Battleship' board game.

Chapter 5

Defensively Equipped Merchant Ships (DEMS) and Convoy Defence

Henry's concern for his shipmates in the Royal Navy extended to the supply lifeline of the Merchant Marine. As convoy protection had been a proven strategy towards the end of 1918, both Royal Navy and Merchant Navy ships were earmarked for additional defensive measures. A standard A.A. configuration was set at a low angle for surface targets like submarines and a high angle for anti-aircraft defence. Weapons included both a 3-inch and a 4-inch gun. The Navy established their own projectiles, such as the rockets from a Royal Navy shore unit, opened in 1941 as an outpost of the Directorate of Miscellaneous Weapons Development (DMWD) on *Birnbeck Pier,* Weston-super-Mare and hence named HMS *Birnbeck*.

Defence of ships at sea had been enhanced during the First World War, but development ceased in 1918. In the face of German rearmament in 1936, the Shipping Defence Advisory Committee was established in 1937 to agree costs for ship owners to install fittings for A.A. guns in time of war. The Defensively Equipped Merchant Ship (DEMS) organisation was created in June 1939 by the Admiralty Trade Division. In the first six months of the Second World War 900 merchant ships were strengthened and fitted with a mixture of weapons, expanding to 3,400 merchant ships by the end of 1940.

If war came to Britain, a significant percentage of supplies and manpower would be imported, with men, goods and ammunition re-exported to support the war effort across the world. This lifeline was formed by the Merchant Navy with the protection of the Royal Navy.

Reflecting the lack of practical combat experience or effective new technology since 1918, very basic gunnery training for ships crews started in July 1938. Crews were a mixed assortment, depending on the skills required to maintain, load and fire the various weapons. Royal Navy HO (Hostilities Only) ratings, known as Acting Gun Layer or Acting Seaman Gunner, were drafted in to serve on a DEMS. The Admiralty ruled that a mercantile rating could earn an additional ninepence a day when embarked as a gunnery rating. Appointed as Inspector of Merchant Navy Gunnery, Admiral Sir Frederic Dreyer was responsible for overseeing DEMS. In 1941, Dreyer initiated a two-day course especially for merchant seamen. By the end of the war, 100,000 merchant seamen had completed the instruction, which comprised both lectures and active demonstrations, including live firing at clay pigeons and aircraft-towed targets.

Alongside the Dome Trainer, converted double-decker buses (see Plate 16) were used as mobile classrooms. This instruction unit would travel to ports country-wide, providing merchant seamen with the two-day course without removing them from their ships.

Until ships' crews were trained, light machine gun crews were posted to ports from the Royal Artillery. Five hundred men were rotated in crews of two allocated to a ship on departure, switching to another that was leaving when the first ship arrived back in port. Skills were concentrated into a Maritime Anti-Aircraft Regiment of Royal Artillery in 1941, renamed the Maritime Royal Artillery (MRA) in January 1943. By 1943, 14,000 servicemen from the MRA were serving at twenty-four British ports.

On 12 August 1942 the Anglo-Soviet Mutual Assistance Pact was signed in Moscow, and on the same day the first convoy to Russia, codenamed 'Dervish', set sail from Liverpool carrying much needed fuel, tanks, aircraft, ammunition and other equipment to the beleaguered Russian forces. Merchant seamen ran the gauntlet of German U-Boats, battleships and bomber aircraft to unload at the Russian ports of Murmansk and Archangel on the Arctic coast.

Merchant vessels travelled in convoys that were escorted by destroyers, cruisers, battleships and aircraft carriers operating from Scapa Flow, all of which required anti-aircraft defensive skills. Provisioning and maintaining the ships of British, Canadian and US Fleets, both convoy escorts and merchant ships, placed a heavy demand on the naval facilities on the Orkney island of Hoy. With the majority of escort vessels requiring refuelling and rearming at sea, priority was also given to training merchant seamen in defending from air attack. Training courses in aircraft recognition and anti-aircraft gunnery were mounted for DEMS crews. A specialised training complex was built at Rinnigill, consisting of Royal Navy 'synthetic' trainers to prepare ship and submarine crews for combat at sea. These provided DEMS personnel with invaluable target identification and tracking experience through combat simulators (see Plate 15).

One of the trainers provided a Role, Yaw, Pitch, Alter Course (RYPA) unit, where a manually operated platform simulated seaborne movement of hard chine or round-bilged vessels. Trainees would operate copies of ship-based anti-aircraft guns and endeavour to fire .22 ammunition at a target card whilst the platform moved aggressively under them.

As the maritime lifeline of supplies to Britain in 1940 expanded across the world, additional gunners and officers were posted to ships from the Royal Navy and Royal Marines. From 1942, the RAF Regiment manned A.A. guns on troopships carrying Royal Air Force personnel. All armed service crew on a DEMS ship additionally signed on as merchant crew under the command of the ship's captain, allowing them to visit neutral countries without arrest or internment. All DEMS Gunners were listed as merchant crew on sailing lists, concealing their skills and the configuration of weapons held by the civilian ship. A typical large gun required up to eight crew, comprising a gun layer, a breech worker, a rammer, a trainer, loader, sight-setter and two men feeding ammunition.

Given the demand on every ship, gunnery skills were spread amongst the crew, both armed forces and civilian sailors. A military non-commissioned officer commanded, with a ship's second mate as a gunnery officer. The newly designed anti-aircraft training took place from 1940 at HMS *Excellent*, the Naval Gunnery School at Whale Island, Portsmouth, using the new Dome Trainer from 1942. A Dome Trainer taught principles of eye-shooting fast-moving aircraft targets in a quarter-sphere dome, representing the arc of the sky. Moving target images were reflected on the Dome interior by a cam-actuated reflecting mirror attached to a 35mm projector which the trainee would endeavour to track using a mock-up ship's anti-aircraft gun.

Dome Trainers were quickly deployed as the standard training aid across Britain at both ends of convoy routes, especially in Liverpool. By the end of March 1944, Liverpool was providing more than 28,000 of the 115,978 gunnery courses in Britain. The Royal Navy shore base in Liverpool, HMS *Eaglet*, trained its own gunnery sailors at the Salthouse Dock with a Dome Trainer next to the Dock Traffic Office which was in use until 1951.

The use of the Dome Trainer by the Royal Navy was illustrated by evidence supporting Henry's invention given to the second Royal Commission in 1948 by Rear-Admiral Sir William Agnew KVCO, CB, DSO:

> During the last war I had experience of the Dome Trainer whilst I was at sea in command of the cruiser HMS Aurora from 1941 to 1943, and later when I was in command of HMS Excellent, the Portsmouth Naval Gunnery School, from February 1944 to September 1945. In 1940 HMS Aurora had only very few short-range anti-aircraft weapons. In 1941, whilst at Scapa, the ship was fitted with Oerlikons, and it became necessary to train the crews as quickly as possible in handing and aiming these weapons. A Dome Trainer was available at Scapa, and I sent my men ashore to be trained in it. In my opinion this training improved the accuracy of the short-range anti-aircraft shooting, and good results were obtained later when the ship was subjected to air attacks in the Mediterranean.

Advanced anti-aircraft training at the RAF Woodvale airfield included live firing on the nearby gunnery range at HMS *Charlotte* with tracer ammunition at targets towed by aircraft.

Air Ministry scientists working at HMS *Birnbeck* for the Directorate of Miscellaneous Weapons Development (DMWD), near Weston-super-Mare, adapted the Parachute Aerial Cable (PAC) rocket system, used by the RAF for airfield defence. This fired a cable into the path of an attacking aircraft, the cable being then held temporarily aloft by a parachute deployed from its upper end. An explosive charge was attached to the lower end so an enemy aircraft dragged a charge up to the wing where it would explode. Just the act of the cable being dragged over the wing could be enough to bring down an aircraft.

DEMS gunner Fred Dent described the deployment of a PAC rocket:

> The officer of the watch pulled a lanyard which fired the rocket up to around 400 feet in the air. The rocket took up a length of wire. Attached to the middle of the wire was a canister containing a hand grenade. Another length of wire was attached to a parachute and the canister. The drag on the parachute and the weight of the spent rocket suspended the grenade canister in mid-air. The idea was that if an enemy aircraft flew into the wire, the explosive charge would be dragged up to the wing and detonate.

Dent joined the East Yorkshire Regiment in August 1940 and then volunteered for the Maritime DEMS. He noted that other soldiers also volunteered to join the Maritime Anti-Aircraft Regiment Royal Artillery as they had wished to join the Navy, but conscription had sent them to the Army. After two weeks of gunnery training on HMS *Satellite* at South Shields, Dent was posted to one of twenty-four ports in Britain, initially for port defence. He then reported for DEMS service on convoy duty.

Lance-Bombardier Smith was attached to the 1st Maritime Regiment Royal Artillery and served on board several Allied merchant vessels between 1941 and 1944 as a DEMS gunner. Defending the Dutch cargo ship *Montferland*, sunk by a German Heinkel 111, Smith was given the fourteen days survivor's leave granted to shipwrecked Allied serviceman.

Both HMS *Glendower* (a Royal Navy shore base at Butlins, Pwllheli in North Wales) and HMS *Wellesley* at Liverpool (formerly the Royal Southern Hospital) were central DEMS bases to train sailors for war service in merchant ships. By 1944 33,000 DEMS gunners had passed out of HMS *Glendower* and HMS *Wellesley*. As the hub of convoy activity, Liverpool, with 1,285 inbound convoys arriving during the war, was at the core of the 'Battle of the Atlantic', defending precious convoys against U-Boats. Five weeks basic training was followed by up to three weeks of gunnery and three weeks of advanced ship skills. The entire range of weapons available on DEMS ships was taught in the final four weeks.

The MRA built up six regiments based at twenty-four ports, staffed by 14,000 men and one hundred and seventy officers. Over 150,000 Merchant Navy seamen were trained as Merchant Seaman Gunners. A range of DEMS training ships and land bases used Dome Trainers. The principal initial deployment was at HMS *Excellent*, the Royal Navy Gunnery School at Portsmouth, where the prototype of the Dome Trainer was built by Henry Stephens on rejoining the Royal Navy Volunteer Reserve. Other Royal Navy shore bases with a Dome Trainer included HMS *Caroline* in Belfast, HMS *Carrick* in Greenock, HMS *Chrysanthemum II* at King's Reach on the River Thames, HMS *Claverhouse* in Leith, HMS *Eaglet* with HMS *Wallace* in Liverpool, HMS *Flying Fox* in Bristol, HMS *President* on the Thames, HMS *President III* at Dedworth Manor, Windsor and HMS *Safeguard* at Southampton.

Henry's private journal for 27 July 1943 confirms that alongside the Dome Trainer, there were a variety of synthetic gunnery training devices used by the Royal Navy at HMS *Excellent.* The Low Angle spotting tables provided 'splashes' around a model ship allied to fire control procedures. Night Lookout tables provided model ships viewed in different light conditions to simulate night visibility. A director on a moving platform fired .22 bullets on a range to represent firing from a moving ship.

The Laying and Training Teacher used a moving projector representing pitch, roll and yaw at sea, projecting on to a semi-circular screen. A gun was laid through a telescope to simulate sea conditions. The Battle Teacher provided gun crew drill in darkness, including realistic gun flashes and explosions from enemy shells, plus sea spray and waves. A portable 'eye-shooting Teacher' was used as a hand-held static gun sight.

Installed at Eastney under the auspices of HMS *Excellent*, a Panoramic Gunnery Trainer was imported from America. Gunners viewed the target through a small peep-hole, and a photo-electric device checked accuracy. This was used for air-to-air gunnery and adapted for ship-to-air instruction. At Eastney, similarly to the Dome Trainer, model aircraft film was projected through a series of mirrors. Spotters used binoculars to judge speed, bearing and angle of sight of targets. A rolling gun platform at Eastney was hydraulically operated to give rough weather experience to gun crews (see Plate 22).

In November 1942 the Royal Navy and the Royal Australian Navy built a miniature tracer-firing range (MTFR) for merchant DEMS and coastal forces, also used by the RAF as a Tracer Trainer Mark I. Naval versions were installed at HMS *Excellent* on Whale Island and HMS *Chrysanthemum II* at King's Reach on the Thames, next to HMS *President.* These tracer ranges used pneumatic pressure guns to fire chrome-plated balls or steel ball bearings which were lit by a spotlight to give a tracer-stream effect. Targets consisted of model aircraft or model E-Boats. Thousands of the McGlashan Type E-3 Aerial Gunnery Trainer (using an air machine gun) were used by the USAAF and the US Navy to train DEMS crews. Cycled by an electronic solenoid and powered by compressed air, steel pellet projectile velocity was up to 600 feet per second. As an alternative, the M9 anti-aircraft machine gun Trainer used two dummy guns to simulate .50 water-cooled guns over a 1:30 range, firing plastic bullets. Electronics added timing for firing, recoil, gun blast and sounds of battle. Three model aircraft were run on wires as horizontal, climbing and diving planes, backed by paper targets to show hits. For night training, the M9 kit included 250-watt ultra-violet light on the gun, with painted fluorescent pellets firing at the fluorescent painted model plane.

The RAF Regiment was formed in February 1942 in response to the Army's attempt to defend airfields on Crete which had resulted in the surrender of a strategic island to the new tactic of German parachute forces. This new RAF service included low-level air defence. With skills honed in a Dome Trainer, the 40mm Bofors L60 (see Plate 10) was the principal weapon of the RAF Regiment's Light Anti-Aircraft squadrons in North Africa, Malta, Italy, the Balkans, Britain and Europe. These were deployed from D-Day through to the cessation of hostilities. The RAF Regiment shot down a rare German Me 262 new jet aircraft in November 1944. During the December 1944–January 1945 Ardennes offensive, the RAF Regiment shot down forty-three German aircraft and damaged twenty-eight others during their attacks on eleven RAF airfields on New Year's Day 1945.

Outside Britain, the Dome Trainer was used by 40,905 Merchant Navy crews in ports of the British Empire (see Plate 19) and the USA. A total of 32,000 merchant seamen and 1,200 Maritime Royal Artillery gunners lost their lives on British merchant ships. For wartime service, 541 men and women were awarded the Silver Lloyd's War Medal for Bravery at Sea, the Lloyd's Meritorious Medal and the Lloyd's Silver Medal for saving life at sea. Some 24,000 members of the Merchant Navy and Fishing Fleets are honoured at the Tower Hill Memorial, London.

Chapter 6

Invention of the Dome Trainer

In 1940 the operational risks for ships attacked by aircraft had become evident. Vice-Admiral Lionel Wells commanded a Home Fleet expedition of seven destroyers, the heavy cruiser HMS *Berwick*, the aircraft carriers HMS *Glorious* and HMS *Ark Royal*, sailing with the battleship HMS *Valiant*. On 1 May 1940 the force was ordered to provide fighter patrols over the ships evacuating troops from Andalsnes in Norway. Attacked by both Junkers Ju 88 and He 111 bombers, Wells ordered that no Royal Navy ships should operate within range of Norwegian airfields used by the Luftwaffe. He reported to the Home Fleet Admiral, Charles Forbes, that aircraft carriers must not be placed at such risk. The Navy had no proven or effective defence against attack from the air until the introduction and deployment of the Dome Trainer.

In anti-aircraft gunnery the most important element of training was to show A.A. gunners how to 'aim off' when engaging an enemy aircraft; in other words, how to aim at a point ahead of the aircraft along its line of flight. This was explained in detail for all Navy gunners in the Gunnery Pocket Book (Appendix F).

As a photographer in civilian life, Henry Stephens initially designed his Dome Trainer to use film taken of dummy attacks by captured enemy aircraft. A cine camera could photograph the aircraft and the camera movements (i.e., panning or elevating) could be accurately recorded. By precisely moving a projector along the same paths as the cine camera, when the resulting film was projected onto the inside of a curved wall it would reproduce the attack for trainee gunners to practise aiming (see Plate 11). The sound of the attacking aircraft and other battlefield sounds, including the noise of the anti-aircraft gun itself firing, would acclimatise the gunners psychologically to the reality of coming under attack (see plates 6 & 7).

Trying to move a projector in the same manner as a cine camera was prohibitively difficult due to its size and weight. With a projector in a fixed position (facing away from the screen), the same result could be achieved by projecting the image of the film onto a gimbal-mounted mirror. This mirror moved freely in traverse and elevation and threw the moving film aircraft image onto a curved projection screen.

In the end, Henry's original idea of filming real aircraft to be projected in the Dome was not feasible since the exact position and range of the aircraft in the air could not be precisely calculated. Therefore, films were made using stop-frame photography in which aircraft models were photographed frame by frame in different positions and ranges, following a pre-calculated and scripted flight plan of an attack. Technicolor Ltd worked with Henry to produce a prototype Dome Trainer and confirmed the initial cinematographic limitations; they also went on to produce the Dome Trainer equipment. The films were also produced by Technicolor, who manually made complicated calculations to determine the flight plan and to enable the profile of the cams for each film to be ascertained and manufactured. Films of German, Italian and Japanese aircraft were produced during the war.

The gimbal-mounted mirror was moved by two thin steel wires attached to two cam-following arms tracing the profile of two cams (one for traverse and one for elevation) that were manufactured in accordance with the scripted flight plan. As only one cable was used for traverse and elevation, return springs were attached to the mirror. The mirror was limited to 180° in traverse and 90° in elevation, meaning that half of a Dome's surface would be used for projection. The rotating cams were driven by the projector's film-advancing motor. Movement of the target aircraft via the cam-controlled mirror were thereby synchronised precisely with the film. One rotation of the cams would equal the length of one film. For longer training sessions, multiple lengths of the same film and further cam rotations could be used. To give a variety of different attacks, a number of different films and their specific pairs of cams were produced.

A third cam (or electrical contacts on a two-cam assembly) indicated a range for the target aircraft, only visible to the instructors. It showed if the gunner was opening fire too soon when the target was still out of range, thus wasting ammunition and leaving the gunner without ammunition at the most effective moment of the attack, and also defenceless.

A synchronised sound track on the film would produce the noise via speakers of the attacking aircraft with its weapons firing and the sound of bombs falling and exploding, together with the noise of the defending A.A. gun. Guns were either a rifle-calibre machine gun or a larger 40mm LAA gun. The machine-gun option gave a continuous five-second burst of fire or a total of five seconds in shorter bursts. This represented the firing period of a Lewis gun with a small ammunition pan (magazine). The larger LAA gun had a total firing period of fifteen seconds. The Dome's smooth, round inner surface had great acoustic qualities and created an incredibly immersive environment.

The target aircraft on the various attack films were produced on a circular film frame rather than the usual rectangular frame. The idea of this was to make it easier to merge the light circular background of the target image into the blue-sky lighting. However, the edge of circular film frame still appeared brilliant and sharp, and to make it merge more effectively with the new scenic projection a 'vignette' was fitted to the target projector to diffuse the sharp edge.

To provide an indication to an instructor of where the trainee gunner should be aiming, a yellow spot was printed ahead of the aircraft on the film. This was the Future Position (FP) of the enemy aircraft. To fit the spot on the same frame of film as the aircraft, spot and aircraft image were pushed to opposite edges of the frame. The yellow spot would not be visible to the trainee, due to either a yellow filter being positioned in the gun sight or yellow filter glasses being worn by the gunner. The FP position also varied depending upon the speed of the target aircraft and the shell velocity of the type of LAA gun. Differing films and cams were used for each type of weapon.

The instructor could see where the gun was being aimed, as an image of the gun sight was projected from a gun sight projector mounted on the gun. This was not visible to the gunner as the actual gun sight would be aligned so that it coincided exactly with the projected gun sight image. When the centre of the image from the gun sight projector coincided with the yellow FP spot, the instructor knew that the gunner was scoring hits as long as the target was within range.

With the advent of the jet aircraft age after the Second World War, and increasing aircraft speed, any Future Position yellow spot needed to be much further ahead of the aircraft. This could not be fitted within the film frame of the target aircraft. It therefore became necessary to have a new separate yellow FP spot projector mounted on top of the main projector. This projected the yellow FP spot onto a new secondary smaller gimbal-mounted FP mirror above the main mirror.

At first this FP mirror was controlled by cam followers, using the existing main mirror elevation and traverse cams, but positioned in advance of the existing cam followers. This then anticipated the aircraft movements and always moved the FP mirror so that it kept the yellow FP Spot in front of the aircraft. This common use of the cams did not always give the correct future position, and so a second set of elevation and traverse cams, calculated for the correct and varying FP were mounted onto the existing main mirror cams assembly complete with their own cam followers. The maximum FP spot distance would be required for a flight directly across the front of the A.A. gun (left to right, or vice versa). For an attack approaching the A.A. gun at 45° the aiming point would be roughly half the above distance.

At one time it was envisaged that the diameter of the yellow FP spot would vary in size according to the range of the target. At greater distances the spot would be two inches in diameter, representing a target more difficult to hit. As the aircraft flew nearer to the gun position the diameter would increase up to eight inches. The size of the spot would be changed by having a variable aperture iris fitted to the front of the FP spot projector which would be driven by the range cam/contacts. However, as the gunner under training would not normally view the yellow spot (unless the instructor allowed him to remove the yellow filter or glasses to emphasise some point), and linking an iris mechanism to the range cams/contacts would add complication, this feature was not adopted.

Henry Stephens also proposed using an invisible pulsed FP infra-red spot (instead of the yellow spot) which could be picked up by a photo-electric cell mounted on the gun. This would register on an instructor's visual device when the gunner was aiming on target and show the hits on target. However, this was also judged to be too complex and expensive. The static yellow filter was therefore retained. Later post-war Domes made by RFD (see plates 37 & 38) did use a pulsed yellow spot. This registered on a photo-electric cell mounted on the gun and aligned with the gun sight which recorded 'on target' and 'hits scored' on an instructor's Gunnery Display Unit (see Plate 12).

The general lighting in a Dome consisted of two fluorescent tubes on the back wall, flooding the whole Dome with an even white light. When an attack was being projected, the general lighting would be switched off and a single low-light blue fluorescent tube would be switched on. This provided an illusion of distance when looking into the blue void of the sky. To simulate low visibility, night or dusk attacks, suitable filters were placed in front of the projector's lens so that an aircraft could be heard approaching but could not be seen until it was relatively close.

To enhance the realism of the Dome Trainer, a landscape or seascape colour slide was projected around the base of the Dome screen surface. The projector was mounted above and behind the gun position so that no shadow was created, and the image was of low enough intensity to merge with the blue-sky lit screen and not interfere with the aircraft target image or yellow FP spot. On later post-war Domes manufactured by RFD, four or five scenic projectors were placed on the floor a few feet away from the radius of the Dome screen, with each projecting part of a 180° panoramic scene.

A cloud/sky projection system designed by Henry, consisting of an inverted glass goldfish-type bowl with two cloud/sky scenes painted on its internal surface, was granted a Patent No. GB707877 (see Plate 9). This was on a tall pole behind the gun position in the Dome and with a light placed within. A commercial cloud projector consisting of a clear cloud-painted disc rotating in front of a projected light was available in later RFD Domes.

In 1945 Henry returned to his earlier concept of filming actual aircraft (rather than stop-frame models) carrying out dummy attacks upon an anti-aircraft position. He invented a 'Photographic Table' that was used to film real aircraft. Whilst filming, the device recorded the range and angle from the camera of the aircraft being filmed. This information could be directly translated into the profile data needed for the elevation and traverse cams that moved the target projection mirror. The 'Photographic Table' marked out these profiles onto a blank cam that could then be taken away and cut out. However, the original standard of film was judged sufficient, and Dome Trainer films produced after 1945 still used aircraft models with stop frame photography.

After the Second World War, Dome Trainer manufacturing was taken over by RFD and films were changed. Instead of a solid dark aircraft image on a pale circular film framebackground, a pale/white aircraft image on a blue circular film frame background was used. In the original films the pale circular film frame background could be seen by the trainee gunner, who then tended to just looked for the pale circle rather than picking out the aircraft image itself. With a light aircraft image, the surrounding darker blue circular film frame background merged much more readily with the blue lit interior of the dome screen, making the aircraft image much more prominent.

The system with two mirrors (the Main and FP) was known as the Double Mirror Column. Dufty Engineering Limited, with Henry Stephens as a director, patented a different type of Double Mirror column to the Technicolor/RFD one. However, this did not go into production, and RFD bought Dufty Engineering with all rights and patents.

Chapter 7

American and Canadian Dome Trainers

On 26 September 1941 the US Navy ordered the units of the Atlantic Fleet to protect all ships engaged in commerce in United States defensive waters. The orders authorised the Navy to patrol, escort merchantmen and attack any German or Italian naval forces.

Both the United States and Canada imported the Dome Trainer technology to train ships' companies, especially those engaged in Atlantic convoys. Land-based Domes were equipped with a fixed gunnery platform. Adaptations for naval conditions included the Royal Canadian Navy at HMCS *Cornwallis* in Nova Scotia adding machine guns mounted on moveable bases to simulate ship movement at sea.

The War Diary of the operations zone under COMEASTSEAFRONT (Command of Eastern Sea Front, USA) from 1 December 1941 to 30 June 1942 refers to defensive training by the Eastern Sea Frontier, including the Dome Trainer:

> Throughout the month efforts were made by the Commander, Eastern Sea Frontier to increase still further the scope and efficiency of our anti-submarine warfare. In the first week of June, the Commandants of all the Naval Districts within the Frontier were directed to set up anti-submarine warfare training centres. To assist the Commandants in this venture, instructions, blueprints and a list of necessary instruments accompanied the directive. These training centres at Boston, New York, Cape May, Norfolk and Charleston were to be equipped with an attack teacher, the Dome Teacher for practice in anti-aircraft machine gun fire, lookout training room and a library and reading room where all available ASW (anti-submarine warfare) publications, both US and Allied, would be readily available to officers of anti-submarine vessels.
>
> At the same time that this directive went out to all activities, the Commander, Eastern Sea Frontier recommended strongly to the Commander, Gulf Sea Frontier that similar training centres should be established in his activity . . . Captain Hungerford was instrumental in developing plans for training bases similar to those British schools he had seen at Halifax and Londonderry. After careful preparation of the ground through preliminary steps, Commander Eastern Sea Frontier sent to his Task Group Commanders in the competent naval districts, a letter directing that each of them begins immediately to establish a

> training centre for ASW, each centre to include the following: (1) Attack Teacher, for use of patrol and escort vessels. (2) Reading Room, which would contain a confidential library of current ASW publications, British and American. (3) Lookout Training Room modelled closely after the one already in use at New London. (4) Dome Teacher, for use training crews in anti-aircraft fire.

On 25 August 1942 an inspection of a naval base at East Boston, Commonwealth Pier No 1 recommended: 'It is the intention to install an Attack Teacher, a Dome Teacher, a night lookout trainer and a confidential publication reading room on the Pier.'

The USS *Bristol* (DD 453) noted in her War Diary of April 1942: 'Moored 27th and 28th at Naval Base, Londonderry. At 0900 on 29th shifted to Naval Pier, Lisahally, (about two miles downriver). Carried out 'harbour training' (ASDIC attack teacher, Dome Teacher, lookout table).'

The War Diary of the USS *Washington* (1200 11 April to 13 April 1942) noted her arrival at Scapa Flow, the Royal Navy base in Orkney:

I. Moored to Buoy E, Scapa Flow. Rigged torpedo defence net along port side. (b) HMS *King George V*, HMS *Victorious*, HMS Du*ke of York*, HMS *Kent* and HMS *Nigeria* stood out. Held searchlight drills Saturday night. Held Divine services Sunday morning.

II. (1200 12 April 1942 to 1200 13 April 1942). (a) Morning of 13th underway for operational area. Exercised at streaming and recovering paravanes. (b) Held the following drills and instructions: (1) Dummy fire control runs (2) Main and secondary battery spotting board drill (3) Loading drill for main and secondary batteries (4) Instruction of one/75 battery in anti-aircraft fire-control and ammunition supply (5) Sent twenty men to 'Dome Teacher' for instruction in 'sight control'. (6) Sent forty marines to rifle range for sighting in and field exercise (7) Sent fifteen men from repair parties to Fire-Fighting School, Lyness.

III. (1200 13 April 1942 to 1200 14 April 1942). (a) Conducting five degaussing calibration runs in afternoon. Moored to Buoy 'E', Scapa Flow upon completion at 1530. Underway Tuesday morning with USS *Wichita*, USS *Wilson*, USS *Wainwright* and USS *Sterrett* for exercises. (b) Held the following drills and instructions (1) Main battery radar tracking on island (2) Secondary battery tracking on anti-submarine patrol plane. (3) Anti-aircraft batteries exercised at repelling simulated torpedo attack by RAF Beaufort planes.

IV. (1200 16 April 1942 to 1200 17 April 1942) (a) Took aboard aviation gasoline. Exercised at searchlight drill in evening, in conjunction with shore searchlight batteries. (b) Friday morning got under way at 0800, and anchored in Berth B2, Scapa Flow for deperming by HMS *Magic Circle*. Rigged connections and sent all watches, clocks and delicate removable mechanisms ashore.

Deperming, or degaussing (wiping a current-carrying cable up and down a hull), temporarily removed a magnetic field from steel ships so that they would not trigger magnetic mines. Contact sea mines were moored or floating with 'horns' made of metal and holding a glass container of battery acid. The base of a horn contained an electric battery without electrolyte. Contact with the horn broke open the acid container, powering the battery to heat a platinum wire in a mercury fulminate detonator and exploding the mine.

This War Diary reflected how, after arriving in Scapa Flow, USS *Wichita* and the other American ships spent several weeks training with their British counterparts. On 28 April 1942 the *Wichita* sailed on a joint operation with the British, assigned to the Allied ships of the Arctic convoys QP 11 and PQ 15. The American ships, named Task Force 99, comprised USS *Washington*, USS *Wichita*, USS *Tuscaloosa* and four destroyers. The British ships were the carrier HMS *Victorious*, battleship HMS *King George V*, a light cruiser and five destroyers. USS *Wichita* and USS *Wasp* returned to Scapa Flow on 29 May after serving protection for the Murmansk-bound convoy PQ 16 and eastbound QP 12. King George VI inspected *Wichita* on 7 June. In June the ships were assigned to protect convoy PQ 17. The convoy's escort included USS *Washington*, HMS *Victorious* and the battleship HMS *Duke of York*, all moored together as recorded in the War Diary of the *USS Washington*.

At Rinnigill, Scapa Flow, Orkney, are the ruined remains of a Night Attack or Torpedo Attack Teacher, inside a building visited by the author in 2015. It is likely that this structure was used by all the crews mentioned in the various war diaries, alongside the Dome Trainer. The circular plaster bowl structure trained ships' crews for night torpedo attacks on enemy shipping. It consisted of a moving bridge mock-up mounted on a circular platform representing the sea, all housed in a building without windows. A lighting system simulated a ship at dawn or evening as viewed from the bridge with various levels of illumination. The target was a model ship mounted on a circular ring, raised or lowered to give distance with limited structure showing. A bearing would be passed to the helm and the bridge moved to the new heading. If illumination was ordered, especially to identify and avoid firing on friendly shipping, the instructors requested a simulated star shell towards the target bearing. A man moved around the outside ring to a place that matched the bearing. A small bulb was turned on and lowered on a string to light up a target. The structure was plywood and painted dark blue with no sky colour.

On 10 and 11 January 1944, the War Diary of Destroyer Division 32 noted: 'USS *Champlin* and USS *Nields* moored at Queen's Dock, Swansea, Wales. During this period Annual Military Inspection was conducted aboard *Champlin and Nields* by Commander Destroyer Division 32, assisted by Boards from each vessel. Training facilities available such as A.A. Dome Teacher and AAMG (anti-aircraft machine gun) firing were utilised.' The experience of USS *Nields* was typical of convoy escorts trained within Dome Trainers. During 1943 and 1944 she protected both Mediterranean and British convoys including UGF-10, GUF-12, UTF-three, KMF-25-A, TU-03 and TU-6. The War Diary for February 1944 of the USS *Daniel T Griffin* recorded:

> Moored port side to USS *Reeves*, Pier 17, Naval Operations Base, Londonderry, N. I. In company with escort Division Six undergoing minor repairs and awaiting rendezvous with [convoy] UC-12. During this period *Griffin* availed itself with excellent training facilities on shore station, Naval Operations Base, including Dome Trainer, (crews on anti-aircraft at Pier 17), Night Lookout Trainer, Attack Teacher, Night Attack Teacher, radio drill circuits, signal drill and convoy duties. Recreational facilities and USO shows considered excellent. Medical needs of crew were furnished by Naval Hospital, Naval Operating Base, which included seven (7) tonsillectomies.

On 3 February *Griffin* recorded: '1305 under way with pilot for refuelling Docks, Lisahally. 1405 Moored alongside USS *Donnell*, birth 'D' Lisahally to take on fuel'. On 7 February *Griffin* was 'under way at 0658 in compliance with Atlantic Fleet Escort Control, Londonderry, Escort order 3-44, joining Convoy UC-12, taking station at position 3 of 6 in escort screen. Base course 26670 T, top speed 10 knots; search area are CO5° T to 225° T.'

Dated 19 January 1944, the War Diary of the Destroyer Escort Division 19 included USS *Amesbury*, USS *Bull*, USS *Rich* and USS *Bunc*h. Deployed elsewhere were USS *Bates* and USS *Blessman*. The Diary records: 'Division 19 moored starboard side, Pier 19, Naval Operating Base, Londonderry, Northern Ireland. On Thursday 20th January 1944, ships of the division carried out upkeep and training. Activities being carried out or attended while at Londonderry are Division Gunnery School, Attack Teacher, Night Lookout Table, Aircraft Recognition, Anti-aircraft Dome Trainer and radio drill with the base.'

Having escorted twenty-six vessels with five other escorts before being relieved by HMS *Lawson* off Torry Island, Division 19 returned to Lisahally. On 19 April 1944 the War Diary continued:

> Division moored at Lisahally, Naval Operating Base, Northern Ireland, receiving commissary supplies and oil aboard. Personnel attended Attack Teacher, NEAT, Tactical Game, Lookout School, recognition school, A.A. Dome Trainer and other schools. CpmCortDiv-20 held Surprise Inspection of all ships of Division during this period, in accordance with Deslant Letter X-8. At 1000/19April, Board of Investigation, Comdr. P.B. Mavor, USCG, Senior member, convened on board to inquire into death of two men by drowning on 7th April 1944.

The War Diary of USS *YP228* dated 3 May 1944 (ref 3/1-31/44) refers to a report from Commander A.W. Moffat, USNR to the Commander, Northern Group. Moffat was ordered to take his ship to Digby, Nova Scotia, and to liaise with Captain J.C. Edwards, Royal Canadian Navy:

> Aboard USS YP228 I arrived at Digby, Nova Scotia at 1100 on April 26th. . . . Driven by Lt-Commander Gage, RCNVR., Operations Officer to the station which is located at Cornwallis, Nova Scotia, ten miles north of Digby on the Annapolis Basin beyond Deep Brook. The establishment HMCS *Cornwallis* has now been chartered as the town of Cornwallis, Nova Scotia, with its own Canadian Pacific Railway station and post office. The present personnel consist of about 7,000 trainee who have been though boot school and are at *Cornwallis* to be qualified in ratings other than communications . . . The gunnery training is particularly impressive. In a building 700 foot long is located every type of gun and turret used in the British Navy up to three-inch twin mounts. The machine guns in the Dome Trainer are mounted on movable bases to simulate ship movements at sea [see Plate 22]. The second floor of the A/S building is equipped with a dozen or more Attack /Dome Teachers complete with sound. Departure was made from Digby at 1500 Q April 27th, for Cutler, Maine. USS YP228 arrived at Bar Harbour at 1200 Q April 28th.

Commander Moffat's visit reflected the fact that the base at *Cornwallis* served as a principal training facility for Canadian forces, serving more than 500,000 students during the Second World War. HMCS *Cornwallis* at Deep Brook was created by the 1942 reorganisation of naval facilities in Halifax, Nova Scotia. This was the largest naval training base for new recruits and naval crews in the British Dominions and Empire during the Second World War, including Stephens Dome Trainers within the HMCN Gunnery School.

On 21 March 1943, the Air Support Group under Air Commodore A.V. Buckley, Royal New Zealand Air Force was involved in operations 'to conduct landing force exercises in Omaha and Kawau Bay areas, North Island, New Zealand at 0900. Held machine gun practice for ships gunners at Dome Trainer on Dock.'

A contemporary secret US Navy evaluation of the Dome Trainer explained its popularity and the effective training of Americans using Henry's invention, even with rudimentary understanding of how it worked:

> This Teacher is primarily a practical and realistic means of training machine gun layers to estimate the correct sight offset for any rapidly moving target at any time it is within effective range. In addition, the gunner learns when to commence and cease firing so that ammunition is not wasted on an out of range or receding target and is accustomed to the rapid and accelerating rates of train and elevation of the target.
>
> All equipment is located at the centre of a hemispherical room approximately twenty-five (25) feet in diameter. A dummy gun, consisting of two grips, a trigger

and a ring sight assembly is mounted at normal gun height and may be moved in both train and elevation. Attached to the dummy gun is a shielded lamp which projects the image of the ring sight and cross wires on the bulkhead. Immediately below the dummy gun is a mirror so mounted that it may be trained or elevated by gearing. A motion picture projector, mounted at an angle to the deck, projects its beam of light to the centre of this mirror. The films used seem to be motion pictures of actual attacks by enemy aircraft.

The exact method of directing the mirror is not known but it is believed that a cam and follow up provide the directive force; a different cam is used for each film. Each film is accompanied by appropriate sound effects such as long-range anti-aircraft fire, heavy machine gun fire, aircraft machine gun fire, aircraft engines and light and heavy bomb explosions, close aboard on board. Above the gunners' head is an indicator which shows the range to the target continuously. The firing key of the dummy gun closes the circuits of a motor-driven set of noise makers which duplicate the sound and rate of fire of whatever calibre gun is selected. Each frame of the film after the target reaches a range of about 1,000 yards is marked with a yellow spot which indicates the correct position of the centre of the sight.

The report continued:

When the equipment is operated the room is illustrated with a blue light. The picture is reflected from the mirror to the bulkhead and travels left or right and up and down at the same angular rate as the subject of the film would. The student sights the target which at first appears as a pin point except in the case of low-level bomb attack on an adjacent ship. From its initial position angle, manoeuvres and later appearance he identifies the type of plane, speed and target angle, then estimates the proper lead off.

As the aircraft approaches, he looks through the sight, puts the target at the proper position. When the target is at the proper range, he presses his key. If fire is opened too soon the dummy gun will cease firing before the attack is completed. If the gunner has selected the correct position of the target on the ring sight and has kept it corrected for the changing attitude of the aircraft the centre of the projected ring sight image will coincide with the yellow spot.

For men who have had no previous instruction in the use of the ring sight, a two-reel instructional film has been prepared which fully explains the use of the sight. For advanced training a yellow filter is placed over the rear sight so the gunner does not see the yellow spot and must use his own estimate of lead and the time to open fire. With constant training, the gunner will instinctively take the correct lead on the sight based on angular velocity of the target rather than

> the more cumbersome method of estimating speed of target and target angle. The student also overcomes the tendency to commence firing too soon caused by the high-pitched drone of the approaching aircraft and the noise of heavier guns. Several films also require a quick shift to another target in the same or different types of attack to train the gunner to disregard possible damage in his vicinity and prevent gazing after an enemy about which he can do nothing.
>
> The Dome Trainer is superior to usual practice firing or tracking drill because the Dome Trainer targets are moving with the same angular speed and in the same direction as an attacking aircraft. In addition, the yellow spot and projected ring sight shows the gun to be hitting or not hitting. Use of the Dome Trainer is not restricted by weather conditions as are many of the training period at machine gun schools. The use of the ring sight is also believed essential, even if tracers are to be used. Fire must be opened close enough to the target to enable the gunner to correct his tracer stream in the very short period that the aircraft is within effective range.

The report included a visit and demonstration of an A.A. Dome Trainer:

> A Dome Trainer simulator was inspected at Malta in a Territorial Army Drill Hall. The Dome was made of plywood on a wooden framework. It was 20ft in diameter, and supported 7ft off the ground. Documents included a 'User Handbook for Apparatus, Dome Training, Version No6, dated 1962. This apparatus is an anti-aircraft gunnery trainer developed on principles similar to the Apparatus Dome Training Version No4. Used in conjunction with a service dome, it provides a substitute for field training with aircraft co-operation when training anti-aircraft gunners on LAA weapons. It provides also realistic gunnery practice under conditions closely resembling those experienced in actual warfare.

Similar to the training at HMS *Chrysanthemum*, in June 1942 the USAAF reported via the Flying Training Command a 'great need' for a tracer trainer, urging the adoption of a British model if American experiments failed. Tests at the Kingsman Army Air Field, Arizona in August 1943 under the 'Pinball' programme involved a B-17 Flying Fortress bomber used for firing dummy ammunition at attacking fighter aircraft in flight. However, the USAAF reported that 'in every case the individual whose tracer appeared to be piercing the target and who might be considered to have high scores received no hits on the target, and in every case the individuals whose tracer appeared not to pierce the target were in all cases the individuals who received hits on the target.' Bespoke film with a tracer attachment was sent to America by Technicolor Films on 20 August 1945.

Canada was an excellent choice for aircrew and gunnery training for home-grown crew and Allied forces. The British Commonwealth Air Training Plan was a wartime agreement to March 1945. At the peak of the war, 94 schools operated 231 sites across Canada, with 10,840 aircraft and 104,113 men and women. Over 3,000 students graduated each month. At a cost of more than US$1.6 billion, 131,553 pilots, navigators, bomb aimers, wireless operators, air gunners and flight engineers were trained in Canada (see plates 13 & 17).

A typical Royal Canadian Air Force site was No. 5 Elementary Flying Training School at High River, Alberta, set up in June 1941 and expanding in November to No. 8 Bombing & Gunnery School. A hundred square miles of land was leased from the Blood Indian Reserve nearby, and Fairey Battle, Westland Lysander, Avro Anson and Bristol Bolingbroke aircraft provided target towing and gunnery bombing practice. No. 8 Bombing & Gunnery School offered training to Observers (8 weeks), Navigators (8 weeks), Bomb Aimers (12 weeks), Wireless Air Gunners (12 weeks) and Air Gunners (12 weeks). As in Britain and America, there was intensive ground and simulator training, rather than flying. Between 1940 and 1942 an Observer in training rated only twenty hours in an aircraft, with air gunners only flying for seven hours.

The gunnery curriculum included learning to load, aim and clean standard .303 machine guns before using the ranges for live firing. As in Britain and America, gunners in Canada moved on to ground-based aircraft turrets with multiple machine guns. Flying experience was in Fairey Battle aircraft shooting at targets on the ground and at airborne drogues towed by Lysanders. To pass, students had to be able to recognise seventy-two different types of aircraft.

Another example of a Royal Canadian Air Force station was at Jarvis, Ontario. This station was home to No. 1 Bombing and Gunnery School from August 1940 to February 1945, and 6,500 airmen were trained here, using turret configurations for Frazer-Nash and Boulton Paul gun camera and .303 standard machine guns.

The Naval Air Gunnery School No 1 at Yarmouth, Nova Scotia, (nicknamed 'Nags'), was unique as it only trained air gunners flying pre-Second World War 'string bag' Swordfish for the Royal Navy`s Fleet Air Arm.

Part of the Royal Canadian Air Force in Britain during the Second World War was No. 6 Group under RAF Bomber Command, using Dome Trainers for airfield defence from 19 November 1942 to 23 July 1945. Records were declassified in April 1986.

On 31 January 1945, Bomber Command Headquarters 'adjusted the list of Dome Trainer responsibilities via a "Secret" Form 348 to HQ for 1,3, 4, 5, 6, 7, 8, 9, 91, 92, 93 and 100 Groups and HQ (Unit), British Columbia with ref BC/S. S8155/Def. A.A. Dome Teacher. It has been decided that Zonal Stations Docking and Bircham Newton be transferred from West Raynham to Langham. It is requested that Appendix 'A' to this Headquarters letter of even reference dated 14th February 1944 be amended accordingly.' Additional orders dated 4 June 1945 added, 'The screening of Dome Teacher gunnery instructors and Projectionists from normal posting has been authorised for a further period of six months, until 1st December 1945.'

With a Dome Trainer, RAF Docking hosted Canadians of No. 407 Squadron and Dutch of No. 320 Squadron, who flew combined operations with Hudson aircraft to attack coastal shipping. At least three aircraft were lost in 1942 for every ship sunk. Docking closed in 1945 but continued to be used for aircrew waiting to return to civilian life, including the actors Richard Burton, Warren Mitchell and Robert Hardy.

RAF Birch Newton was another base used to attack the Dutch coast and Friesian Islands. Squadrons included No. 235 Squadron (Blenheim), No.500 Squadron (Anson and Hudsons), No.415 Canadian Squadron and No. 524 Squadron, flying Wellington bombers against E-boats. No. 320 Dutch Squadron (Hudson) and No. 407 Canadian Squadron (Hudson) were shared with RAF Docking. Birch Newton closed for operations in December 1962, ending a long and distinguished RAF service of more than forty-four years involving more than eighty flying units.

Gunners of all nationalities recorded their various experiences of a Stephens Dome Trainer:

> 'One particular film sticks in my memory. Stuka dive-bombers did a circuit of the Dome, then turned towards the gun. A few moments later when they were nearly overhead, they started to peel off. They shrieked into their dive straight at the guns. As the first flattened out and went overhead I could almost count the rivets in its fuselage. The 'crump' of exploding bombs filled the air.' (Tom Wright, No. 222 RAF fighter squadron, based at Hornchurch, who came to Langham for a week's A.A. course in 1943) (see plates 14 & 23)
>
> 'The object of the exercise was to check out those who were so affected by the screaming noise of the aircraft and the sound of the shots coming from the enemy that they ducked. I was top of the class but found this to be of little use when two years later I was demobilised. Who wants a top gunner in civvy street?' (Ken Roe, 2nd class Coxswain on an RAF Rescue Launch, Dome Trainer on the Isle of Man)
>
> 'The men found it very intriguing, new and exciting. Much more realistic than shooting at towed targets just going across in front of you. In the Dome the whole point was to pick up the enemy aircraft and shoot it down before it dropped its bombs- not after it had gone away.' (Alan Eade, Dome Trainer instructor, Lieutenant in the Norfolk Yeomanry [TA] at Langham Dome 1956–68)
>
> 'We had ten or eleven different films to practise different things. The men took it very seriously. They were in full uniform with all their equipment. They operated the gun as they would have done in the field. It was very realistic. There was the true gun sound 'bang, bang, bang' as the gun fired. Very, very noisy.' (Ron Williams, Dome Trainer instructor [TA] using a Bofors gun in a Dome Trainer)

'The main lights went down and quietly at first came the sound of an aircraft, but from which direction? Left, right, ahead, behind, above? When the targets appeared and one opened fire the row was unforgettable – the clatter of a Browning, plus the engine's guns and bombs.' (Mr Ellison of Luton, Flight mechanic 1941–46, Dome Trainer at RAF Fairford)

'I can well remember obtaining 47 hits out of 600 rounds. We could have happily spent our entire camp in there, it was such tremendous fun for us youngsters.' (Ronald Mells of Liss, ATC Cadet, Dome Trainer at annual camp at Lee-on-Solent in 1945)

However, wartime use of Dome Trainers was coming to an end. On 25 February 1945 Bomber Command Headquarters sent a 'Secret' Postagram to the same Groups and Headquarters: 'It is requested that Appendix 'A' to this Headquarters' letter of even reference dated 4th February 1944 be amended as under: To Ipswich, add Bentwaters. To Hornchurch, add Andrews Field and Chigwell. To Stradishall add Great Dunmow, Rivenhall and Wethersfield. From Andover, delete Worthy Down. From Inverness delete Fearn.'

On 26 May 1945, the Group 76 (RCAF) base at Topcliffe sent a reallocation of Dome Teacher training to Dalton, Wombleton, Dishforth, Skipton, Leeming and Topcliffe:

> Commencing Monday, 4th June 1945 and continuing until further orders: Mondays – Topcliffe. Tuesdays – Dalton and Skipton. Wednesdays – Dishforth. Thursdays – Wombleton. Fridays – Leeming. (Saturdays and Sundays excluded).
>
> Each station will send 10 students per day with the exception of Dalton who will send two students and Skipton who will send eight students. Students will report to the Dome Teacher at 09.00 hours and will be dismissed at 16-30 hours. Nearest railway station is Topcliffe. They will bring knife, fork & spoon. The mid-day meal will be provided by 76 (R.C.A.F.) base. Stations will be responsible for all transport arrangements. Copies to 6 & 7 Groups).

On 13 July 1945, Bomber Command Headquarters a further Postagram to the same Groups and Headquarters:

> The undermentioned list of 16mm Dome Teachers which will be closed with effect from 1st August 1945 is given for information: Ayr, Biggin Hill, Carew Cheriton, Cambridge, Carlisle, Chipping Warden, Cranwell, Desford, Driffield, Halton, RAF Holmsley South, Netheravon, Northolt, Odiham, Pershore, Peterborough, Pocklington, Portreath, Spitalgate, Templeford, Ternhill, Watchfield, Yatesbury. (2) It is requested that where Dome Techer instruction is affected by these closings down, Groups will notify this Headquarters by

> 20th July 1945 of any suggestions that they may have to re-ordering of Stations in the Group area.

However, with the advent of the Cold War between the West and Soviet Russia, gunnery training demand continued after the end of the Second World War. The United States Army Combat Forces Journal No. 3 in October 1952 reported that Fort Blix, Texas was using similar techniques to the Dome Trainer, saving a fortune in live ammunition costs:

> At the Anti-aircraft Artillery Replacement Training Centre at Fort Blix, Texas, trainee-gunners 'fire' their weapons at airplanes 'flying' across a motion picture screen – and save the government about $835,000 a month by not shooting up live ammunition. The electronic equipment they use was developed by the British Navy during the Second World War. At Bliss it is used with both .50 calibre machine guns and 40mm guns. When an airplane 'flies' across the motion picture screen the complex electronic equipment established a correct 'lead' invisible to the gunner.
>
> When it is 'fired', tracer projectors go into action, showing the line of fire in correct relationship to where the gun is fired. The special projection system and special glasses worn by the gunner give the gunner a perception of distance that is exactly like he sees when firing live ammunition at an actual target. To further simulate actual firing conditions, the gunner hears both the sound of the attacking aircraft and the gun firing. There is even a recoil. The electronic system records 'ammunition' fired so that the gunner can check on his accuracy.

In Europe, training of aircrew and gunners commenced from the start of the war in September 1939. Walter Henry Layne (known to his friends as Wally) recorded his experiences as RAF aircrew, training at RAF Penrhos in Wales (see Plate 18):

> Divided into squads of six, the training of Air Gunners at 9 Bombing and Gunnery School consisted of a six-week course. Flying kit was issued along with a white flash to put in the airman's cap that denoted he was a trainee. Student airmen were promoted to Leading Aircraftsman (LAC) and were awarded a badge of a propeller to wear on a uniform sleeve.
>
> Alongside air gunner films, students covered classroom training in aircraft recognition, map reading, mathematics and basic navigation. All aircrew had to be familiar with pyrotechnics and all of the types of armament used with a variety of different weapons systems, especially the British Browning .303 machine gun. Weapons had to be dismantled and reassembled with blindfolds in under two minutes.

At Penrhos, training huts were equipped with Boulton Paul and Frazer-Nash turrets with a spotlight on to a cinema screen and realistic gunnery noise. Another gunnery choice was a drum-fed Vickers 'K' gas-operated .303 machine gun. Special buildings held the nose, upper and tail gun turrets of Bomber Command aircraft. Gunners practised maintenance, loading and firing the two or four guns of the highly manoeuvrable Frazer-Nash, Boulton Paul and Bristol gun turrets. Fully glazed turrets were operated by either electrical or hydraulic power, normally provided by aircraft engines. The ground-mounted training turrets were fitted with cine cameras which recorded the accuracy of the student's shooting and showed whether the gunner was firing high or low in relationship to the target.

At Penrhos, live firing used a portable gun turret mounted on rails, firing at a moving wooden aircraft. Six students flew in a Whitley bomber. They fired a single machine-gun-fitted front turret, then the four guns in the powered Frazer-Nash rear turret. Every fifth round was loaded with tracer. A 7 per cent hit ratio was considered successful and was calculated on the number of hits to shoot an enemy aircraft down.

Wally qualified as an Air Gunner in February 1941 and was shot down over Germany in September 1943 as part of the crew of Lancaster Mk.III JA708. After sixty-four missions, Wally spent the remainder of the war as a prisoner.

A disused Dome Trainer is at the decommissioned RAF Pembrey Airfield (see Plate 30) in Wales, where in 1941 Polish Air Force Squadron 316 was formed. Pembrey was home to No. 1 Air Gunners School, training with Bristol Blenheim, Vickers Wellington bombers and Spitfires. Pembrey witnessed the inadvertent capture of an intact German fighter. On 23 June 1942, a Focke-Wulf Fw190 landed there in error after a battle over the Bristol Channel. Oberleutnant Armin Faber, adjutant of III fighter Gruppe of JG2, had been involved in a dogfight with Spitfires of 19 Squadron and the Czech Wing over South Devon. Disorientated, he then mistook the Bristol Channel for the English Channel and, short on fuel, landed at Pembrey, believing it to be a Luftwaffe airfield in the Cotentin Peninsula, Normandy. Faber was piloting the latest enemy fighter, the Focke-Wulf 190A-3, only seen flying in France.

Henry's private journal on 27 July 1943 records the deployment of the first 148 Dome Trainers, including installation of the prototype Dome Trainer at HMS *Excellent*, the Royal Navy Gunnery School at Whale Island, Portsmouth. Admiralty Home stations ordered forty-one, with Admiralty Overseas stations ordering forty and four spares. Royal Air Force ground defence ordered thirty. The Army Small Arms School ordered a prototype for Port Said, followed by twenty-seven for the Army Anti-Aircraft force in Britain and four units for the Army overseas. In 1945, cams and films for the Dome Trainer produced by Technicolor in Britain were sent to Alexandria, the Middle East, Gibraltar, Malta, America, Algiers, Karachi, Sri Lanka (see Plate 19) and Canada.

Chapter 8

Air-to-Air Gunnery – Operation Pinball in the USA

With the entry of the United States into the Second World War in 1941, both naval anti-aircraft defences as simulated by the Dome Trainer and airborne gunnery training became crucial for their inexperienced aircrew in all fighting theatres. Over occupied Europe and Germany, whilst the RAF's Bomber Command pursued night bombing raids, the US Army Air Force's Eighth Air Force's B17 Flying Fortress's and B24 Liberator heavy bombers carried out attacks on the enemy in daylight, initially without any protection from fighters once over land.

Training soon revealed the challenges of moulding a fighting machine from civilians. Following the statement, 'If God wanted us to fly, he would have given us wings', the American Army Air Force from 1941 suffered non-combat losses of men and aircraft in meeting the demand for more and more aircrew and equipment. In training alone, according to the USAAF Statistical Digest from December 1941 to August 1945, the US Army Air Force lost 14,903 pilots, aircrew and assorted personnel and 13,873 aircraft in the United States. A thousand planes vanished when travelling from the United States, and 43,581 were lost outside America, including 22,948 on combat missions and 20,633 by non-combat causes.

Built in August 1934 to match the US Army Air Corps' requirement for a large multi-engine bomber capable of carrying a 'useful bomb load' at an altitude of 10,000ft with a top speed of at least 200mph, the B-17 Flying Fortress became one of the most famous bombers for its dangerous and unescorted daylight bombing raids over Europe. The American actor Clark Gable was an officer of the Eighth Air Force and trained as an aerial gunner on B-17 bombers. He was asked to make a film to recruit aerial gunners and headed a six-man film crew. He flew five combat missions as an observer-gunner during May to September 1943 and narrated the film *Combat America*, released in 1945. It was an account of aerial combat over occupied Europe and a testament to the Eighth Air Force aircrew and ground crew in England.

However, despite carrying up to thirteen machine guns, Flying Fortress combat losses were catastrophic, with 4,750 B-17s lost to enemy action. In a June 1943 raid on Kiel and Bremen, twenty-six bombers were shot down and 260 aircrew were lost. Twenty-two of the downed planes carried inexperienced gunners and crews. In July,

German fighters destroyed 128 bombers. American crew claimed 545 German fighters that July, but this was adjusted down to only forty due to multiple guns from several planes claiming the same target. In a single raid of B-17 bombers over Germany in August 1943, sixty aircraft out of 376 were lost, a rate of 16 per cent, as well as 600 aircrew.

October 1943 saw the worst loss rate for the American Eighth Air Force in Europe of the entire war: 2,448 aircraft flew combat missions and 172 were lost. On 'Black Thursday', sixty bombers were lost, leading to a halt on long distance raids until December 1943, when the long-range P-51 Mustang fighter aircraft came into service. The chance of a B-17 crew completing a 25-mission tour was less than 30 per cent. Flak defences accounted for over 50 per cent of the USAAF's combat losses during the war in Europe, destroying almost 5,400 aircraft.

Over 4,000 bombers and fighter aircraft were shot down by Luftwaffe fighters, but American commanders were sceptical about the effectiveness of airborne gunnery defences. American bombers in the European theatre of operations used 26 million rounds of .50 ammunition in 1943, and 36 million rounds in 1944. In October 1943 the ammunition expenditure was 633,000 rounds per operational day, calculated as nearly 12,000 rounds for every enemy aircraft claimed to have been shot down by air gunners. American fighters calculated 2,800 rounds per enemy aircraft destroyed. Clearly, effective and realistic training had to be transformed!

In April 1943 Colonel Putnam, commander of the 306th Bomber Group, said that four gunners needed to fire simultaneously at an enemy fighter to have a 50 per cent probability of destroying it. Putnam estimated that one in ten of the gunners who only theoretically had a firing opportunity actually opened fire. Colonel Milton from the 308th Bomber Group said that defensive guns were often more a hazard than a protection, due to the danger of 'friendly fire' in the dense formation of planes required to ensure mutual protection.

The first American attack in Europe was by twelve B-17s of the new Eighth Air Force on 17 August 1942. RAF squadrons with sixty Spitfire IXs provided outward escort, and seventy-five escorted them home. Apart from slight damage from anti-aircraft guns, all the aircraft returned, with half their bombs landing near the railway marshalling yards at Rouen-Sotteville in France. None of the 144 machine guns on the twelve aircraft scored a hit during three attacks by Messerschmitt Bf109 fighters.

At the beginning of the war, as in the Dome Trainer, aircraft gunnery sights were a simple ring and bead type in which a gunner had to maintain constant eye contact. Accuracy depended on the gunner's skill in calculating deflections (the swerving path of fire towards the target), and it was extremely difficult to hit a moving target. A critical error in early training tactics was the assumption that attacks were expected from the rear of a bomber. The speed of the bomber would then be subtracted from the speed of the fighter, and closing speed was much reduced, allowing easier deflection and target hits. However, in combat they now faced the German tactic of head-on attack, in which the bomber's speed had to be added to the closing speed of a fighter. This gave very little realistic time to score hits.

Ring and beads were replaced by an optical reflector sight that avoided deflection errors by placing the reticule on the target. At the end of the war gunners were equipped with gyroscopically predicting or compensating sights to greatly improve accuracy. Early B-24 Liberators were fitted with a top turret, a nose gun, a tail turret and guns in waist positions. With waist positions always open and very limited heating, gunners suffered hours of flight up to 24,000ft at zero temperatures.

Early gunnery training was by use of shotguns mounted on the back of moving platforms, or more sophisticated gun camera and projection screen trainers, such as the Jam Handy and Waller trainers. Similar to the Stephens Dome Trainer, the Jam Handy was a portable unit with a gun camera which fired at film of moving targets. The more sophisticated Waller trainer was used to train four gunners simultaneously. Two operated turrets and two used remote aiming devices. The entire fixed training unit was housed in odd-shaped buildings to accommodate the cinema screen. Turret gunners used the Sperry ball turret, the Martin and Sperry upper turret, the Consolidated B-24 tail turret and a similar Emerson nose turret.

US students were given 288 hours of training in 1942; forty-four hours for the ring and bead, reflector, telescopic and compensation sights; eight hours for training of range accuracy; twelve hours on a Jam Handy trainer; and six hours on the Waller trainer.

Demand was insatiable. Nearly 20,000 American air gunners had been trained by July 1943, rising to a further 57,000 in the next six months. The Las Vegas Army Airfield trained 600 gunners and 200 pilots every five weeks. The more realistic training was by using live gun cameras to 'fire' at attacking fighters from the gun positions of medium and heavy bombers. However, as the scoring and correction of accuracy had to wait for the negatives to be printed after the flight, it was ruled as unsatisfactory.

A secret American project was therefore authorised to train air-to-air gunners by shooting 'frangible' bullets (a mixture of lead and plastic) from a bomber aircraft in flight at an armoured manned attacking fighter aircraft. Described by pilot Ivan Hickman in *Operation Pinball*, the target aircraft selected was the Bell P-63 Kingcobra fighter as an armoured flying target. Painted bright orange for extra visibility, and with a red nose light that was supposed to flash when hits were registered, these were flown with extra armour and a reinforced canopy. B-17 gunners fired at the P-63 with 'frangible' bullets that would disintegrate on impact with the Pinball's thick plating. Sensors located throughout the fuselage detected hits, triggering a light in the propeller spinner so gunners could tell when they had scored hits.

The 'Pinball' target aircraft, the P-63, was not judged suitable for European combat apart from supplies to Soviet forces under Lend-Lease. Designated as a RP-63A (restricted from combat use), five prototypes became known as 'Pinballs'. A further ninety-five RP-63As were ordered, followed by two hundred RP-63Cs in early 1945. In addition to the armour plating, over a hundred microphones were installed to indicate hits on a counter in the cockpit. A red light replaced the nose cannon in the propeller spinner and flashed every time the sensors recorded a hit by a frangible bullet.

The Pinball project was designed by Major Cameron Fairchild, based at Harlingen in 1942, who proposed non-lethal 'frangible' bullets. The initial idea was to use glass bullets, which would break apart and splinter upon hitting anything solid. Fairchild enlisted help from Professor Paul Gross and Professor Marcus Hobbs at Duke University. The US Army Ordnance Department, responsible for development of all weapons and ammunition, argued that any bullet that was truly frangible would not have the same ballistic characteristics as real ammunition. However, supported by the Bakelite Corporation and Duke University, Gross and Hobbs created a .30 calibre bullet made of lead and Bakelite (an early plastic) which could be fired from a modified machine gun. The bullet did not penetrate the armoured metal panels from 40ft.

The training of aerial gunners to operate defensive gun turrets and guns of the medium and heavy bombers of the USAAF began in June 1941. The first gunnery school opened at Las Vegas, in the Nevada desert. The site enjoyed good flying weather, with uninhabited land for gunnery practice. Aerial gunnery schools also opened in Arizona at Kingman and Yuma, in Texas at Harlingen and Laredo, and at Tyndall Field, Florida. A school for gunnery instructors opened at Buckingham Field, near Fort Meyers.

Early basic target recognition was based on the 'W.E.F.T.' format, a reminder to a gunner to look at 'Wings, Engines, Fuselage and Tail', and covered known German, Italian, British, Russian, Japanese and American aircraft profiles. However, as in the Stephens Dome Trainer, gunners spent too long trying to identify aircraft in the few seconds before a potential attack.

This system was quickly replaced with the 'Renshaw' flash tachistoscope. A series of images were flashed very rapidly on a screen for only 1/100th of a second, to create subliminal recognition of objects that were imprinted on the mind. Adopted by the US Navy to train 285,000 cadets, a Renshaw Recognition System (RRS) officer was posted to every US Navy ship from 1943.

Target aircraft were selected to match German equivalents. A single-engine fighter with a liquid-cooled engine would resemble the German Messerschmitt Bf 109s attacking American bombers in Europe.

The Army Air Force staged a demonstration of the new programme in March 1945, and training was ordered at all seven American gunnery schools. Adjustments were constantly required as gunsights were recalibrated for the lower velocity and different trajectory of frangible bullets. The lead and plastic caused guns to jam, and a danger was that real ammunition could become mixed in with the practice rounds. One Pinball pilot returned with a cracked 38mm armoured windscreen.

Armour was extended to protect the engine cooling intakes on the final version of the Pinball, RP-63G's. Additional 'hit' lights were added on the fuselage and wings. Thirty-two Pinballs were delivered before production was cancelled at the end of the war, during which 11,000 Pinball missions were flown, using 13 million rounds of ammunition.

Chapter 9

Synthetic Land and Air-to-Air Training Devices

All military forces provided training solutions. These covered every aspect, from single-axis guns operated by a pilot to gunners firing in an arc around the aircraft in more flexible defence. Films like *Memphis Belle*, *Catch 22* and *Masters of the Air* (2024) depict realistic challenges faced by gunners in combat.

Before the Second World War, the RAF experimented with trainers for air gunners with free guns mounted on scarf rings or in turrets. The gunner aimed at a moving spot of light on a curved wall. This was the Spotlight Trainer and later the Advanced Spotlight Trainer. Nash and Thompson made a still projector, with the spotlight moved by electric motors or hydraulics, whereas the Stephens Dome Trainer projected onto a moving mirror. One hundred and thirty of these air--to-air gunnery trainers were employed by the RAF.

The Spotlight Trainer was improved with work from the National Institute for Industrial Psychology (NIIP), a civilian scientific association. They made a driving simulator with model cars and in 1939 promoted a pilot trainer to the Air Ministry. The NIIP devised a system named the 'Turret Gun Sighting Trainer' (TGST) and used a 20-foot diameter hemispherical screen mounted on edge, similar to a modern radar dish. This was made up of a steel framework with a white dished fibrous plaster screen and housed inside an existing building.

At the centre and in front of the screen was a 10-foot-tall steel framework tower fitted with a hydraulic Frazer-Nash gun turret. Above this was a gimbal-mounted 16mm target projector that projected directly onto the screen. Movement of this was controlled by elevation and traverse cams that were driven by the projector motor and therefore directly synchronised with the film being projected.

The equipment was demonstrated to the RAF and the Admiralty at RAF West Freugh near Stranraer on 27 November 1940, with formal adoption by the Air Ministry on 16 December. Stanhope Engineering in Cricklewood, North London were paid £12,600 to build 'Turret Gun Sighting Trainers'. Production was increased to included 341 of the later more simplified 'Standard Free Gunnery Trainer' (SFGT) (see Plate 8), which were without cams to move the projector. In the SFGT an operator followed a diagram on a card showing what movements of the projector were required to move it so the target aircraft flew along the correct path.

Although the Air Ministry and the Ministry of Aircraft Production asked the NIIP to develop a mechanism for making films for the TGST, the existing Technicolor films used in the Dome Trainer with a yellow future spot were preferred. The irony is that Technicolor had seen the NIIP equipment for making model films at HMS *Excellent*.

A floodlight mounted on the projector gimbal illuminated the screen, with a diffuser to merge this light into the general illumination. A frame fixed in front of the floodlight (consisting of a metal plate on a rod) blanked off the centre of the floodlit area. A corresponding rectangular aperture frame was fixed in front of the projector. The attacking aircraft film filled the small area, with the aircraft on the film being dark on a lighter background. As the frames were adjusted away from the lens of the projector and flood lamp with a diffusing effect, the two became a single image.

The gun turret in the tower was fitted with a graticule projector to illustrate the aiming point of the gunner on the screen, the gunner looking through a reflector sight. This was fitted with a yellow filter in front to hide the correct yellow future position spot. An instructor pressed a button to register the number of hits from the shots fired. For distraction and realism, the air gunner would hear the loud sound of their aircraft engines through loudspeakers on either side of the turret, and of the turret twin guns when firing. Films consisted of targets of Messerschmitt 109 and Junkers 88 for attacks on front or rear turrets.

The instructor on the SFGT was moved above the gun turret on the projector platform, which was fitted with a console of switches and displays. The instructor pushed a button when he considered the gunner was on target which calculated a display of hits achieved.

The SFGT used both the hydraulic Frazer-Nash and the electrically operated Boulton Paul turrets without guns and fitted with dummy sights. The sights simulated could be either the reflector sight or a gyro gun sight. Graticules of either sight would be projected onto the screen by the still projector on the turret.

After time the SFGT floodlight principle was discontinued, although the image was still projected through an aperture which gave a diffused edge to the frame. A mirror under the aperture reflected the range of the aircraft, which was marked on the film, so that it appeared on an opaque screen which could be only seen by an instructor. For aircraft recognition films a name of the aircraft replaced the range.

Attached to the turrets on the SFGTs was also a 'skyscope' projector, which consisted of a clear dome painted inside with sky colours, and an internal light threw a skyscape onto the screen. This projector had a pendulum attached to it to give the effect of aircraft movement. If the trainer was in a blister hangar, the screen could be cylindrical with a radius of 33 feet.

Aircraft (friend or foe) identification films for the Stephens Dome Trainer and the TGST/ SFGT included the North American P-51 Mustang, Curtiss P-40 Kittyhawk, Bell P-39 Kingcobra (as used in the Pinball project), the American carrier-based Grumman Martlet (British) or F4F Wildcat (American). Other aircraft included a Vought V-156-B1 Chesapeake, Douglas A-20 Boston, North American B-25 Mitchell and the Lockheed P-38 Lightning. Friendly aircraft gunners were encouraged not to fire at included a Vultee A-31 Vengeance, a British Bristol Beaufighter, Hawker Typhoon, Hawker Hurricane, De Haviland Mosquito or Supermarine Spitfire. Other unwelcome targets included a Westland Lysander or the Handley Page Hampden. German aircraft targets included the Focke-Wulf Fw190, Junkers Ju88 or the Junkers Ju87. Faster options were offered by the German Messerschmitt Bf109 and Bf110, Dornier Do217, Messerschmitt Bf210 and Heinkel He126. Other target films depicted drogues and combinations of a Junkers Ju88, Focke-Wulf Fw190, Messerschmitt Bf109 and Bf210.

A different design by Group Captain Alfold and the NIIP at RAF Jurby on the Isle of Man used an arc-shaped screen. The screen was cylindrical, 10ft high and with a radius of 90ft. Aircraft images were projected onto this screen with up to twelve turrets positioned in front of it. By July 1942 this project was cancelled.

'Turret Gun Sighting Trainers' and 'Standard Free Gunnery Trainers' were housed in Turret Trainer buildings which could contain single, double, triple or more trainers.

RAF North Creake in Norfolk has the remains of a Single Turret Trainer building used to train aircrew gunners who flew Short Stirling and Handley Page Halifax aircraft. Tall narrow windows were set alongside a large doorway with a high grill for ventilation. From May 1944 RAF North Creake was the base for Squadrons from 100 Group RAF Bomber Command which flew operations to counter German radar tracking of RAF bomber streams, under the project led by Professor Jones.

The remains of a Double Turret Trainer building are extant at RAF Davidstow Moor in Cornwall. Operational from late 1942 for the rest of the war, it was the highest RAF airfield, at an altitude of 294 metres, and suffered frequent poor weather. The base was used by Coastal Command with Wellington, Warwick, Beaufighter, Liberator, Flying Fortress and Hudson aircraft used to attack U-Boats and enemy shipping, and Walrus aircraft in the Air Sea Rescue role.

The No. 9 Air Gunners School at RAF Llandwrog on the western Welsh coast was established in January 1941 but disbanded in mid-1942; it used Whitley and Anson aircraft. On the airfield there are the remains of a Triple Turret Trainer, reflecting the sophistication of gunnery training required.

Wales has a long association with Polish aircrew. On 15 February 1941, RAF Pembrey saw the formation of 316 (Polish) Squadron. At Pembrey there is a disused Dome Trainer which was as part of No.1 Air Gunners School, training with Bristol Blenheim and Vickers Wellington bombers, and Spitfires. On the southern Welsh coast, Imperial War Museum records show Sergeant Kazimierz Sawicz was instructing fellow Poles (see Plate 18) of No. 18 Operational Training Unit (soon to be No. 301 (Polish) Bomber Squadron) on the .303 Vickers K-type gas-operated machine gun at RAF Penrhos in July 1940.

In America, training equipment included the sophisticated multi-gunner Waller gunnery trainer, brought into use after Pearl Harbor was attacked in December 1941. Over 1,000,000 gunners were qualified with this trainer by 1945. Compared to the single projector of a Dome Trainer, the Waller Trainer was far more complex and sophisticated. Five 35mm projectors were used for the films and four for the scoring unit. Gunners sitting across from a semi-spherical screen used dummy guns with vibrating handles to represent recoil. When the trigger was pressed, headphones gave a high-pitched tone to confirm the correct point of aim. A score was kept of the bullets fired, hits when in range, hits when aimed correctly and hits when both in range and aimed correctly. Sights included a Mark 9 collimator sight, Sperry and Martin turrets, Sperry ball turrets, G. E. fire control stations, different mountings for 0.50-calibre and 20mm guns (with and without lead-computing sights) and a Navy Mark 51 Director. Waist-position guns on US aircraft did not use a turret but fired a single 0.5 machine gun mounted onto the aircraft. Gunners for the B-29 aircraft used three pedestal-type G. E. Directors and one ring-type director.

An engineer on the project was asked to describe the Waller technology:

> Oh, that's easy. You take the end of the Triborough Bridge [linking New York via Queens, the Bronx, and Manhattan over the East River] and put four men on it with their feet dangling in the air. Add a console like a church organ, and behind that photocells, amplifiers, levers, scanners and a lot of other things. Take the Perisphere from the World's Fair, cut it into four pieces, push the end of the Triborough Bridge into one of the pieces and you have a Waller Gunnery Trainer. It's just as simple as that.

The US Link Celestial Navigation Trainer was used to train navigators and bomb aimers. It consisted of a replica bomber aircraft fuselage mounted on top of a rotating tower. all within a surrounding projection screen. The interior of the fuselage represented a bomber aircraft with positions for pilot, navigator, radio operator and an instructor. As well as training navigators, bomb aimers could also be instructed on this trainer. The pilot flew the simulated aircraft by instruments, while the navigator, with his own instrument panel and chart table, gave directions by observing the projected ground terrain and the stars in the projected night sky.

Additional US navigation training using star locations was carried out with a Hagner Planetarium, students sitting inside a set of rings that represented a celestial map, called an armillary sphere.

RAF Navigators were not radio operators as they were not involved in directions via voice or Morse code. Their role with navigational radio measures was receiving and interpretating information sent to them on instruments mounted above their chart table. The Radio Operator would pass any 'fixes' to the navigator that were transmitted to the aircraft from UK ground stations plotting their position from the aircraft radio transmissions.

From 1942 RAF Bomber Command aircraft began to use radio navigation aids in the form of a system called 'Gee'. The system involved radio signals being transmitted from two known UK base stations. By measuring the time difference between their reception by an aircraft, a navigator was able plot the aircraft's location. It had an accuracy of a few hundred metres at 350-miles range.

British efforts to disrupt similar tools used by German bombers en route to bomb British targets became known as the 'Battle of the Beams' and were led by Professor R.V. Jones, assisted by the code-breakers at Bletchley Park.

Typical radio training technology included the 'Harwell Box' trainer, named after RAF Harwell, where radio training started. The trainer consisted of a small cubicle which simulated the actual space on an aircraft and housed the radio equipment. Within the cubicle were speakers which emitted engine noise and the occasional sound of machine guns firing. Signals arrived via a wire, and beacons provided bearing practice. A version of the Harwell Box was mounted on a gimbal arrangement which swung the entire unit to simulate an aircraft in flight.

To train RAF bomb-aimers, the Vickers-Bygrave Bombing Teacher gave a realistic simulation of what to expect when airborne over an enemy target. An aerial photograph of a target was projected downwards onto a white floor, representing a scale of 1 to 200,000 and covering 1,600 square miles from a height of 9,000ft. The projector moved in various directions to illustrate wind pressure on the aircraft. From an elevated steel platform 12ft high the trainee aimer issued instructions to the pilot to ensure that turns were flat, to avoid disrupting the vertical bomb sight in the nose of the aircraft. When the bomb release was triggered, calculations were made to indicate the landing point of the bomb.

USAAF bomb-aimers were also expected to man guns on the way to a target. Crews specified for the B-29 and B-32 (very heavy bombers flying against Japan) required two fully qualified bombardier-navigators. A B-29 required a third pilot tasked with acting as a flight engineer.

Chapter 10

The Portobel Dome Trainer

A direct evolution of the Stephens Dome Trainer became the Portobel (see plates 20, 21 & 22), named by Charles Stanley Bell, a fellow officer in the RNVR who had seen the Stephens Dome at HMS *Excellent*. Bell designed a miniaturised self-contained projection unit with a balloon canvas dome inflated by an air pump which could be quickly erected by a team of six and transported in a three-ton truck. Training came to the students.

Charles Stanley Bell was commissioned in the RNVR in 1940 after having served for a year with the RAF in 1925, when he undertook flying training. He was posted as an instructor to HMS *Glendower*, a Navy gunnery school set up at an ex-Butlins holiday camp in North Wales. Before the introduction of specific DEMS gunnery training, Bell experimented with different ways in which to train anti-aircraft gunners. A local firm made aircraft models which Bell ran along a wire in front of a gunner, who aimed at them with a moving spot light.

As Inspector of Merchant Navy Gunnery, Admiral Dreyer met Lieutenant Bell in 1941 and transferred him to his staff. Bell reduced the size of equipment in the Stephens Dome, using a 16mm projector to replace the 35mm projector of the early Technicolor domes. Bell wanted to have the projector gimbal-mounted and project direct onto a screen, not via a mirror as in Henry's design. However, HMS *Excellent* vetoed this idea as they wished to retain projection via the mirror and use existing Technicolor cams. Bell then adapted simple bicycle chains and gears to take the drive from the projector to the cams.

After a visit to RFD in Godalming, Surrey which made barrage balloons, Bell dispensed with the idea of a fixed dome structure and worked with RFD to create an inflatable dome. This 20ft diameter dome was made up of a hemispherical screen inside a sealed envelope made of two-ply balloon fabric. A low-pressure air pump kept the fabric inflated, with an airlock for entry and exit and relief valves to release excess pressure.

The first 'Portobel' dome was demonstrated to Admiral Dreyer and staff from HMS *Excellent* at RFD Godalming on 6 May 1942. A contract was placed by the Admiralty with Bell and CB Projections for two experimental domes (contract No CP/2A/434 31/42) on 12 May 1942, including one for trial at HMS *Excellent*. Bell filed a patent for the portable Dome Trainer on 1 October 1942 (Patent No 586,870). As well as an anti-aircraft training dome the patent included diagrams of an air-to-air trainer, which consisted of a nearly complete sphere with projector and trainee gunner mounted in a central tower.

After testing on 22 September 1942, a contract was placed with CB Projections on 10 May 1943. The Admiralty ordered 110 units without projectors and 45 spare dome envelopes for £122,000. Technicolor provided 1,376 films for Portobel Domes.

After 1945 the Portobel Dome Trainer was enhanced by RFD (having taken over production of Dome Trainers from Technicolor and CB Projections) and was tested and recommended for use by the Army's School of A.A. Artillery at Ty-Croes between October 1949 and February 1950. This was designated Trial G.282. The report's summary stated:

> The apparatus Dome Trainer No 4 Mk.1 was a 30ft diameter portable Dome Trainer for use by the Army. It was developed from the earlier 20ft diameter model used by the Royal Navy, and the prototype required several minor modifications. When these had been carried out, the apparatus proved to be an efficient and reliable training device. The complete apparatus could be carried in a three-ton General Service vehicle and be erected in approximately two hours by six men, either in the open or under cover. The fully loaded vehicle was tested over all types of road surfaces for 700 miles, and the equipment suffered no damage. The training facilities provided were identical to those provided by a static Dome Trainer.
>
> To assess the value of the equipment as a portable training device it was taken to the drill hall of a L.A.A. Territorial Regiment. On two drill nights it was used by the regiment and was considered by the officers to be a very valuable and economic training device, in that it saved transporting their men to the nearest static installation Dome 90 miles away.

On 19 May 1950 the War Office accepted this recommendation to adopt the portable A.A. system. The recommendation was sent to HQ Anti-Aircraft Command, Stanmore, the School of Anti-Aircraft, Manorbier, the School of Artillery, Larkhill and the London military liaison for the American, Australian, New Zealand and Canadian Armies.

The United States Army Combat Forces Journal No. 3 in October 1952 reported that the USA in Europe had adopted the 20ft inflatable Portobel, a smaller and portable derivative of the Dome Trainer with similar characteristics. The presentation system (the projector, mirror and cam assembly) was less bulky, using a smaller 16mm projector. An entire Portobel would fit into a three-ton Bedford lorry. The assembly and strike-down instructions were in strict number order for six men, only requiring that the No. 1 person had experience of setting up and taking down a Portobel inflated Dome. The others followed their numbered instructions strictly in sequence. The Portobel was tested and adopted by the Americans as described in Journal No.3:

> The Anti-aircraft Artillery Journal reports that the 34th A.A.A. Brigade in Europe has adopted the British-built 'Portobel' machine gun trainer. It is designed to provide M16 and M55 quadruple calibre .50 machine gunners with practice in tracking targets with speeds of up to 500 miles an hour on any type of course. The apparatus consists of an airtight fabric dome 30 feet in diameter and 20 feet in height which is fully inflated when in use. Instruction is carried out inside the dome, the internal pressure of which is about one millibar greater than the external barometric pressure.
>
> The interior of the dome is illuminated to represent the sky and finished with a white rubber surface which makes a good screen. A 16mm projector throws pictures of attacking aircraft onto a motorised mirror which moves in azimuth and elevation while reflecting on the inner surface of the dome. A yellow spot becomes visible when the aircraft comes within range of the gun. If the gun has been aimed correctly, the reticle should coincide with the yellow spot on the film. This spot is normally not visible to the gunner as they wear spectacles which filter out the yellow colour.

Five months before Journal No.3 published the American adoption in Europe, the Portobel was announced to the British public by the *Illustrated London News* (see plates 21 & 22). On 7 May 1951 cinemas featured a Royal Navy crew training in Portsmouth, filmed by Pathé News:

> Believe it or not, these men are going to the pictures. But the film they will see is quite out of the ordinary, for this is a portable Dome Trainer. Inflated by air, the dome contains training devices for anti-aircraft and naval gun crews. One side of the Dome serves as a cinema screen on which films of aircraft in flight are projected. The targets are followed in the gunsights by the practice gunner. As the projector starts running, the target film is thrown on to a mirror which reflects the image on to the dome, and noise effects are produced to simulate battle conditions. At the end of the exercise, all results are recorded.

Chapter 11

Royal Commission on Awards to Inventors - History

Disbanded after the First World War, the second Royal Commission on Awards to Inventors was re-established by Royal Warrant under the chairmanship of Lord Cohen in May 1946. Their task was to accept recommendations only from H.M. Treasury or other government departments to assess and confirm any awards to be paid for the use by, or on behalf of, the Crown of inventions, designs, drawings or processes, particularly in connection with the war effort. The Commission began hearing claims in February 1947 and completed a final hearing in December 1955, having ruled on 440 submissions.

In 1953 the Royal Commission reported on progress and gave a general survey of the principles which guided its decisions and particulars of the important claims dealt with up to 8 November 1952. Since February 1947 the Commission had sat in public on 278 days and disposed of 325 cases, of which 255 were withdrawn after being referred to the Commission, proving that the procedure adopted to enable any claimant and the government department involved to set out a case in writing had led to the settlement of many difficult cases without recourse to a hearing. The major part of the Commission's task had been completed.

To assist in determining which cases should be referred, the Chairman created an Investigating Committee to carefully examine all claims. This sub-committee dealt with 280 claims, many of which comprised several inventions which had to be considered separately. Sums totalling approximately £616,770 had been awarded since the establishment of the second Commission. Most awards were on an *ex gratia* basis, whereby the claimant had no legal right to payment but relied upon the bounty of the Crown. Under this heading, for example, the Commission awarded a total of £94,600 to the inventors of radar installations, including £50,000 to Sir Robert Watson-Watt.

A further series of awards for £23,300 was recommended for the inventions (known as 'degaussing') used on ships to counteract German magnetic mines. Other claims concerned the 'Fido' project for dispersing fog from airfields, the 'Leigh' light for aircraft used in anti-submarine warfare and the 'Morrison' table shelter for air-raid protection. The Commission also dealt with several legal claims based on the use of patents, acting in lieu of the High Court. One of these concerned stabilising gear for reducing the rolling of ships, earning the claimants £27,500.

The regulations used in 1919 were judged to be too restrictive. All servants of the Crown were then debarred by service regulations from obtaining the grant of a patent in respect of any invention they might have made, unless they had obtained the permission of the proper official authority. If permission were given, it was only on condition that the patent should be assigned to the Crown. No Crown servant, therefore, whether a member of the military or a civilian, could claim under Head 1 of the Royal Warrant. The only route was to request their case might be considered for an *ex gratia* award.

The Commission was tasked to look at reward recommendations under four headings. Head 1 covered claims against the Crown under patent law for inventions already used by the Crown. The Deputy Chairman and three other members were delegated to examine a very large number of such claims, and each was judged as either outstanding, with some inventive merit, of dubious merit or of no merit. A typical example was a claim concerning a novel 'sticky' bomb. Used by the Crown as contractors for the assembly of components, the claimants had devised and patented a special adhesive. Their contract with the Crown stipulated that no other rewards would be made beyond the original payments. However, the Commission ruled that the claim had some inventive merit, and an award was made.

A second case was reviewed in which manufacturers of a Sten gun sped up the process by including rifling when barrels were made. No award was granted, as the improvement of manufacturing speed allowed additional sales to be made. The inventor of joints for concrete roads was given an award to reflect both existing and future use by the Crown. Described as a competitor to the Stephens Dome Trainer, the Commission reviewed a claim for a 'fly plane predictor' for naval anti-aircraft gunnery. This was dismissed as there was no evidence of any wartime use. The design moved to production only after hostilities ceased.

Head 2 was changed from its 1919 definition to allow the Commission to accept recommendations from the Treasury regarding the terms of any agreement or proposed agreement between the owner of an invention or design and any government department. This now included claims of use by an Allied Government with the prior approval of the British Government. A further change was to add 'including a servant of the Crown', to emphasise that employment by the Government was no disqualification for an award under Head 2.

The second Commission had more detailed powers to deal with both patented and unpatented inventions. An example was a claim for improvement of fresh water stills for lifeboats. The invention was patented but judged unsuitable by the Ministry concerned, so the inventors sold through a private firm, whereupon the Crown adopted and extensively used the invention and the Commission ruled favourably on an award. A second case concerned the use of obturators required by the Crown for breech-loading guns. These are devices that retain the extreme pressure of an exploding charge when the breech is closed. An award of 5 per cent of the projected sale of obturators for the life of the patent was made.

Normally, Head 2 was used for claims for inventions agreed but not yet deployed. A unique exception was made when the Ministry of Supply and the Treasury requested that the Commission consider an award to Frank Whittle (who made no claim) as the inventor of revolutionary jet engine and gas turbine technology. From an initial design in 1929, whilst a cadet at the RAF College in Cranwell, Whittle spent twenty years designing and refining his inventions. With remarkable tenacity of purpose and undeterred by formidable difficulties and failures, Whittle finally succeeded in the face of official opposition and the vested interests of obsolete manufacturing companies. In 1935, as was normal commercial practice, Whittle formed Power Jets Limited and was granted commercial licences for Britain and overseas sales, subject to a share of profits paid to the Air Ministry. Evidence was provided on behalf of the Crown that because of Whittle's efforts a radically new Meteor jet aircraft was deployed by the RAF. This provided Britain with a military and technical lead in aircraft and gas turbines of at least two years. In 1944 the British government purchased the rights to Power Jets Limited, offering Whittle £46,875 for his shares. However, declaring himself a patriot, Whittle freely gave all his shares to the government. Lord Cohen therefore recommended an *ex gratia* payment to him of £100,000.

Head 3 covered the majority of claims as noted by Cohen. As in Head 2, the scope was amended from the 1919 brief to include 'claims for inventions used by an allied Government' and added 'including a servant of the Crown'. Inventions had to show both novelty and ingenuity. A claim for a welding machine used to construct the sections of the Hamel pipeline for use in Operation Pluto, the fuel lines for D-Day, was accepted as of exceptional utility, but it was ruled that the standard welding processes employed disqualified it from being an invention. The Swiss company that invented the insecticide DDT (dichloro-diphenyl-trichloroethane) in 1942 found themselves under German control, but the chemical was only deployed by the Germans for agricultural purposes and control of moths. Although the invention had been 'made known to and used by an enemy country', the Commission granted an award in recognition that the company had independently notified the British by diplomatic channels of its properties. The British used the chemical around the globe for safeguarding the health of troops against typhus, malaria and other epidemic diseases in wartime, whereas the Germans did not. An award was justified as helping the British war effort.

All Head 3 claims had to be for independent inventions that were later notified to the Crown and used in wartime service. Success often has many parents, as illustrated by the arguments to identify the true inventor of the tank in the First World War. Churchill, as First Lord of the Admiralty, ordered the creation of a Landship Committee in February 1915 to investigate the development of armoured fighting vehicles on the Western Front. The Committee's existence was concealed from Lord Kitchener at the War Office, and from the Board of the Admiralty and the Treasury, all of whom were expected to block any such invention. The three members were a Director of Naval Construction, an officer from the Royal Naval Air Service Armoured Car Squadron and an engineer Colonel from the Naval Brigade working on transport for the Royal Navy Division. A series of experiments in September 1915 led to the construction of an armoured vehicle. The first tank was named 'Little Willie', followed by 'Big Willie,' designed to cross wide trenches, and the invention was quickly adopted by the Army.

Mr Bede Bentley made a claim in 1920 for £300,000 as the inventor of the tank. Evidence on his behalf was provided by Churchill, but the case was dismissed. Thomas Kerr wrote on 24 November 1925 to Churchill, claiming that he had had the first idea for a tank, and Churchill had been told this by a Major Valentine Fleming, with whom Kerr had served. Charles Darbey wrote from Dublin in December 1925 to Churchill, claiming that his idea for rotating ship torpedo screens, sent to the Admiralty in 1914, was used to create tanks.

A more credible claim came from an Australian, Lancelot de Mole, who conceived his innovative designs working with heavy transport in Western Australia in 1911. De Mole had submitted plans to the British War Office in 1912 and submitted a claim in November 1919. Included in the evidence was a letter written from Perth to Lord Kitchener, the British Secretary of State for War, on 19 September 1914 by G. W. D. Breadon, a civil engineer who became Commissioner for Munitions in India. Breadon promoted de Mole's invention, described as a 'travelling caterpillar fort', confirmed de Mole's previous design submission and explained what this new weapon could achieve, two years before tanks appeared on the battlefield at the Somme. He wrote:

> The question of armaments being of paramount importance to armies engaged in this great war, may I suggest your placing the plans, specifications, and model, submitted by Mr. Lancelot de Mole in 1912, before a committee of experts, with a view to the adoption of travelling forts against the German forces. In my humble opinion no deadlier or more efficient war engine could be used than de Mole's caterpillar fort, which can travel over broken ground, climb embankments., span canals, streams and trenches with the greatest of ease, and which, if armoured and manned with small quick-firing guns and maxims, will quickly turn the most stubborn of armies, even if they be most strongly entrenched.
>
> A line of moving fortresses – no dreamer's fancy, but an idea which can be materialised – adequately supported by artillery, will carry everything before it, and save the infantry. I trust that you will appreciate the value of my suggestion. Should you require the services of Mr. L. de Mole kindly request the Western Australian Government to communicate with Mr. H. J. Anketell, resident engineer, Department of Public Works, Perth – Yours, etc., G. W. D. Breadon.

The first British Royal Commission on Awards to Inventors, presided over by Mr Justice Sargant, declared:

> De Mole made, and reduced to practical shape, as far back as the year 1912, a very brilliant tank invention, which anticipated, and in some respects surpassed, that put into use late in 1916. Counsel for the Minister for Munitions specifically admitted: 'De Mole's suggestions would, in the opinion of present advisers, have made a better article than those that went into action.' The Chairman said to him: 'Your suggestion is sent to the Government in 1912 and 1915. Then it gets pigeonholed. That is your misfortune, but not your fault.'

De Mole's submission to the government certainly anticipated the later machines, but his were much earlier than the accepted design from other inventors submitted in 1916. His brilliant and original designs were shelved and forgotten until the expediency of wartime allowed others to successfully promote similar concepts. Whatever its merits, the case was dismissed as any awards were judged as outside the scope of the Commission, which ruled only on designs used in warfare. After the ruling, De Mole wrote to Churchill on 26 November 1925 enclosing his evidence to show Bentley was not the inventor.

Considering such restrictions, the new 1949 Commission adjusted the scope for Head 3, to allow claims where an individual demonstrated an 'extraordinary brilliance' in their invention, even when the claimant carried out the work entirely as official employment. All Head 3 claims had to demonstrate that the invention possessed 'exceptional utility', with the qualification that practical evidence must be given of its value in actual use in the prosecution of the war. An individual who demonstrated 'dogged perseverance and persistence' in the face of official discouragement merited a special bounty from the Crown, as demonstrated in the case of Frank Whittle. An award of £12,000 was granted to Sir Donald Bailey, who persevered from 1936 (alongside his full-time job at the War Office Experimental Establishment) with his independent design of the Bailey Bridge. By January 1941 all the accepted tubular bridge designs had failed under combat conditions, and Bailey once again promoted his own detailed unit panel construction. By November 1941 his bridge had been successfully deployed to fighting units. His award reflected operational deployment for prosecuting the war, excluding peacetime commercial value.

Finally, claims under Head 4 to the Cohen Commission revealed previously secret designs, especially when exchanged between governments rather than individuals.

Once the Commissioners disbanded, in 1957 Lord Cohen published a 'Compendium of the principles and procedure adopted by the 1946 Royal Commission in assessing compensation and making awards'. He recorded 729 claims made to the Royal Commission, of which 287 were rejected and 440 were considered. Government departments submitted 318 claims to the initial Investigating Committee, of which 258 were rejected and 54 were reviewed by Lord Cohen. He detailed the effectiveness of the Commission but hoped that such wartime rewards would never again be necessary.

Cohen explained that the principal setting for the great majority of claims was Head 3: 'applicable to cases of use or alleged use by any Government Department or, with the approval of a Government Department, by an Allied Government (other than a Dominion Government and the Government of India) of inventions, designs, drawings or processes which, though the inventor, author or owner thereof (including a servant of the Crown) may not possess any monopoly against the Crown or any statutory right to payment or compensation, may, nevertheless, appear from their exceptional utility or otherwise to entitle such inventor, author or owner to some remuneration for such use.'

Chapter 12

British Defence – Radar and Radio Beams

As a civilian in 1939 before his return to the Royal Navy, Henry Stephens experienced the horrors of the Blitz on London in 1940, and subsequently being bombed by aircraft at Whale Island in Portsmouth whilst developing the Dome Trainer. He was aware from his First World War experience that training to destroy aircraft over a target in a Dome was only effective in practice if there was sufficient warning of an attack, together with its direction and range. Secret detection by early British radar provided such warnings. A first task for the Commission on Awards to Inventors was reviewing rewards for assisting the development of radar to Professor John Randall, Doctor Henry Boot and Professor James Sayers.

In the First World War, Zeppelin airships and large biplane bombers were used for long-range bombing of Britain, against limited defences. By the 1930s aircraft flew faster and higher, permitting widespread aerial bombardment of all targets. However, the key to building both defensive and offensive measures lay in the physical aircraft themselves. In 1923 H.M. Signal School noted that radio programmes were disrupted by planes flying nearby, and the Post Office observed in 1931 that radio reception was constantly interrupted by low-flying aircraft. In 1922 Marconi undertook similar research to propose using reflected radio waves to detect ships as an aid to navigation at night and in poor weather.

In anticipation of future combat, the Air Ministry established in 1934 the CSSAD (Committee for the Scientific Survey of Air Defence), chaired by Sir Henry Tizard, to improve air defence. By January 1935 rumours were spreading of a German 'death ray' capable of destroying cities with radio waves. Harry Wimperis, the Director of Scientific Research at the Air Ministry, asked Robert Watson-Watt, a British pioneer of radio direction-finding and radar technology, to investigate building a British version of such a death ray, to be used specifically against aircraft.

Watson-Watt started his career in radio physics at the Met Office, building an accurate method to predict and track thunderstorms using the radio signals given off by lightning. By the 1920s he had developed this into high-frequency (long-distance) tracking of radio broadcasts. High-frequency direction finding, usually known by the abbreviation HF/DF or its nickname, 'huff-duff', was used to give a compass bearing to locate enemy radios which are sending messages. This technology was critical to locate radio transmissions from and between Nazi U-Boats, triangulating location, direction and speed. Contemporary reports estimated that 25 per cent of all successful attacks on U-Boats were directed by huff-duff, which was also useful to locate friendly aircraft as a navigation aid. A 'pip-squeak' transmitter was added to friendly aircraft, automatically sending a steady tone for fourteen seconds each minute, although it blocked radio operations whilst broadcasting the DF signal.

Calculations by Arnold Wilkins showed that a death ray device was impossible to construct. However, Wilkins remembered the civilian radio service being disrupted by aircraft in flight and therefore proposed that radio waves might be capable of detecting aircraft. Wilkins's idea was presented by Tizard to the CSSAD on 28 January 1935. On 26 February 1935 Watson-Watts arranged a secret demonstration with two receiving antennae set six miles from a BBC shortwave broadcast station at Daventry.

Only three people were allowed to witness the birth of radar: Watson-Watt, Wilkins and Albert Rowe. A member of CSSAD, Rowe was another eminent British physicist who later played a major role in the development of radar. A clear signal was repeatedly reflected up to eight miles, bounced from an RAF Handley Page Heyford heavy bomber. On 2 April 1935 Watson-Watt received his patent on a radio device for detecting and locating an aircraft. By May 1935 Wilkins had set up further research at Orford Ness, a peninsula on the Suffolk coast, and by June 1935 aircraft were being detected at up to sixteen miles, ranging up to sixty miles by December. Five stations were ordered to defend London.

As part of this programme prior to the outbreak of war in 1939, Randall and Boot quietly visited these secret radar stations to establish that a Barkhausen tube could detect radio waves. With higher performance demands, in February 1940 they assembled and tested a radical new design. This was the cavity magnetron, subsequently adopted to generate high-power pulses in radar equipment. A third scientist, Professor Sayers, worked on the existing klystron device, before switching to help Randall and Boot improve the magnetron. Sayers solved a significant operational problem in Randall and Boot's original device by designing a 'strapping' technique. The Sayers design was so novel that repeated German attempts to copy captured cavity magnetrons from destroyed Bomber Command aircraft all failed.

Over a million cavity magnetrons were manufactured, including those licensed to the United States under Head 4 claims. All three claimants assigned their Letters Patent to the Admiralty, although as civilians, they were not under any service regulations. The Commission awarded £36,000 to each man, finding the 'inventions attributed to these three claimants were of outstanding brilliance and were of exceptional utility for offence and defensive purposes.' Apart from other claims and £200,000 paid to inventors of radar in 1945, the Commission reviewed twenty-five claims over forty-four days. A total of £94,600 was paid to the radar teams involved, with £50,000 going to Sir Robert Watson-Watt.

Watson-Watt was sent to the United States in 1941 to advise on air defence after Japan's attack on Pearl Harbor. After the war, in 1956, he was caught speeding in Canada by hand-held radar and said, 'Had I known what you were going to do with it, I would never have invented it!'

Breaking the German secret radio codes allowed the British to read most of the German military radio traffic. The code-breakers at Bletchley Park were instrumental in providing information about German use and development of radio, radar and radio beam navigation systems. This enabled the scientists and the services to develop measures to counter enemy aircraft attacks that used radio navigation beams to direct them to their targets.

In his book *Most Secret War*, published in 1978, Professor Reginald Victor Jones explained that the development of radar had a long history. Jones was a British physicist and scientific military intelligence expert who played an important role in the defence of Britain in the Second World War, including evaluating and deploying defensive and offensive technology. He led what was described as 'The Battle of the Beams', one of the first modern electronic warfare campaigns against attacking aircraft. Between 1943 and 1945 Jones worked with Tony Flowers and the code-breakers at Bletchley Park on Colossus, a set of computers with thermionic valves (vacuum tubes) to solve cryptanalysis of the Lorenz cipher. Colossus was one of the first programmable, electronic, digital computers, given instructions by switches and plugs rather than a stored program.

Amongst other secret projects, Jones was tasked to counter German technologies, including a secret radio navigation beam system called *Knickebein* which guided German bombers to their targets. The RAF special duties 100 Group of Bomber Command at RAF Creake, formed first in November 1943 in Norfolk, provided a squadron to build and test electronic warfare and counter-measures equipment alongside Professor Jones. They also flew aircraft within a bomber stream, interfering with German ground and airborne radio and radar defence measures.

Knickebein was an evolution of the pre-war commercially available *Lorenz* blind-landing system. This was a civilian radio beam navigation system broadcast from an airfield and received by approaching aircraft up to a maximum of 20 miles away. The German system relayed two powerful radio beams by secret code that intersected over a target. A navigator heard Morse code dashes if they flew to the left of the beam, or dots if they strayed to the right. Using radio traffic messages decoded by Bletchley Park, Jones predicted the transmission frequencies. On 21 June 1940 an RAF search aircraft intercepted radio signals in this frequency range. By October 1940 the RAF had built fifteen jamming stations code named 'Aspirin', which replaced or bent the German dot signal with a more powerful but totally false British beam.

Once *Knickebein* was discarded, the Germans deployed the *X-Gerät* system. A transmitter sent four beams. An automatic bomb-release command was remotely triggered when passing over where three beams crossed. This new navigational aid was used by the lead target-marking unit of the Luftwaffe, with flares and incendiaries to mark targets for other bombers. However, based on their own limited experience of finding targets, RAF Bomber Command soon formed a similar target-marking group, the Pathfinder Force.

The 'Bromide' radio beam jammer was built by Jones to defeat the *X-Gerät* system. By 1941 he was developing further jammers against the next radio beam system called *Y-Gerät*, or *Wotan*, named by the Germans after the one-eyed Norse god. Using information from Resistance units in occupied territory, radio traffic ciphers decoded by Bletchley Park and targeted photographic reconnaissance, Jones identified the specific location of Nazi transmitter beacons in Europe. These used a beacon transponder to calculate range between the *Y-Gerät* station and a German bomber, sending encoded radio course corrections (cracked by Bletchley Park) to the navigator.

The BBC television transmitter at Alexander Palace in north London, was requisitioned, and renamed 'Domino' was used to re-broadcast the *Y-Gerät* range signal. A second Domino was installed at Beacon Hill near Salisbury, causing German ground station receivers to lock on to the British jammer instead of the *Y-Gerät* transponder in the German bomber. Range measurements therefore became completely inaccurate, and this led to the *Y-Gerät* system being discarded. Due to the addition of barbed-wire fences and civilian exclusion zones, the secret radar sites were later identified by specific photographic flights as high-value targets, with each added to raids in preparations for D-Day.

Lady Luck was smiling on Britain in May 1941. Three Heinkel bombers were shot down before their crew could destroy the equipment for measuring a bearing beam. Their capture helped to disrupt this by continuous wave jamming.

Success against German technology was further enabled by the audacious capture of an enemy Würzburg radar equipment by a new style of soldier. In 1942 Jones planned a remarkable and successful first parachute Commando and Royal Navy raid on a site at Bruneval in France. The raiders collected new secret German radar equipment with full instructions, and kidnapped a German operator. Captain John Frost led Operation Biting, winning a Military Cross, and the raid proved the viability of this new force that became the Parachute Regiment. Once promoted, Major Frost is better known for spearheading the 1st Airborne Division's assault on the bridge at Arnhem as part of Operation Market Garden in September 1944. In 1976, he was played by Anthony Hopkins in *A Bridge Too Far*.

Jones's investigation of continuing heavy losses by Bomber Command was partly resolved in July 1944 by a gross navigational error by a German Junkers Ju 88 *Nachtjäger* (night fighter). Flying from Holland to Germany, the pilot mistakenly landed at RAF Woodbridge. The latest top-secret passive electronic monitoring systems called *Naxos* and *Flensburg* were revealed. Jones proved how German attacks were using RAF aircraft IFF (identification friend-or-foe) transmitters as the Ju 88 had special aerials to track IFF transmissions.

Jones theorised that strips of metal foil falling through the air might overwhelm radar systems, producing false echoes, and in early 1942, Telecommunications Research Establishment (TRE) researcher Joan Curran explored the idea. She concluded that a system whereby bundles of aluminium strips were dropped at intervals from an aircraft could blind enemy radar with false echoes. The radar-blocking metal strips system was codenamed 'Window'.

On 9 May 1943, a defecting German aircrew landed their Junkers Ju88 night fighter, fitted with the latest German radar, at RAF Dyce, near Aberdeen. Using this aircraft with its radar against a Wellington bomber, Jones demonstrated the jamming disruption caused by the aluminium strips. The strips were cut to a length appropriate to the radar wavelength being used.

Initially, Window was not employed for fear that if used, once the Germans knew of it, they would develop their own version and thereby blind British radar. The Germans had already independently created a metal strip radar-blinding system called '*Duppel*' but were also worried about its deployment. Permission was given to commence use of Window in July 1943, since a more recent British centimetric radar could more readily cope with any use of similar tactics by the Luftwaffe. Window was first used in Bomber Command's week-long series of raids on Hamburg as part of Operation Gomorrah in July 1943. Swamping of German radar enabled bombers to drop their bombs with little resistance and consequently fewer aircrew losses.

However, by the winter of 1943/44, RAF Bomber Command losses were devastating. German night fighters had been fitted with new *Schräge Musik* (jazz music) upward-firing auto cannon, allowing an approach to an unsuspecting bomber from below and outside the gunners' field of view. By 1944 a third of German night fighters were fitted with these upward-firing cannon. An attack by a *Schräge Musik*-equipped fighter came as a complete surprise to the RAF bomber crews.

In a raid over Nuremberg on 30 March 1944, 820 Lancasters and Halifaxes formed up from ten squadrons in No. 1 Group, eight squadrons in No. 3 Group, seven squadrons in No. 4, twelve in No. 5, nine in No. 6 and twelve in No. 8 Pathfinder Force Group. Fifteen night-fighter Mosquitoes flew to engage German night fighters. Ninety-four aircraft were shot down over Germany and Europe, each bomber with a crew of seven. Over six hundred beds and bunks were empty the next day.

As early as 1943, gunners reported that aircraft were being attacked from below. However, senior figures in the RAF refused to believe these reports until detailed examination of the damage inflicted on the aircraft that returned clearly showed that the attacks were carried out in this way. A defence against the *Schräge Musik* attacks was to use Mosquito night fighters with the heavy bombers, since Mosquitoes picked up radar transmissions from German night fighters.

A high proportion of British bombers were fitted with 'H_2S' ground-mapping radar for navigation and target location. Bombers were fitted with a tail warning radar named 'Monica' which detected the presence of German night fighters. However, both radars generated signals which could be detected by enemy radar tracking systems on board their night fighters. Night fighters were thus led to the target, and bomber losses increased.

On 13 July 1944 a Junkers JU88G-I night fighter mistakenly landed at RAF Woodbridge, Suffolk due to the crew mistakenly following a reciprocal course. This aircraft was carrying the very latest radar and radio equipment in the 'Lichtenstein SN-2' radar, and 'Flensburg' (for detecting 'Monica') and 'Naxos' (for detecting 'H_2S') radar detectors. The crew said that the operation of 'Naxos' was of very little use, while 'Flensburg' was able to home in on individual aircraft's 'Monica' radar. After this revelation 'Monica' was removed from all RAF bomber aircraft, while 'H_2S' was allowed to continue in use, as the 'Naxos' system was seen to be of virtually no use.

Jones and his staff were responsible for deception measures against German long-range weapons as part of the Twenty Committee. Based in Room XX of the Admiralty and using captured German agents who agreed to work for the Allies, this preserved anonymity and secrecy. It is no coincidence that the Roman numeral for twenty is a double cross.

Chapter 13

V1 and V2 Weapons and the Proximity Fuze*

The initial aim of the Dome Trainer had been to allow A.A. gunners to experience the sound and fury of attack by aircraft at different heights and speeds. However, specific new technology was required to ensure successful destruction of targets such as the V1 flying bombs.

Alongside Henry Stephens and his family, Londoners suffered all the horrors of bombing during the 1940/41 Blitz, with the 'Little Blitz' of early 1944 causing further damage. People believed the war would be entering its final phase after D-Day, despite rumours of Hitler's secret weapons. However, such weapons were known. Between June 1944 and March 1945 London came under attack by Hitler's V1 flying bomb and later the V2 ballistic rocket missile vengeance weapons.

During the previous twelve months, Jones and his staff had been warned about this new V1 weapon (codenamed 'Diver' by the British) by the French Resistance and photographic intelligence. The overall campaign against Hitler's 'V' weapons was given the code name 'Operation Crossbow' by the Allies. On 17 August 1943 a massive bombing raid by 600 RAF heavy bombers, codenamed Operation Hydra, attacked the Nazi research facility developing these weapons at Peenemünde on the Baltic coast, putting back the introduction of the V1. Bombing of launch sites in France also further delayed the V1 being brought into use.

The 'Flying Bomb' or V1, named after the initial letter of the German word *Vergeltungswaffe*, (weapon of reprisal) has often been called the original cruise missile. It was a pilotless gyro-guided pulse jet, with a ton of high explosive in the nose. Each one was launched from a metal ramp pointing towards London (and also Portsmouth and Southampton). The initial launch speed of the V1 was set by a connection to a piston in a tube within the launch ramp. High-pressure steam propelled the piston and V1 up the ramp, with the piston dropping away after leaving the launch ramp. The imparted speed brought the Argus pulse-jet engine up to full efficiency, with the V1 able to climb to 3,000ft and achieve a speed of around 400mph.

---

* The term 'fuze' is used when referring to a more sophisticated ignition device incorporating mechanical and/or electronic components, such as a proximity fuze for an M107 artillery shell or a magnetic or acoustic fuze on a sea mine.

When the small propeller (a vane anemometer) in the nose completed a set number of rotations for the range required, the V1's two explosive dive mechanisms fired. These put the rudder and elevator into a neutral position and released two spoilers that dropped down from the underside of the tail plane. This had the effect of putting the bomb into a sudden dive. The abrupt negative 'G' force starved the engine of fuel, leading to the characteristic silence as the pulse-jet engine cut out. This sudden silence warned everyone below that it was time to take shelter. This new weapon was quickly christened 'Doodlebug' or 'Buzz Bomb'.

During the night of 13 June 1944, a new and unfamiliar sound was heard in the sky over Kent, and three times over London. The first V1 to strike Britain hit Swanscombe in Kent. Witnesses described the sound of it as being like a motorbike with a broken exhaust. Others said they had seen an enemy plane with flames pouring from the tail. These were the first V1s.

The first flying bomb to strike London hit Grove Road, Mile End, East London on 13 June, killing six people, injuring forty-two and damaging houses and the local railway bridge. On 18 June a second weapon struck Peckham, and on the same day forty-eight people were killed when the Air Ministry in the Aldwych was hit.

One of the worst V1 incidents was the destruction of the Guards Chapel at Wellington Barracks on 18 June. The church had been rebuilt after incendiary bombing in the Blitz and was packed with people. The impact caused the roof to collapse onto the congregation, creating rubble up to 10 feet deep. A hundred and twenty-one Guardsmen and civilians were killed, with 141 seriously injured. The Bishop of Maidstone, officiating, was untouched as the altar portico protected him from the blast.

The bomb left only the apse of the Chapel intact. Professor Jones, working on countering the V1 and V2 in the nearby MI6 office at 54 Broadway recalled: 'One lasting impression I had was that the whole of Birdcage Walk was a sea of fresh pine leaves. Trees had all been stripped and I could hardly see a speck of asphalt for hundreds of yards.'

Elmers End bus garage in South-East London took a direct hit on 18 July, killing seventeen people. On 28 July a V1 struck Lewisham town centre, causing major damage to shops including Woolworth's and Sainsburys and devastating the crowded market. Altogether fifty-nine people were killed. A V1 hit a full restaurant in the Clockhouse area of Beckenham on 2 August, when forty-four people were killed. Fourteen shops and forty-two houses were destroyed. Croydon became the area most heavily bombarded by V1s. It was struck 141 times in 80 days, destroying 1,500 homes and damaging 54,000 more. Over 200 people were killed.

Many Londoners decided that leaving for the night and returning for work in the morning was the safest option. By mid-July 15,000 people were leaving the city each evening. Deeper air raid shelters were opened along the Northern Line, and up to 8,000 people spent the night in the stations at Belsize Park, Camden Town, Stockwell, Clapham North, Clapham Common and Clapham South.

Three lines of defence were put in place against the V1: fighter aircraft over the English Channel, anti-aircraft batteries in Kent and barrage balloons on the North Downs and around London. From 20 July there was a reorganisation of the defences, with the anti-aircraft guns moved to the coast where they could have a clear field of fire out over the sea with added gunnery radar. Fighters attacked V1s over the English Channel. Barrage balloons were set as a final defence of London.

Standard British anti-aircraft guns stood little chance of hitting these fast-moving missiles. However, a new type of anti-aircraft shell fitted with a proximity fuze was now deployed. Gunners were also assisted by newly-developed automatic gunnery tracking radar and an electronic fire control computer.

To attack the V1s in the air required the fastest available fighters, including single-engine planes like the Hawker Tempest V, the Griffon Spitfire Mk XIV or the P51 Mustang. Only the de Havilland Mosquito twin engine fighter was fast enough to directly engage a VI in flight, but attacking a V1 was hazardous if too close to the explosion or the resulting debris. One method of destroying a V1 was to fly alongside it and position the aircraft's wing below it. Raising the wing without contact with the V1 interfered with airflow over the wing and tipped it up. This disrupted an internal gyro and crashed the V1.

V1 attacks launched from France continued until 1 September, when launch sites were overrun by Allied forces. From 9 July, V1s were also air-launched towards London from under the wing of Heinkel 111 bombers. Over 400 V1s were launched by this method before the last was fired on 5 September, after which the Luftwaffe were forced to retreat to Germany. On 16 September, air-launched V1 attacks recommenced, with aircraft based in Holland and Germany. These continued until 14 January 1945. Finally, from 3 March 1945, longer-range V1s with a reduced warhead were ground-launched from Holland until 26 March.

Between June 1944 and March 1945, 10,492 V1s were launched at Britain. Of these, 2,340 hit London, causing around 6,000 deaths, approximately 18,000 injuries and the loss of tens of thousands of houses and other buildings. The A.A. guns, fighters and balloon defences were successful in destroying 4,261 V1 missiles. The worst period was the week commencing 25 June 1944, when 125 V1 flying bombs hit south London.

As well as killing people and inflicting many injuries, a V1 could cause huge amounts of blast damage to buildings. The bomb exploded at ground level and generated a blast for over 600 yards. Statistically, each V1 accounted for one death, with the main result of the V1 campaign being damage to morale and massive blast damage to property.

By 1944 Professor Jones had taken on further responsibilities as a V2 rocket expert for the Cabinet Defence Committee (Operations). He noted that the general target setting was aimed at Tower Bridge. By September 1944 most of the V1s were being shot down before they reached London. On 7 September Duncan Sandys, Chairman of the War Cabinet Flying Bomb Counter-Measures Committee, famously proclaimed that the 'Battle of London' was over. He was sadly mistaken.

One day later, on 8 September, with no siren or warning, a huge explosion rocked Staveley Road in Chiswick, South-West London. A V2, Hitler's much vaunted ballistic missile, arrived after a flight time of five minutes from Wassenaar, Holland. The rocket weighed 13 tons with a 1-ton warhead and arrived via the stratosphere at the supersonic speed of 3,000mph. Three people died, seventeen were seriously injured, and the blast reduced rows of houses to rubble. Because of its supersonic speed there was no audible warning of a V2. The rocket detonated with a large explosion, then came the roar of its passage, due to the sound catching up with the missile's supersonic speed, and finally there was the 'sonic boom' of it breaking the sound barrier. There was no defence against the V2 in flight. A second V2 rocket landed minutes later in Pernod Wood, near Epping, but without causing any casualties.

The V2 rockets were launched from compact mobile launchers with fuel tankers for the liquid ethanol and liquid oxygen rocket propellant, together with launch and control systems. Units could fire, often from avenues or clearings in forests, then move to a new location, launching again within two hours. It was virtually impossible for aircraft to locate, attack and destroy launchers. Destroying rail and road communications and likely storage areas were the only way to stop V2 attacks.

The *Daily Herald* on Saturday, 11 November 1944 reported the official acknowledgement of the existence of the new V2 rocket, nicknamed 'the flying gas main' as all strikes had up to then been officially explained as explosions caused by gas leaks. However, civilians found shards of metal debris from the rockets up to nine feet long and were suspicious of the government story.

The Deptford History Group recorded one of the worst V2 strikes:

> The F. W. Woolworth store in New Cross Road, Deptford on Saturday 25th November 1944 was blessed with mild weather. Morale was high as the Allies pushed on towards Berlin. Word swept New Cross that Woolworth's had received 144 tin saucepans. A queue built up quickly to buy such scarce items. Mums, grannies and even soldiers waited patiently. Every full-timer was at work on the busiest day, supported by Saturday boys and girls, mostly just fourteen years old, topping up their pocket money. At noon the Council's manual workers clocked off after collecting their wages from Deptford Town Hall, opposite the store. Many went shopping.

On Walcheren Island off the coast of Holland, a select group of German dignitaries was celebrating. They had arranged drinks to mark V2 rocket number 250, which was duly dispatched. It malfunctioned and exploded above St Paul's Cray in Kent. No one was hurt.

At 12.15 the second break sounded at Woolworth's and the next wave of store staff headed upstairs for a cooked lunch in the canteen. The train cleaners from New Cross

Station on the Southern Railway slipped off early, hoping to get a hot drink of Bovril at the 'Woolies' Tea Bar. The pile of saucepans near the back tills was going down. In Holland, rocket number 251 was launched. The Deptford History Group continued:

> Suddenly, without warning, at 12.26 the V2 rocket hit the rear of the flat roof of the Woolworth store. After a moment's silence the walls bowed, and the building exploded. The Royal Arsenal Co-operative Society store next door and the queue of people waiting for a tram in the street outside were caught in the inferno. As the dust settled, shards of glass and debris stretched ankle-deep all the way to New Cross Station, half a mile away. It is believed (at the time) that the station had been the target.
>
> In the hours that followed local people helped the emergency services remove the rubble by hand. As it was cleared, the full horror became evident – 168 people died, both customers and staff, and 122 were injured. Just one person survived inside the store. These terrible losses would have been even worse if traffic problems had not caused a suspension of the tram service along New Cross Road a few minutes before the attack.

From 8 September 1944 to 27 March 1945, V2 rockets landed in Chiswick, New Cross, Islington, Deptford, Smithfield Market, Stepney and Orpington, killing 535 people. As the Allies advanced through Belgium to close off German supplies via Antwerp, the port was attacked with both V1 flying bombs and V2 rockets. Over 1,600 V2 rockets were launched against Antwerp. The last eleven V2s were fired from Germany to disrupt American forces crossing the Rhine via the bridge at Remagen.

The V2 strikes on Britain continued until 18 September, when the launch sites in Holland were in danger due to the Allied Operation Market Garden's thrust into Holland to capture the road and bridges up to Arnhem. When the Allied operation failed, firing from Holland continued. On 27 March 1945 the final V2 was launched against Orpington in Kent, causing twenty-three deaths.

From the first V2 on 8 September 1944 to the last on 27 March 1945, a total of 3,172 rockets were launched at Britain, France, Belgium, Holland and Germany, of which 1,358 fell in the London area. The threat from these weapons finally ended in 1945 as the Allies advanced into Holland and Germany, capturing the launch sites.

The senior designer of the V2 was Wernher von Braun, based at Peenemünde. He was top of the Black List, the code name for those German scientists and engineers planned for immediate interrogation by the Allied military. In May 1945 von Braun surrendered his staff of technicians to the Americans. His technical interrogators included Leonard S. Snell. a leading British rocket engineer, who was later chief designer of Rolls-Royce Limited and awarded several patents as one of the inventors of the Concorde's Rolls-Royce/Snecma Olympus engines.

As part of Operation Paperclip, the captured German scientists and technicians were secretly moved to the United States, along with about 1,600 other staff. Von Braun worked for the United States Army on an intermediate-range ballistic missile, developing the rockets that launched the United States' first space television satellite, Explorer 1, in 1958. In 1961 President John F. Kennedy appointed von Braun to lead Saturn 5 and deliver the Apollo 'man on the moon' project. He described himself as a patriot during the war who had answered his country's call; if he had not, someone else would have done. He said, 'The V2 flew very well. The only trouble is that it landed on the wrong planet.'

Reflecting his contribution to victory through intelligence work during the war, Professor Jones was made a Commander of the Order of the British Empire in 1942 and a Companion of the Order of the Bath in 1946. His other awards included the Duddell Medal and Prize (from the Physical Society) in 1960 and a Fellowship of the Royal Society in 1965. In 1994 he was made a Companion of Honour. He was also honoured by the US Government with the Medal of Freedom with Silver Palm in 1946 and the Medal of Merit in 1947. The CIA created the R. V. Jones Intelligence Award in 1993.

Ironically, Professor Jones had worked at the Cavendish Laboratory with a German physicist called Carl Bosch, whose father was President of I.G. Farben Industrie, winning the 1931 Nobel Prize for high-pressure chemistry. Bosch returned to Germany in 1936, designing the radio beam system used for the V2 rockets and interpreting captured British radio devices, many designed, paradoxically, by Professor Jones.

I.G. Farben was the German chemicals company allied to the Nazis which manufactured the Zyklon B gas used to murder prisoners in the death camps. In the First World War, their development of the Haber-Bosch process for nitrogen fixation compensated for Germany's exclusion from the Chilean nitrate trade, producing synthetic nitrate as agricultural fertiliser and explosives such as gunpowder, dynamite or TNT. In the Second World War, I.G. Farben developed processes for making synthetic petrol and rubber from coal, contributing to Germany's ability to wage war without access to any major oil fields. The I.G. Farben trial was the second case brought against leading industrialists of Nazi Germany for their conduct during the Nazi regime. The defendants were all directors of I.G. Farben.

Claims under Head 4 to the Cohen Commission revealed previously secret designs. Head 4 was used by the United States government under the 'Interchange of Patent Rights and Information', signed in August 1942 and extended in March 1946. Other significant details were designs for gyroscopic gunsights, submarine detection devices, self-sealing fuel tanks and plastic explosives. All were grouped under Head 4 claims.

In September 1940, after a secret conference with Winston Churchill, Sir Henry Tizard led the British Technical and Scientific Mission delegation to the United States and Canada in September 1940, at the height of the Battle of Britain. Tizard, as chairman of Britain's Aeronautical Research Committee, was fully involved in the early development of British radar and understood the wartime advantages to be gained from a superior radar system. The team was authorised by Winston Churchill to share British secrets in return for massive American industrial resources to manufacture items for wartime use.

The collection of ideas, blueprints and prototypes is often described as some of the most valuable cargo ever brought to America. British researchers made significant discoveries, but effective use by mass production was impossible under restricted wartime conditions in Britain. In particular, the newly invented resonant-cavity magnetron was disclosed to the Americans, a device already well beyond their ability to generate the high-power microwaves used in sophisticated radar. Secrets included details of the new Frank Whittle jet engine and the Frisch-Peierls memorandum (British Tube Alloys) project on the feasibility of an atomic bomb. The British also disclosed the technical details of the Chain Home early warning radar stations, but this was identical to the American Navy's long-wave CXAM radar. Alongside the initial Dome training for anti-aircraft gunners, destruction of an airborne target could be greatly enhanced by the anti-aircraft shell containing a proximity fuze. This detonated when the radar system within the shell detected the proximity of a target.

A design for the radar proximity fuze (also known as the VT fuze), which came into use later in WW2, was so important that it was kept secret at a similar level to the atom bomb project or the D-Day invasion. The use of these proximity fuzed shells was restricted initially to locations and situations where the enemy could not recover them and uncover the inner workings. The American development of the proximity fuze greatly improved the effectiveness of anti-aircraft gunnery, with the shell exploding at the closest point to the target. The fuze contained vacuum tubes (radio valves) rather than electronic circuits. These had to survive a 20,000 'G' force acceleration and being spun by the gun barrel rifling to nearly 30,000 rpm, generating an immense centrifugal force. Within the shell the fuze was packed with a detonator and batteries into a space the size of a milk carton.

American Admiral Lewis Strauss described the technology: 'One of the most original and effective military developments in the Second World War was the proximity, or "VT", fuze. The proximity fuze must be listed among the very small group of developments, such as radar, upon which victory depended.' During the Pacific battles, all American weapons loaded with VT fuzes were banned over land to avoid the Japanese discovering the technology.

By 1945, Royal Navy gunners were instructed on setting the correct fuze and tracking this by radar as explained in the Gunnery Pocket Book (Royal Navy (1945) in Appendix F. This drill was for high-angle guns against aircraft, setting fuzes correctly.

Working for a defence contractor, American Julius Rosenberg stole a working model of an American proximity fuze and delivered it to Soviet intelligence. He also sent details of the Manhattan project supplied by his brother-in-law to the Soviets, helping them to develop their own nuclear weapons.

PART III

The Hearing

Chapter 14

The Royal Commission on Awards to Inventors - Henry Stephens

On 5 March 1947 the Royal Commission on Awards to Inventors (Cohen Commission), received an application (see Plate 4) from Lieutenant Commander Henry Stephens, seeking recognition and reward as the inventor of the Dome Trainer. The hearing was set for 5 April 1948 under Head 3, file number 168, claims 6, 44, 413 and 471. Decisions were delayed until 28 May 1948 due to rivals claiming a right of invention.

The first documented trainer was a basic prototype built by Lieutenant Colonel G. F. Haszard, who served in the Royal Marines from 1914 to 1934, and Brigadier Vere Ronald Krohn of the Royal Artillery. Whilst instructing at an Army Anti-Aircraft school at Biggin Hill in 1926 they built a 'miniature anti-aircraft range', which used basically the similar principles as the Dome Trainer. A crucial difference was that the reflective surface holding the aircraft image was operated by hand. The shell impact point was shown by a static projector when the trigger was depressed. Unlike the Dome Trainer's realistic sound, they used silent film but made attempts to create separately generated sound.

The Admiralty Research Laboratory spent approximately £1,500 on this project, with Haszard and Krohn taking out British Pat. No. 273,385 of 1926 for their invention. The Royal Commission ruled that Lieutenant Colonel Haszard had no claim for contribution to the Dome Aiming Trainer as his invention did not move beyond a prototype, failed further tests and was therefore was not deployed in wartime.

Since there were two other claimants for recognition and award, Henry compiled a private journal to illustrate his legal claim from concept to entry into service as effective training for anti-aircraft gunners. This journal has been granted to the Imperial War Museum (see Plate 4). In this journal, Henry noted:

> The Royal Commission on Awards to Inventors under the Chairmanship of Lord Justice Cohen, heard my claim on April 5, 6, 7 and 8, 1948.
>
> Appearing for the Crown:
> Mr Bevan (Counsel – instructed by the Admiralty and Treasury Solicitor)
> Captain Alan Campbell O.B.E., R.N. (Witness)

Commander R. Clarke R.N. HMS Excellent (Witness)

Representing myself were:
Mr Pat Graham (Senior Counsel) and Mr Everington (Junior Counsel)
Messrs Kilburn & Strode (Patent Agents)

The following witnesses were present in court to give evidence on my behalf:
Admiral Sir Frederic Dreyer. GBE, KCB, CB.
General Sir Frederick Pile, Bt, GCB, DSO.
Rear Admiral Sir W. G. Agnew. KVCO, CB, DSO.
Captain J.C. Davis, OBE., R.N.
Commander Guy Phelips, R.N.
Commander Pigon, R.N.
Technical officer P.W.T. Forrow (HMS Excellent)

Henry made his claim on Form Three (Head 3) as the inventor of the Dome Trainer and associated technology as follows:

Form Three. Statement of Claim under Head (3) of the Royal Warrant dated May 15th, 1946, i.e., claim in respect of use by any Government Department or with the approval of a Government Department by any Allied Government (other than a Dominion Government and the Government of India) of any invention, design, drawing or process not conferring a monopoly or any statutory right to compensation. When completed, this form should be sent in duplicate to the Secretary, The Royal Commission on Awards to Inventors, Somerset House, Strand, W.C.2 and a copy should be sent to the Government Department concerned.

The Claimant should give details of his claim under the following heads:

RCAI 1. Name and address of the Claimant:

Henry Christian Stephens, 64a. Carlisle Mansions, Carlisle Place, London, S.W.1.

Description: Photographic Expert.

If the Claimant was at any time in Service of the Crown, full details of such service should be given. Joined the Navy 1913. Released 1919. Re-joined 8th July 1940. Released 25th December 1945. It is to be emphasised that at the date when the invention, the subject of this claim, was made and first put forward, the Claimant was not in the Service of the Crown.

RCAI 2. Name and address of any Solicitor or Agent authorised to act for the Claimant.

Kilburn and Strode, 31-33 High Holborn, London, W.C.1.

RCAI 3. Particulars of invention, design, drawing or process in question.

The Dome Trainer [see plates 6 & 7], (a device for teaching Anti-Aircraft Shooting) and its various developments. Briefly, a cinema film is taken of an attacking aircraft (or is made up from pictures of a model) together with a record of the movement of the camera in elevation and azimuth. The film is projected on to a hemispherical roof of a room, the projector being automatically moved in the same way as the camera was moved when the corresponding pictures were taken, the optical systems being so chosen that the aircraft appears completely realistic not only in elevation and azimuth, but also in size and therefore apparent range, and in attitude [see Plate 11]. The realism is completed by a sound track and loudspeakers reproducing the sounds of dive bombing, machine gunning, anti-aircraft fire and so forth. Schedule three follows:

Schedule three. The pupil is placed at the controls of a gunsight near the centre of the Dome. A spot of light (or a graticule) is also projected on the Dome at the actual point at which the pupil is aiming and another spot, invisible to the pupil but continuously visible to the instructor appears at the correct point of aim so that faults are apparent to the instructor and class. After joining the Service, the Claimant developed the above and in addition made and developed other inventions which are now in use or are still being developed, including the following: The 'Photographic Table' is a device which, as a camera (or part of its optical system) is moved to follow an actual aircraft, serves to record the movements made.

That known as 'Background Scenic Effects' involves the arrangement of projectors to project on the Dome a background scenic panorama. That known as the 'Future Position Spot' (FP) an arrangement for projecting on to the Dome a spot at the correct position of aim for a fast-moving target, which may be outside the frame of the picture from the main projector.

The 'Hit Recorder' [see Plate 12] is a device which records the number of shots fired, the number of hits, the number of near misses, and the number of bursts of firing, and switches off the firing control when a certain number of rounds have been fired. The Future Position Spot and the Hit Recorder were protected by British Patent Application No. 4876 of 1946 in the names of the Claimant and Mr. E.T.J. Tapp jointly.

In early Dome Trainers, the number of hits on target that the trainee gunner achieved was visually determined by the gunnery instructor watching the performance. By pulsing the yellow FP spot projector beam, when the trainee had sights on the correct Future Position and was firing, a photo-electric cell mounted on the gun and aligned with the sights and correctly tuned in would pick up the pulsed beam and register hits. On a control panel the number of 'shots' fired would be recorded and, of those, using the above system, the number of 'hits' on target recorded. The equipment could be switched between recording 450 rounds per minute for a 20mm gun or 90 rounds per minute for a 40mm gun, together with the appropriate sounds produced by the gun noise amplifier.

RCAI 4. Particulars with full names and addresses of any other parties interested in the invention, design, drawing or process as assignees, licensees or otherwise:

None (Other than Mr Tapp's rights as co-applicant in Patent Application No. 4876 of 1946 on the Future Position Spot and Hit Recorder)

[Author's note: On 27 July 1951, Mr Ernest Tapp was released from this claim by Henry Stephens on payment of £250 to Henry for work done on four Dome Trainer films for the Admiralty].

RCAI 5. Particulars of alleged use by any Government Department, giving, as far as possible, nature, extent and period of use and brief details of any personal services rendered by the Claimant to the Department in connection with the subject matter of the claim:

The Dome Trainer has been employed from 1941 by the Admiralty, RAF Regiment, and the Army, and is still in use. The Claimant has no data concerning the exact numbers used in this country, and abroad, but believes, that they number at least 300, and that the average cost of the equipment embodying his inventions amounts to at least £3,000 each. His invention was also embodied in the Portobel arrangement, but again he has no information concerning the number and cost of these devices. He also believes that the invention was communicated to the United States Government and was used by them, for example, in the 'Waller' trainer.

Regarding the services rendered by the claimant, the Claimant was originally advised to re-join the Navy as being the quickest way of ensuring that the invention might be considered and adopted. Later developments and work done by the claimant were therefore partly recompensed by his Navy pay. In view of the fact that his rank and pay were only that of Sub-Lieutenant [see Plate 2] (11 shillings per day), from July 1940 to October 1940, a Lieutenant (13 shillings and 6 pence per day) from October 1940 to August 1942, and an acting Lieutenant Commander (25 shillings per day) from August 1942 to December 1945, it is thought that some further recompense is due to him for his later development work and for the additional inventions referred to above. After his release he was retained by the Ministry of Supply for six months to work on development of the Future Position Spot, and the Hit Recorder, for which he received £300 to cover out of pocket expenses as well as services.

RCAI 6. Particulars of disclosure of the invention, design, drawing or process which it is alleged has led to use by a Government Department or by any Allied Government:

The Claimant thought out this invention very early in 1940, as a civilian, and worked on it in his spare time. In May 1940, while still a civilian, he put forward his idea to Commander Guy Phelips, R.N. of the RN. Photographic School, Tipnor, whom he had known for some years. Commander Phelips advised that the best method of bringing it immediately to the notice of the responsible Naval Authorities was for the claimant to join up and put his idea forward to his first Commanding Officer. Through Commander Phelips he re-joined as an R.N.V.R. Officer. Schedule 6A follows:

He received his appointment on July 8th, 1940, as Temporary Probationary Sub-Lieutenant R.N.V.R. to R.N. College for instruction. Acting on Commander Phelips' advice he submitted his broad proposals to Commander Doyley, Commander of the College who placed them in front of Captain J.C. Davis, O.B.E. during the first week of his appointment. 6B follows:

15th July 1940.
To: Commander J. Doyley & Captain J.C. Davis, R.N. College, Greenwich.
Sir,
I have the honour to submit the following two suggestions for your consideration.

A. Cinematograph Films of aircraft attacking a ship and projected in a room with a concave ceiling for training A.A. guns crews and Control Officers.

If cinematograph films were taken of aircraft attacking a ship (either of actual attacks by enemy aircraft or by our own from data collected from enemy modes of attack) from the deck of a ship, and these films were projected the same size as seen by the naked eye, the film being run at the same speed as taken on to the concave ceiling of a room (this could be done at little expense by fixing projection screens at the required angle), Then to an A.A. guns crew or control officers situated in that room, the attack would

Right: **Plate 1.** The inventor of the Dome Trainer, Lieutenant Commander Henry Christian Stephens, RNVR (1940). (Author collection)

Below: **Plate 2.** Lieutenant Commander Henry Christian Stephens' commission into the RNVR (1940). (Author collection)

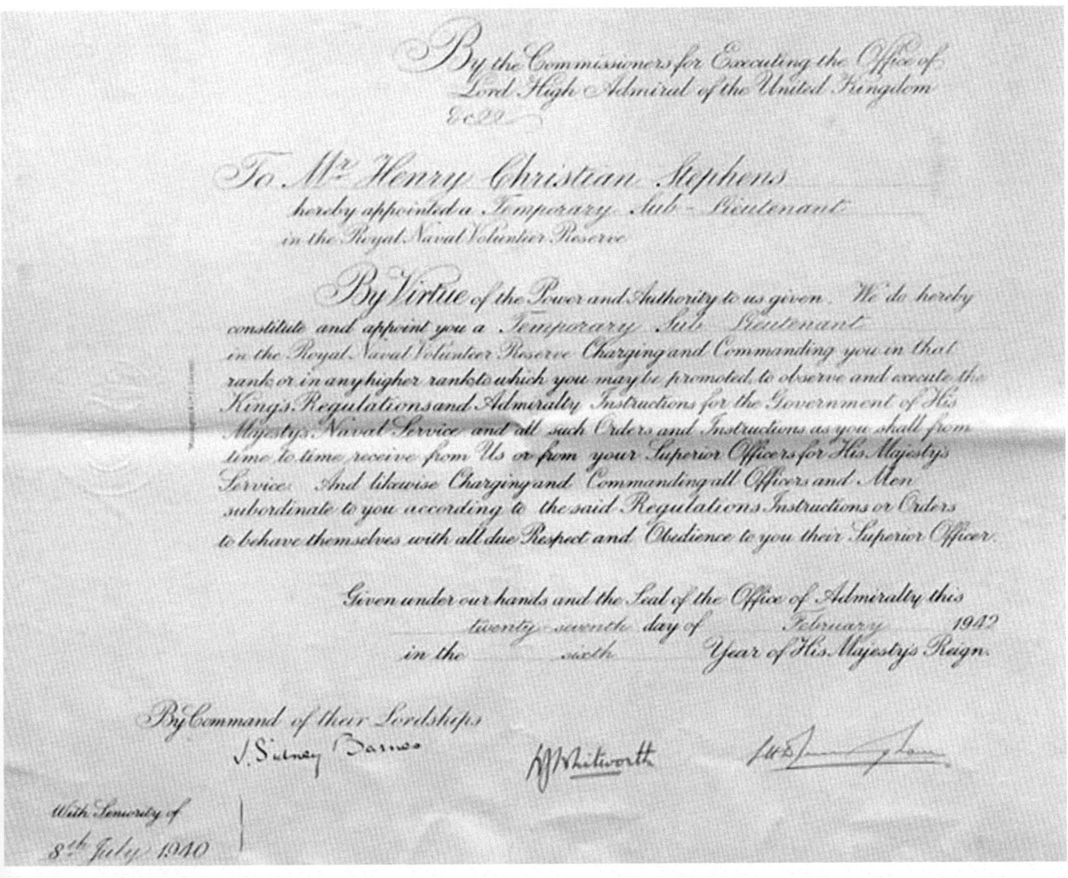

By the Commissioners for Executing the Office of Lord High Admiral of the United Kingdom &c.

To Mr Henry Christian Stephens hereby appointed a Temporary Sub-Lieutenant in the Royal Naval Volunteer Reserve

By Virtue of the Power and Authority to us given We do hereby constitute and appoint you a Temporary Sub Lieutenant in the Royal Naval Volunteer Reserve Charging and Commanding you in that rank or in any higher rank to which you may be promoted to observe and execute the King's Regulations and Admiralty Instructions for the Government of His Majesty's Naval Service and all such Orders and Instructions as you shall from time to time receive from Us or from your Superior Officers for His Majesty's Service. And likewise Charging and Commanding all Officers and Men subordinate to you according to the said Regulations Instructions or Orders to behave themselves with all due Respect and Obedience to you their Superior Officer.

Given under our hands and the Seal of the Office of Admiralty this twenty-seventh day of February 1942 in the sixth Year of His Majesty's Reign.

By Command of their Lordships
J. Sidney Barnes

With Seniority of 8th July 1940

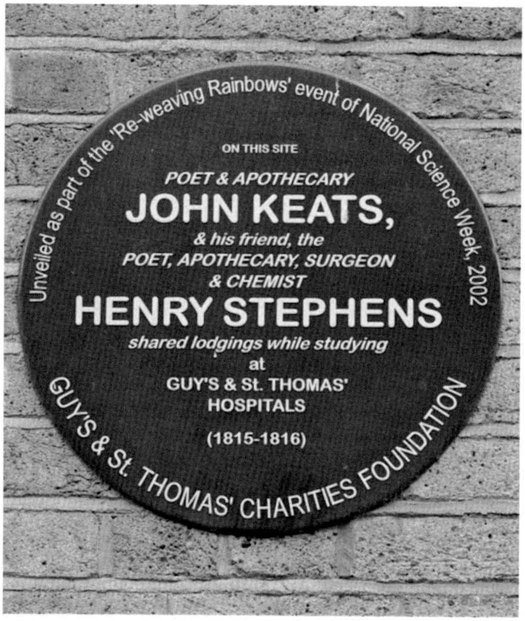

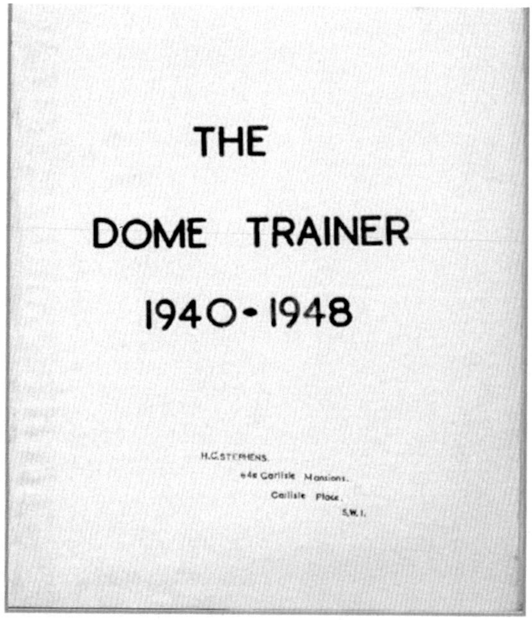

Above left: **Plate 3.** Blue plaque commemorating Doctor Henry Stephens and John Keats (poet), Stamford Street, London (2002). (Author collection)

Above right: **Plate 4.** Private journal of Lieutenant Commander Henry Christian Stephens, held by the Imperial War Museum. (Author collection)

Plate 5. Henry Charles 'Inky' Stephens (February 1841 – July 1918), the successful heir to the ink business. As well as a businessman, he was also a Member of Parliament.

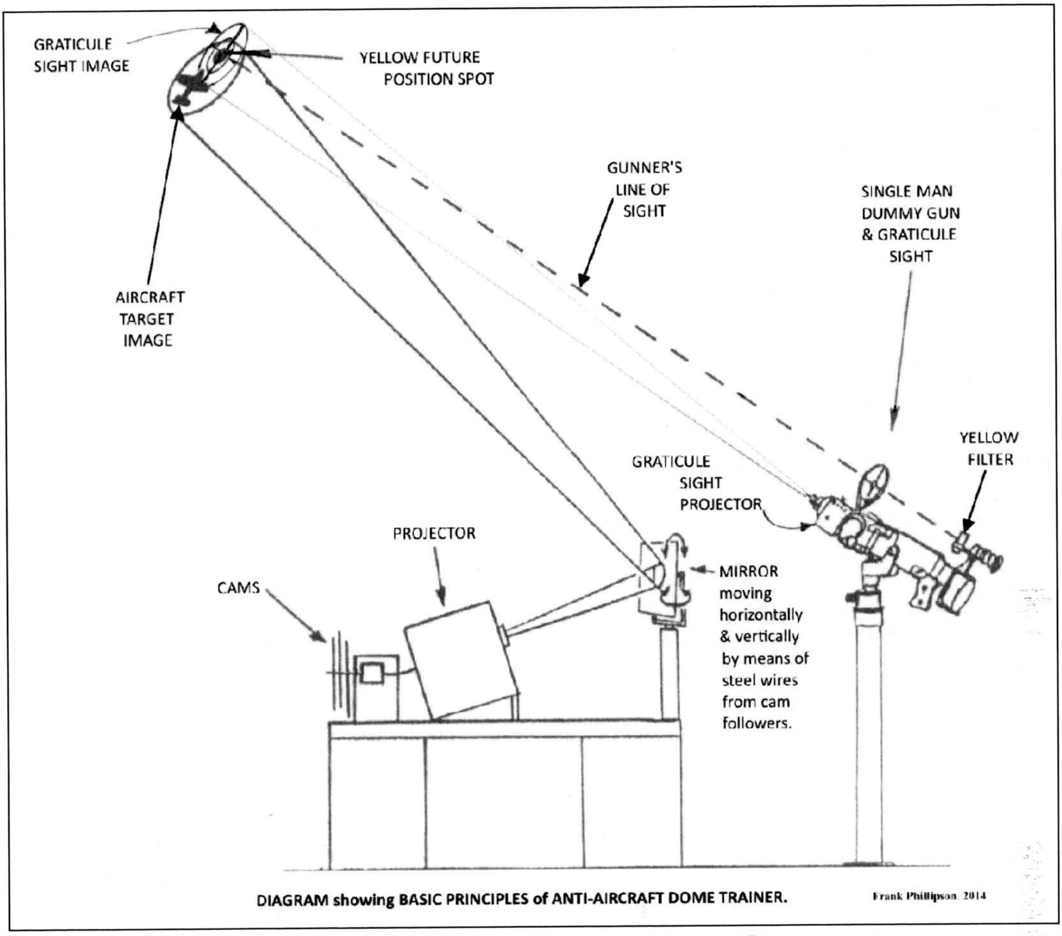

Above: **Plate 6.** Dome Trainer anti-aircraft concept design. (Frank Phillipson, reproduced with permission)

Right: **Plate 7.** Dome Trainer electrical design. (Frank Phillipson, reproduced with permission)

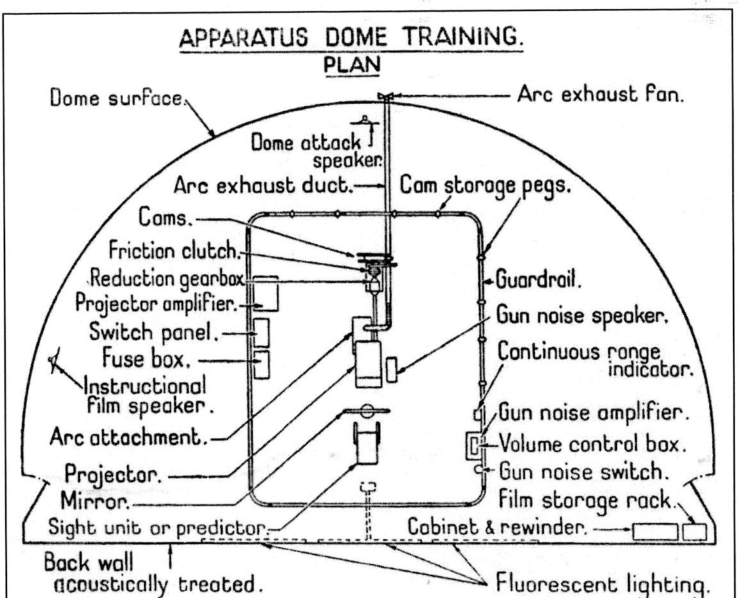

FIG. I

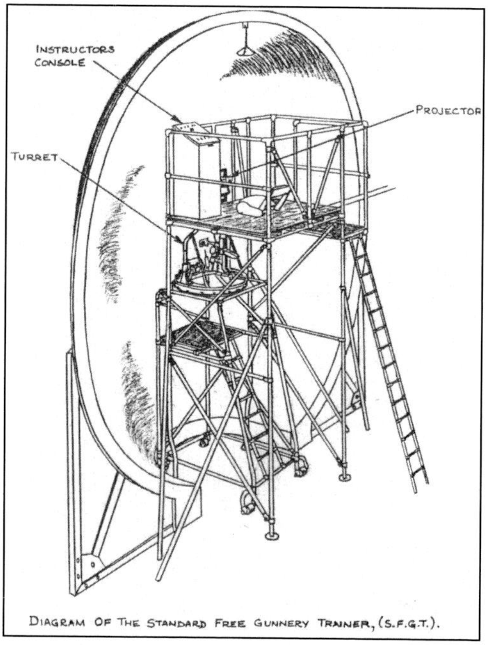

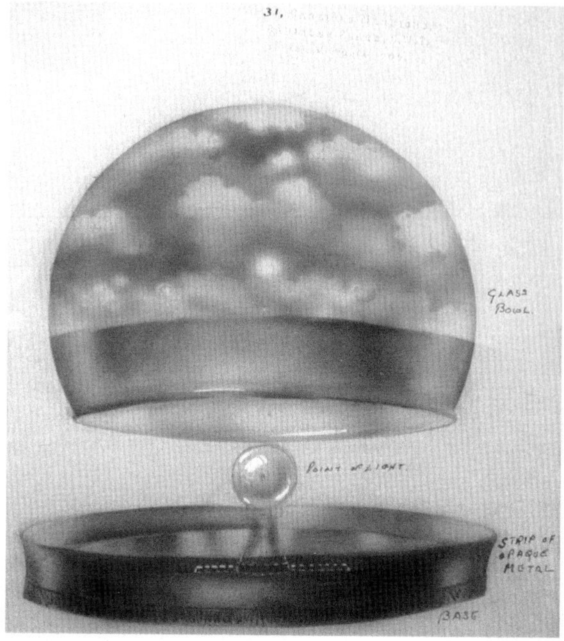

Above left: **Plate 8.** Standard Free Gunnery Trainer drawing, from Henry Stephens' private journal. (Author collection)

Above right: **Plate 9.** Interior Dome Trainer, in a watercolour fishbowl sky design, from Henry Stephens' private journal. (Author collection)

Above left: **Plate 10.** Dome Trainer dummy Bofors 40 mm gun design. (Author collection)

Above right: **Plate 11.** Dome Trainer Projection and mirror. (Author collection)

Plate 12. Dome Trainer "shot and hit" recorder designed by Henry Stephens. (Author collection)

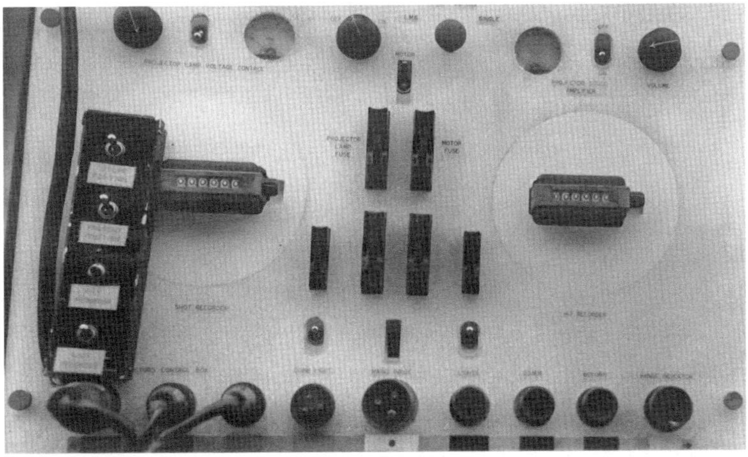

Plate 13. Royal Canadian Navy gunners in Dome Trainer. (Canadian War Museum, Ottawa, reproduced with permission)

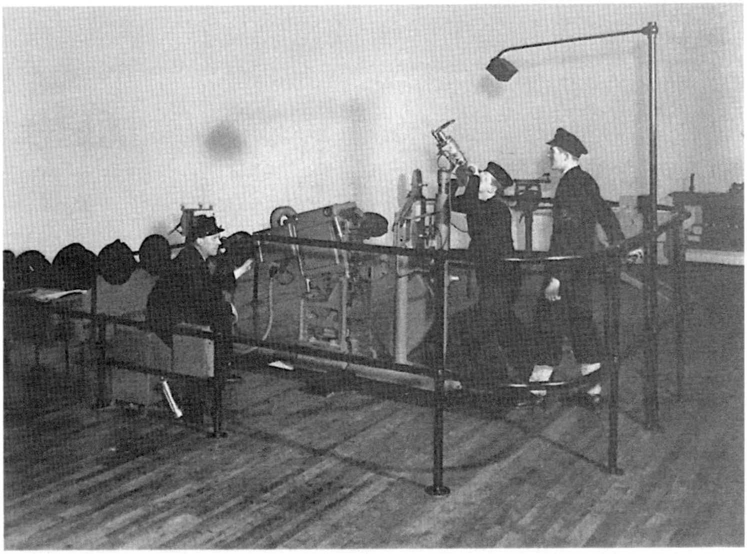

Plate 14. British gunners in Dome Trainer. (Langham Dome images, reproduced with permission)

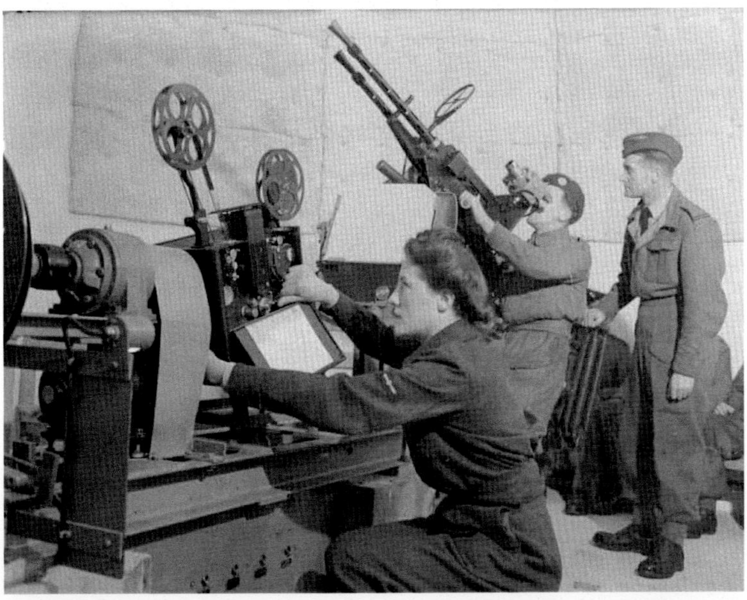

Plate 15. Belgian Merchant Navy (Defensively Equipped Merchant Ships – DEMS) gunners, 1944. (Imperial War Museum, reproduced with permission)

Plate 16. DEMS bus trainer, Devonport, Royal Navy (1940). (Imperial War Museum, reproduced with permission)

Plate 17. Canadian gunners in Dome Trainer. (Canadian War Museum, Ottawa, reproduced with permission)

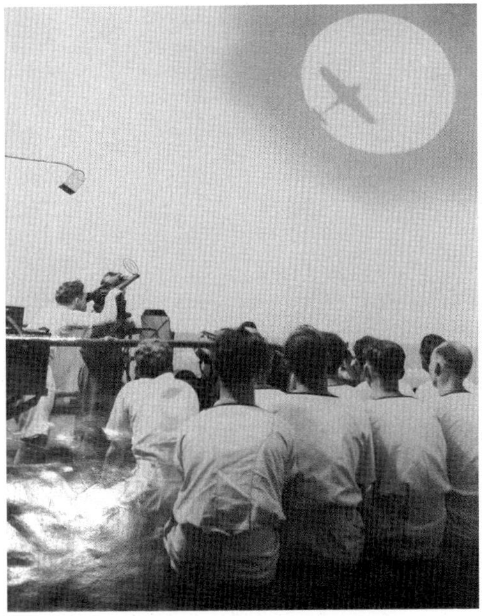

Above: **Plate 18.** Polish air gunners at RAF Penrhos, Wales (1944). (Author collection)

Right: **Plate 19.** Merchant Navy gunners in Dome Trainer, Columbo, Ceylon (Sir Lanka). (Author collection)

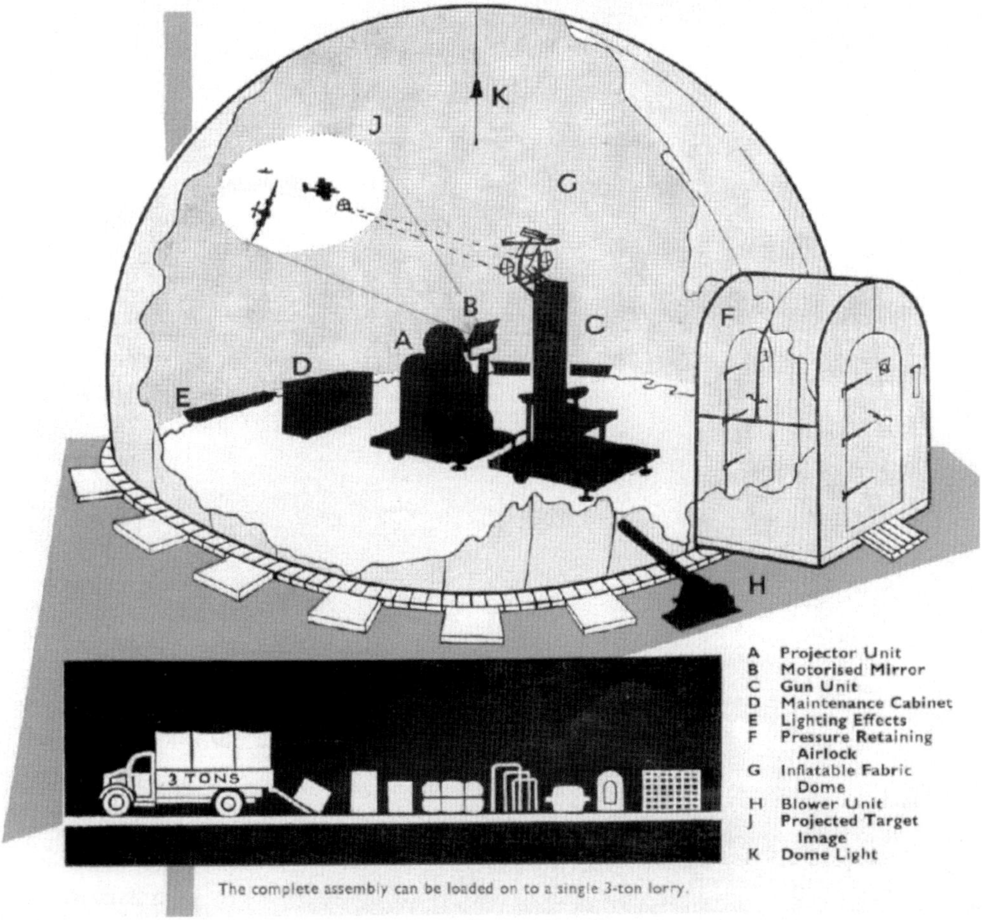

Plate 20. Portobel Dome Trainer packing design for 3-ton truck. (Frank Phillipson, reproduced with permission)

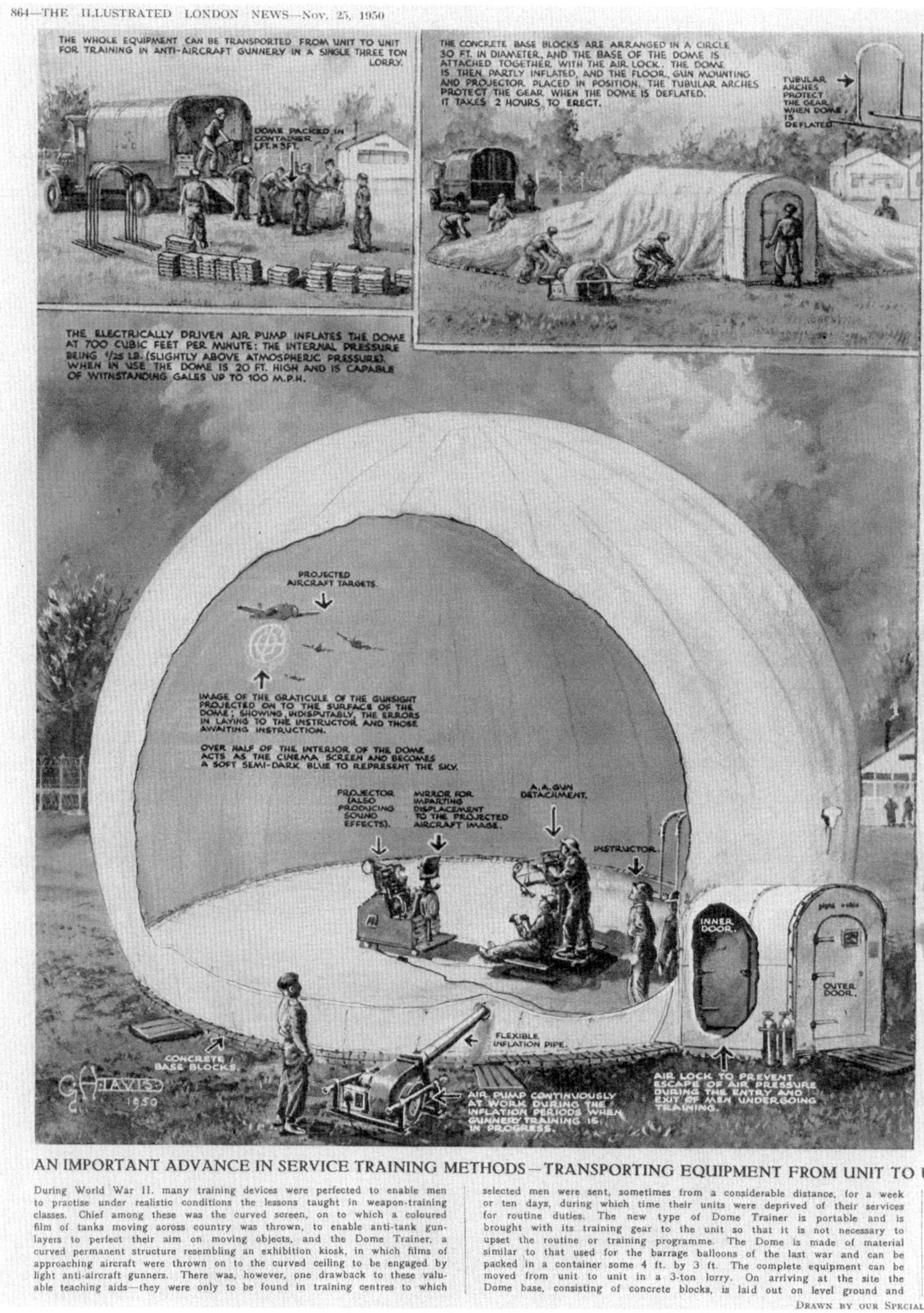

864—THE ILLUSTRATED LONDON NEWS—Nov. 25, 1950

AN IMPORTANT ADVANCE IN SERVICE TRAINING METHODS—TRANSPORTING EQUIPMENT FROM UNIT TO U

During World War II. many training devices were perfected to enable men to practise under realistic conditions the lessons taught in weapon-training classes. Chief among these was the curved screen, on to which a coloured film of tanks moving across country was thrown, to enable anti-tank gun-layers to perfect their aim on moving objects, and the Dome Trainer, a curved permanent structure resembling an exhibition kiosk, in which films of approaching aircraft were thrown on to the curved ceiling to be engaged by light anti-aircraft gunners. There was, however, one drawback to these valuable teaching aids—they were only to be found in training centres to which selected men were sent, sometimes from a considerable distance, for a week or ten days, during which time their units were deprived of their services for routine duties. The new type of Dome Trainer is portable and is brought with its training gear to the unit so that it is not necessary to upset the routine or training programme. The Dome is made of material similar to that used for the barrage balloons of the last war and can be packed in a container some 4 ft. by 3 ft. The complete equipment can be moved from unit to unit in a 3-ton lorry. On arriving at the site the Dome base, consisting of concrete blocks, is laid out on level ground and

DRAWN BY OUR SPECIAL

Plate 21. *The Illustrated London News* (1950) showing a portable variant of the Dome Trainer. The Portobel was made of inflated barrage balloon material, smaller than a fixed Dome and carried from base to base in a 3-ton truck with a construction crew of six. (Author collection)

Nov. 25, 1950—THE ILLUSTRATED LONDON NEWS—865

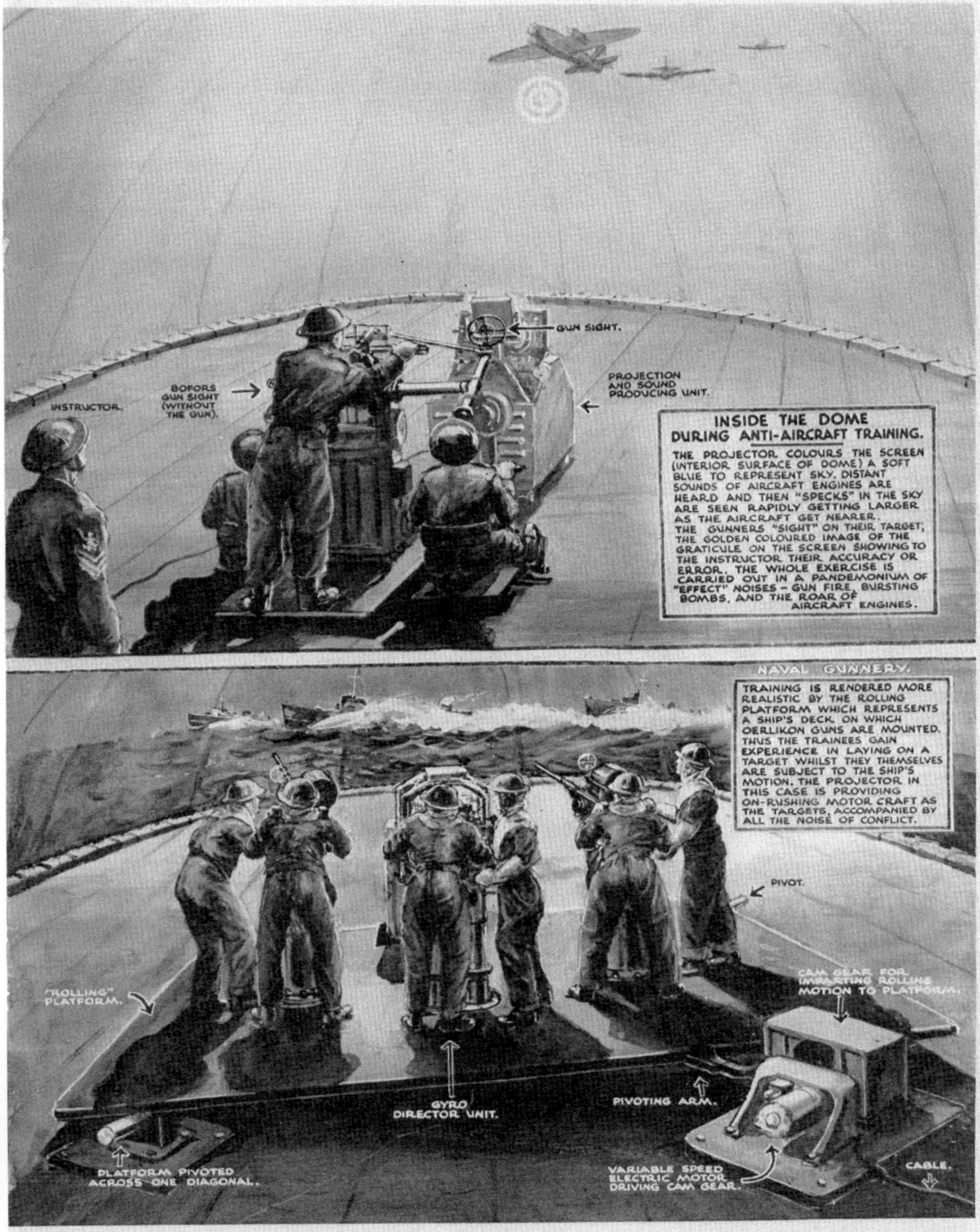

INIT: THE PORTABLE INFLATED DOME TRAINER FOR ANTI-AIRCRAFT GUNNERS AND NAVAL GUN CREWS.

the fabric, air-pump, air-pipe and air-lock are attached. The Dome is then inflated and in about two hours the trainer is ready for use. The Dome remains with the unit as long as it is required and then can be quickly dismantled and taken on the lorry to the next unit. Though the Dome is inflated, and kept at little more than atmospheric pressure within, it is said to be able to withstand winds of 100 m.p.h. force. The whole of one side of the interior of the Dome serves as a cinema screen upon which films of aircraft in flight and motor torpedo-boats are projected as targets. Attached to the projector is a mirror for imparting displacement to the target-image equal to that made by the cameraman as he "followed" the target as the film was taken. In addition, the image of the gunsight is thrown on to the screen in bright light so that the instructor and those awaiting their turn can see the errors in laying as the aircraft approach and pass overhead. The gunner engages his target amidst all the pandemonium of modern war, for the noise of aircraft engines, the chatter of machine-guns and the detonation of bombs are reproduced by the sound apparatus in the projector. Naval gunners can also benefit from the Dome Trainer, and a new rolling platform has been produced which is illustrated for the first time above.

ARTIST, G. H. DAVIS.

Plate 22. *The Illustrated London News* (1950) showing the new Army and Navy variant of the Stephens Dome Trainer. The Navy edition had a pivoting floor to replicate a ship rolling and pitching at sea. (Author collection)

Above: **Plate 23.** Restored and painted Langham Dome Trainer, Norfolk (2014). (Author collection)

Below: **Plate 24.** Langham Dome, Norfolk (2019). Queen's Award for Voluntary Service (QAVS). (Patrick Allen, reproduced with permission)

Above: **Plate 25.** Langham Dome, Norfolk (2022). The interior after restoration. (Author collection)

Below: **Plate 26.** Langham Dome, Norfolk (2024), with Spitfire mounting. (Author collection)

Plate 27. Mildenhall Dome, RAF/USAF base, Suffolk (2022). (Author collection)

Plates 28 & 29. Miss Evelyn Stephens with Dermot (Dermie) O'Gormanon (above left) and her husband, Michael Ward-Thomas (above right) at their wedding in 1955. (Author collection)

Above: **Plate 30.** Pembury airfield Dome Trainer, Wales. (Author collection)

Right: **Plate 31.** Langham Dome Trainer Airfield memorial, Norfolk (2022). (Author collection)

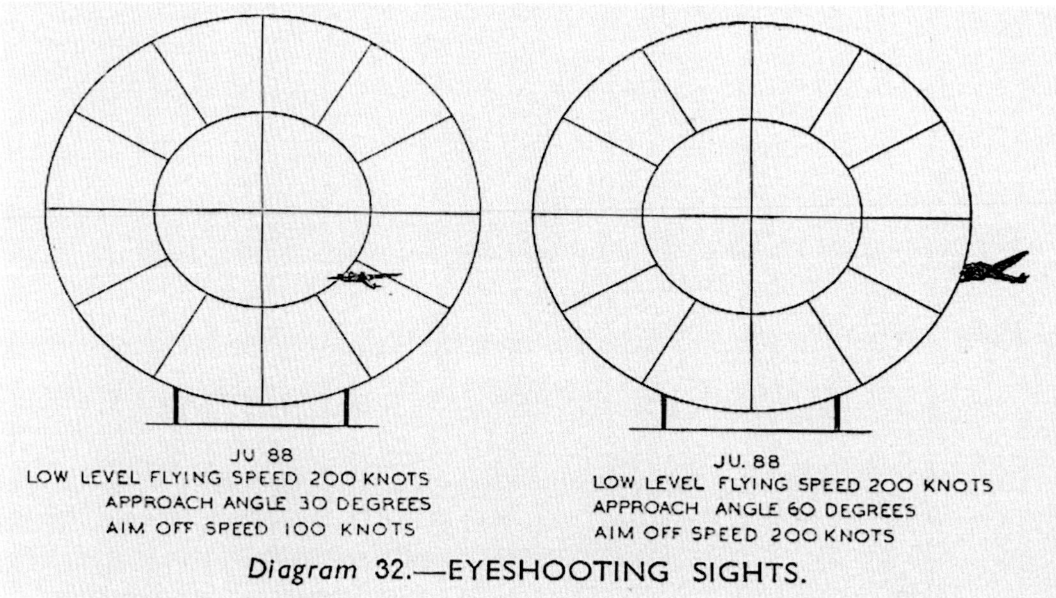

Plate 32. Eye Shooting target – B.R. 224/45. *The Gunnery Pocket Book* (1945).

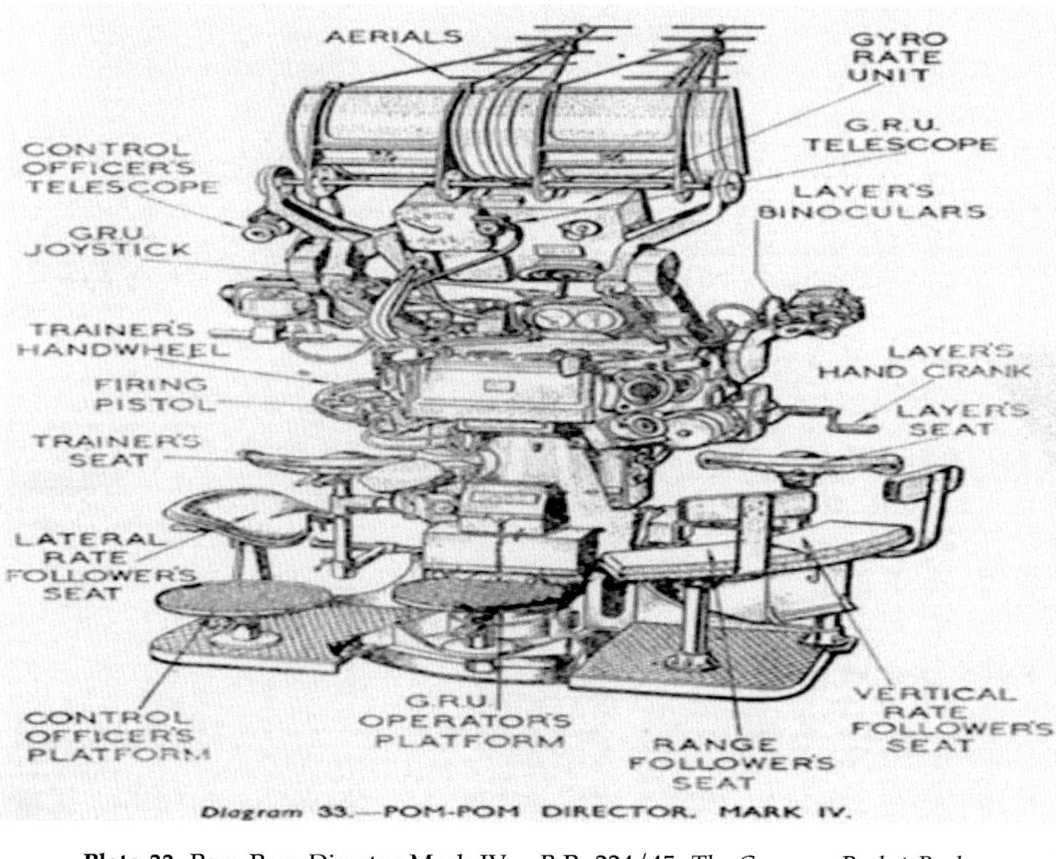

Plate 33. Pom-Pom Director Mark IV. – B.R. 224/45. *The Gunnery Pocket Book* (1945).

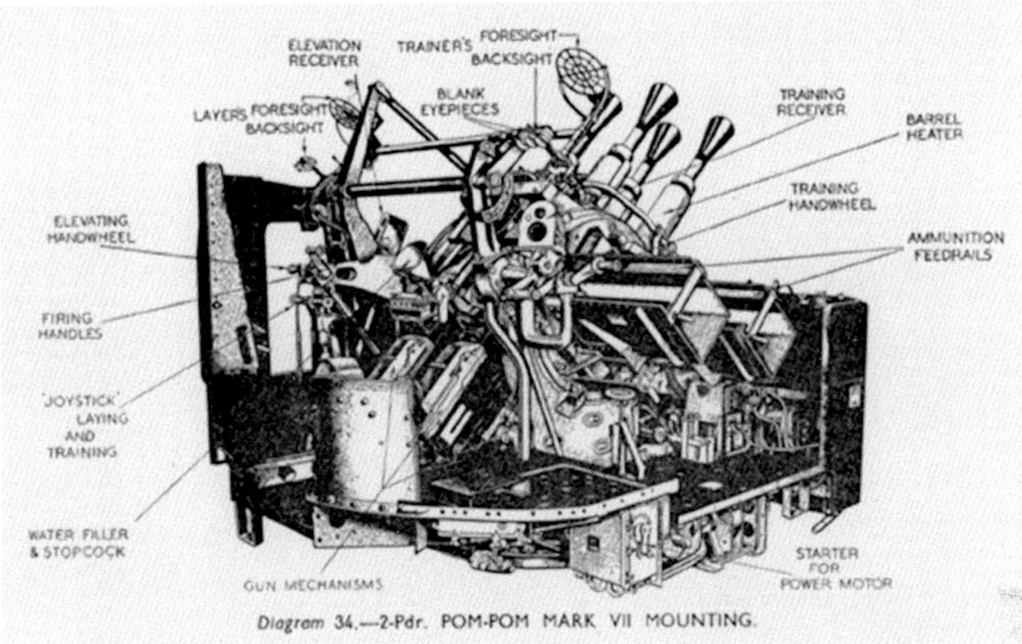

Plate 34. 2-pounder Pom-Pom gun. Mark VII mounting – B.R. 224/45. *The Gunnery Pocket Book* (1945).

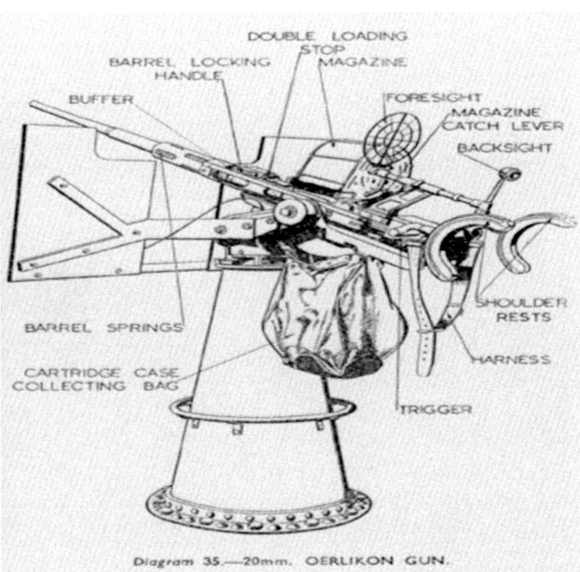

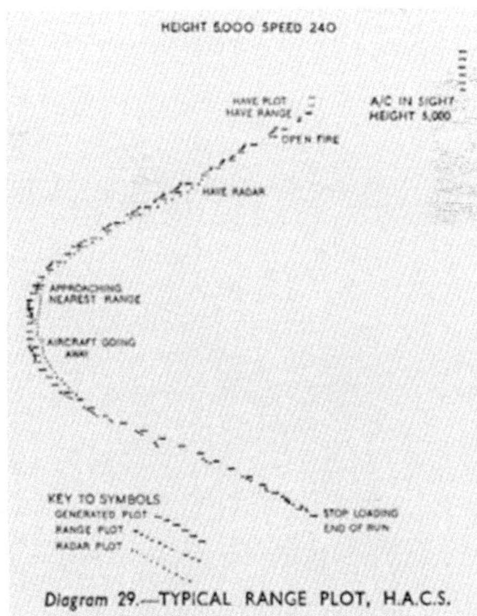

Above left: **Plate 35.** 20mm Oerlikon Gun – B.R. 224/45. *The Gunnery Pocket Book* (1945).

Above right: **Plate 36.** Principals of Deflection – B.R. 224/45. *The Gunnery Pocket Book* (1945).

Plate 37. (*above*) Mid 1960s' 40 ft Dome cinema (RFD Godalming), 20mm Oerlikon, and with calibration dots (*below*).

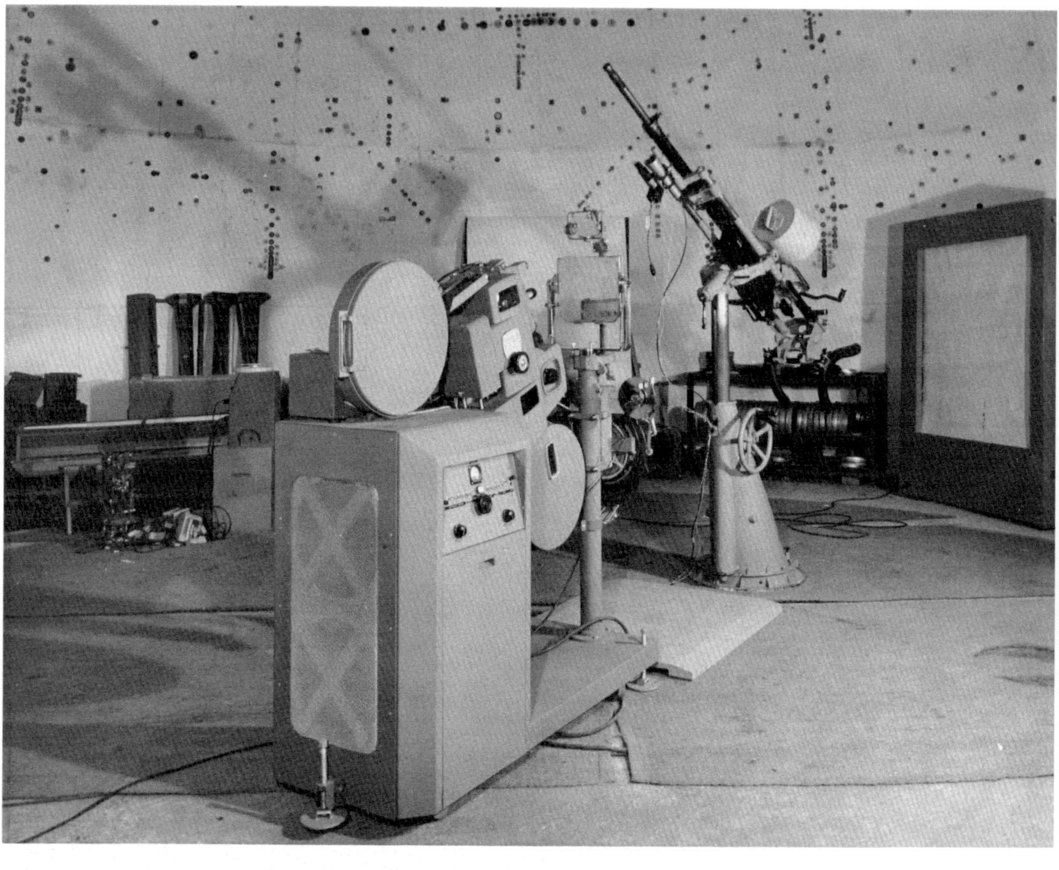

appear to them exactly as under actual conditions, the dive bomber diving and machine gunning - machines passing - hiding behind and breaking through clouds, etc. Sound effects could be used with advantage.

B. For increasing the efficiency of propaganda from the Royal Navy.
That the naval photographers in the service should receive instructions as to how to take pictures that are good propaganda and the type of pictures that will be of use in keeping up the morale of the public, as at the present time they have no idea whatever in this, to my mind, important branch of photography. If one or two officers who understood this work were attached to the R.N. schools of photography and taught the men how to take and what constitutes good propaganda pictures, then when the men were appointed to their respective ships, through the R.N. Photographic Section, instructions could be sent to them to take a picture or series of pictures from time to time that will be in conformity with the news etc. This is too large a subject for me to write fully on, but I would be pleased to explain this idea in more detail should you wish to see me on this matter. Having related to this type of work for the past ten years I feel very strongly that good propaganda from the Service would be a tremendous help to the civilian population of this country at the present time, who are relying entirely on the Royal Navy for their safety and the successful result of this war.

I am, Sir,
Your obedient Servant,
Sub-Lieutenant H.C. Stephens, R.N.V.R.

The claimant was instructed, with Lieutenant Commander Pigou, R.N., to visit various experts to confirm the practicability of the scheme. HMS Excellent was visited on August 6th, 1940, and other experts on ensuing days.

[Author's note: Lieutenant Commander Pigou was Henry's brother-in-law, married to his elder sister Agnes].

Captain Davis then instructed the claimant to make an Official report, which was dated 14 August 1940. 6C follows:

14 August 1940
To Captain J.C. Davis, President R.N. College, Greenwich, from Sub-Lieut. H.C. Stephens, R.N.V.R.
Official study for a Dome Trainer
Sir,

I have the honour to submit the following proposal for giving a sound practical training to the A.A. personnel of H.M. Ships, whereby the accuracy of defence against both long and short-range attack from the air may be improved. At the same time enabling the A.A. personnel to become used to the psychological effect of dive bombing and machine gunning by the enemy. The suggestion is that various forms of enemy attack are carried out by our own aircraft on a pre-selected position where cinematograph cameras are installed.

It is proposed that this should be at Eastney.

The pictures obtained would be projected on to the walls from the central position of a cupola, in such a way that, to an observer (situated at the centre of the cupola), the apparent size and speed of the pictured aircraft are the same as in the real attack.

To give an example: When an A.A. Control party are carrying out an exercise in the cupola they will see waves of enemy bombers circling round the horizon and approaching for attack. One wave closing right in from one side to attack, the Dive Bomber breaking away from formation and coming straight down at them - machine gunning - then passing overhead and away; followed by the next wave of machines approaching from the other side and carrying out their attack.

All the time, the machines appearing and passing at the same size and speed as they would see in actuality - with the resultant shell bursts of the defence appearing in accordance with the orders given for the direction of fire by the Control Officer who is being exercised in the cupola, as explained in later paragraph.

For Long Range Training: The whole of the A.A. Control Personnel with their equipment (who would, on actual service, be viewing the attack) should be stationed round the central position on the floor of the cupola. The R.F. Director and O.O.C. with the aid of certain correcting cams for parallax, will be able to perform their function and register correctly on the target in the cupola, as they would on the actual aircraft.

The reasons for this are given in the following paragraphs.

1. Correct Method of Photographing and Reprojecting Image on Cupola. If an air attack is photographed by a kinematograph camera and the picture reprojected on a suitable concave dome, the projector speed being the same as the camera speed, a spectator of the projected picture would see the attacking planes at the same apparent size and travelling at the same apparent speed as in the real attack as seen from the position of the camera. (It is necessary to have the equivalent focal lengths of the projection and camera lenses identical within close limits.)

2. Giving the Necessary Stereoscopic Image to Range finder for Obtaining Range cuts. If two such cameras aligned parallel to one another be run in synchronism to photograph the attack, and if proper care is exercised to get exact registration of frame to frame both in negatives and in prints, then, using a pair of projectors also aligned parallel and running in synchronism and projecting the right-hand picture into the left-hand, the conditions observed by range-taker are as follows: - subject to the mechanical quality of the apparatus being satisfactory the angle at which an object is projected into the rangefinder corresponds exactly with the real angle of the object as seen by the camera.

The range-taker therefore, will get the same results for his ranges as he would using the same rangefinder on the actual target from the position of the camera.

Conclusion arrived at by 1 and 2. If, therefore, we combine the two parallel cameras of the second paragraph with the camera of the first paragraph, also with axis parallel to the two mounted on the same beam so as to follow the same action, and have the three cameras running in synchronism, then, on projecting three pictures also in synchronism the mean picture will be thrown on the dome for the spectators to see and the left and right pictures thrown into the rangefinder for the range-takers.

To show the position of shell burst relative to the aircraft it is proposed to project (with a suitable time lag) a flash by a member whose angular position is determined by that of the gun at the word 'Fire', and at a time lag from the word 'Fire' corresponding to the fuze length range time of flight.

It is further suggested that the different ranges might be simulated by projecting a position of actual shell burst at a variable magnification determined and automatically set from the fuze setter.

Short Range Analysis. Each original attack should be ranged on from the long base RF at Eastney, which automatically gives a plot in the A.A. School, whilst the photographs are being taken.

For short Range Attack: Short Range A. A. weapons to be placed close round the central position on the floor of the cupola. The range plot from Eastney should be supplied to the film printer, and from this, a continuous record by commentator could be made of the ranges for analysis purposes. Analysis can be reached by means of projecting a spot of light appearing in the correct position in relation to the plane and the gun. Details of the necessary electrical circuit are not yet worked out. This will eventually prove efficient practice for tracer.

Sound effects. With reference to dive bombing and general short-range attacks, including machine gunning, it is proposed that sound effects should be run in conjunction with the film.

General remarks and Information. It is suggested that for each of the three cameras we use a 23mm lens on the 35mm sound frame. This would give an angular field 40 degrees square. It is suggested that it is impracticable to increase this angle as there is no commercially available lens to cover 35mm film of shorter local length than the 24mm in question. It is proposed to hire cameras and sound recorders and to use 1,000 feet spools giving an eight-minute run at 32 frames per second.

It is suggested that the best type of screen for the cupola is a semi-specular one mounted on a wooden frame, and the radius be not less than 60 feet. The cupola being built of canvas and wooden frames, this would in no way be a large item of expense. It is required to record in some manner the angular motions of the camera both in elevation and training and reproduce these very exactly in the projector. One suggestion for a method is that an electrical device, for example one in which variable elevation causes variable capacity in a condenser which, in its turn, causes a variable frequency from an oscillator. The output could be fed into a sound recording camera and the result would be like an ordinary sound track. In projecting the picture, similar apparatus working backwards ought to be capable of reproducing the original motion of the camera. Two tracks will be necessary, reproducing the original motion of the camera. Two tracks will be necessary, one to control the elevation and the other to control the training angle. We want expert advice on this, which the Admiralty can supply. It is estimated that, provided there is no delay with the elevation and training angles mentioned above, we could start making pictures in six weeks.

Professor Warmisham of Messrs. Taylor, Taylor and Hobson Ltd., and Mr Oliver of Technicolor have been kind enough to give me fifteen and a half hours of their time discussing this proposal, and they are both agreed that this project can be carried out optically and photographically within limits of error which are negligible as far as the present system of HA gunnery is concerned. I respectfully suggest that the services of Professor Warmisham are retained in this matter, as he is the highest authority in this country on the cinema lenses, etc. which will be needed. At the same time, Mr Oliver should be retained on the photographic side, as only he has the knowledge and plant in this country capable of working to the very exact limits required. Both these gentlemen are extremely interested in this project, and I feel sure will work whole-heartedly for its success.

I am, Sir,
Your obedient servant.
Sub-Lieutenant, R.N.V.R.

The claimant was then sent to HMS Excellent to discuss the proposals further, with a report from Captain Brind as follows:

A.A. Training – use of modern cinematography and sound production.
From: Captain, HMS Excellent, Portsmouth.
Date: 24th August 1940.
To: The Commander-in-Chief, Portsmouth. (Copies to: The Director of Training and Staff Duties Division. The President, R.N. College, Greenwich, S.E.10.)

1. A scheme has been proposed by Sub-Lieutenant H. C. Stephens, R.N.V.R., of the Royal Naval College, Greenwich, whereby full use can be made of modern principles of cinematography and sound production to evolve a realistic indoor A.A. Range.
2. Attacks of all types can, it is claimed, be represented exactly as seen by the naked eye in practice and the full sound effects of own and enemy action, with a suitable

commentary, can readily be added. The control apparatus on which personnel are to be trained is mounted in the centre of the Teacher and details have been worked out whereby accurate instruction can be given in aiming, spotting and range taking, both for long-range gunnery and for close-range.

3. Since facilities on shore for outdoor instruction against aircraft targets are now often difficult to obtain (due to instruction on flying and to the limited capacity of the A.A. ranges) it is strongly recommended that this scheme should be built as soon as possible, with the close-range gunnery problem being studied first.
4. It is realised that the provision of a structure large enough to house the Teacher may present difficulties, but, in the case of the pilot model, it should be possible to utilise a film studio or some similar building.
5. In connection with the development of this Teacher, I have also had conversation with certain members of the film industry about instructional films, and particularly those for naval A.A. Gunnery. I am convinced that a very great deal could be done in a short space of time to improve A.A., training, both ashore and afloat, if the full resources of the civilian film industry, with all its technical and psychological knowledge and drive, were mobilised to help.
6. The urgent need for A.A. Instructional Films, for example to teach eye-shooting, tracer-observation, spotting and similar subjects, has long been felt. The fact that these films have not been produced is due firstly to the fact that the R.N. School of Photography is already working to full capacity on other commitments and secondly that a Gunnery Officer, with first-hand experience of modern training, would be required to devote his whole time for several months to the work.
7. It has been suggested to me by Mr. W. Oliver of Technicolor Films Ltd., that first-class instructional films could be produced almost immediately, using the minimum amount of Service effort and the maximum amount of civilian effort, if a selected team of civilians from the film industry could be allowed to work in direct co-operation with the A.A. Range, Eastney, for the production.
8. Mr Oliver impressed me as being exceedingly alert, intelligent and genuinely enthusiastic that the film industry should contribute its best to the war effort, suggesting that we have at hand in the industry potential resources which have not been tapped and which can readily be used at once without occupying the time of military personnel or other war production urgently required for other purposes.
   I am not able to check his bona fide nor his credentials to speak for the industry, but he claims to be in a position to utilise that part of the industry which is equipped to work with very exact accuracy and to be able to do so with the one aim to press on with war work with economy to the country's military and financial effort.
9. I venture to suggest that if restrictions and formalities could be removed, so far as is practicable, and if HMS Excellent be allowed to deal directly with the selected firm or organisation with such guidance and advice as the Admiralty may consider

necessary, much valuable time could be saved and a strict check kept on the films produced.

10. I recommend most strongly that steps to initiate such a procedure should now be taken and that the work of making the films should be commenced as soon as Admiralty approval is given.

[Author's note: A consequence of this report on 24 August was that the invention was recommended for immediate adoption in a letter by Admiral James, Commander-in-Chief, Portsmouth, dated 27 August 1940].

A.A. Training - Use of Modern Cinematography and Sound Production.
Ref: HMS Excellent No.1351/1 of 24th August 1940
From Portsmouth (No.4375/8570. Admiralty of 27th August 1940. (Copies to: President, R.N. College, Greenwich. HMS Excellent).
Forwarded for the early consideration of Their Lordships and recommending that formalities be dispensed with and Captain, HMS Excellent, told to get on with the project at once.
Admiral W.M. James
Portsmouth. 27th August 1940.

[Author's note: Henry was appointed to the staff of HMS Excellent at their request during the construction of the first Dome, which was erected in the old Racquets Court at Whale Island. On 21 March 1941 a secret contract was placed by the Admiralty with Technicolor to construct a Dome and the appropriate films].

The Director of Naval Contracts, Royal School, Landsdown Road, Bath
Quoting: - C.P.Br. 2D/30385/41.
25th March 1941.
<u>SECRET</u>
Gentlemen,

I must refer to your discussions with the Captain, HMS 'Excellent', Portsmouth, concerning the 'Dome' Cinema Aiming Teacher for Anti-Aircraft Instruction which it is desired to erect and equip at Whale Island, Portsmouth, brief particulars of which are attached, and to request that you will now put the necessary work in hand as early as possible.

It is desired that you will forward as soon as you are able to do so a quotation for the work and the contract is placed with you on the understanding that you and your sub-contractors agree to satisfy the Admiralty as to the reasonableness of the prices to be paid for the work and to afford all facilities considered necessary by the Admiralty for that purpose. Your quotation should specify precisely and in full detail the various items included in the work. It is also requested that you will state the names and addresses of the firms with whom you propose to place sub-contracts for any portion of the work.

The contract is subject to the general conditions shown on the enclosed Form 17 so far as they are applicable and to the following special conditions.

Form 171C will also apply to the contract. This form is furnished in duplicate, and it is requested that you will sign and return one copy to this Department.

(I) All work is to be executed to meet the requirements of the Captain, HMS 'Excellent', and will not be accepted until it has been approved by his or his duly authorised Representative.

(II) British Subjects only shall be employed in connection with the execution of the work under the contract.

(III) No communication whatsoever concerning the contract is to be made to the Press and no publicity of any kind is to be issued.

(IV) The work carried out under this contract and all information obtained concerning anti-aircraft fire and methods of training shall be regarded as secret and the contractor undertakes that neither he nor any of his employees engaged on the work carried out under this contract will communicate or cause to be communicated any information whatsoever concerning or resulting from the work carried out under this contract without the written permission of the Admiralty. If information is solicited by any unauthorised person an immediate report shall be made by the Contractor to the Admiralty giving all relevant particulars including, if possible, the name and address and Occupation of the enquirer.

Attention: Messrs. Technicolor Ltd., Bath Road, Harmondsworth, West Drayton, Middlesex.

Attention is called to the Official Secrets Act 1911 to 1929 and to The Defence (General Regulations) 1939.

(V) The contractor shall comply, as regards work to be performed within the boundaries of any Naval Establishment with the Rules, Regulations and Requirements in force for the time being for such Establishment. The contractor shall not be under any liability in respect of damage caused by fire to any property of the Admiralty at such Establishment unless the damage shall be caused by any breach by the contractor of the provisions of this clause which would have been avoided by reasonable supervision.

(VI) The contractor will be responsible for the maintenance of his employees whilst at a Naval Establishment.

(VII) The contractor shall indemnify the Admiralty and all Officers, Servants and Agents, or the Admiralty, against all claims resulting from the death of or injury to any of the Contractor's personnel or from loss of or damage to any effects or apparatus belonging to the contractors or to any of his personnel while such personnel is employed on work in connection with this contract wherever such work may be performed, whether in a Naval Establishment or in a ship afloat or elsewhere.

Clauses (I) to (VII) shall also apply to any sub-contracts which you may let in connection with the work.

In addition to the above conditions the following special conditions shall apply to the films produced under the contract.

The price quoted for the films shall include the supply and delivery to the Captain, HMS Excellent, Portsmouth, of one 35mm picture negative, one 35mm. sound negative, the positive cutting copy and one 35mm positive print, together with 'protective master' copies of the negative. The contractor undertakes that all drawings, diagrams, documents, negatives, positive prints and cuttings in connection with the films shall be specially safeguarded and allowed to pass through as few hands as possible in the execution of the work and when not actually in use will be kept under lock and key. Background noises in the films are to be reduced to a minimum by the use throughout of noiseless recording. Absolute clarity of speech is essential. Stock used for the positive prints shall have been coated not more than six months prior to the date of acceptance of the tender. The words 'Admiralty, Official, Crown Copyright Reserved' surmounted by the Tudor Crown are to be embodied in the titles. A 35mm specimen copy of this marking will be issued to the contractor, if required, on loan, without charge, on application to The Officer-in-Charge, R.N. School of Photography, Tipnor, Portsmouth. The name of your firm is to be shown on the bottom of the titles, below the 'Crown Copyright Reserved' marking, in the form 'Produced and Photographed by Technicolor Ltd'. The titles of the films and the reel numbers are to be inserted at both ends of all reels both positive and negative; these markings are not required for screen display but are to be of a permanent character and may be printed or perforated.

All the negative and positive material used in these films and all rights of exploitation and other rights therein shall become the property of the Crown including all copyright whether in the pictures or in the sound which shall be Crown Copyright vested in the Controller for the time being of His Majesty's Stationery Office. Negatives and positive prints shall not be used by the contractor for any purpose other than that of carrying out work in connection with this contract. All film material both positive and negative not included in the accepted pictures shall become the property of the Admiralty and is to be delivered suitably packed and carriage paid to The Officer-in-Charge, R.N. School of Photography, Tipnor, Portsmouth, on acceptance of the film. If sent by post the package is to be registered.

Please acknowledge receipt of this letter.

I am, Gentlemen,
Your obedient Servant,
(SGD) P.D. SYKES.
Director of Navy Contracts.

C.P.2D/30385/41
Brief Particulars of the 'Dome Teacher'

Erection of the Dome
Dome to consist of a half hemisphere, of radius approximately 25 feet, to be erected inside the Old Racquets Court, Whale Island. The centre of the Dome to be at a height of approximately 5 feet above the present floor level. Means to be derived by suitable flairs and curvature of the Dome surface where it meets the floor, also be extending the wing structure, to preserve the illusion of distance when targets are at low angles of sight or near the edge of the Dome. Internal surfaces of the Dome to be suitable for projection of coloured cinematographic films. Illumination of Dome lighting and ventilation of building, and lockers for films, to be provided as necessary.

Films.
(a) The following attacks are to be filmed for the first set: -
three low level bombing attacks on own ship at different heights
three low level bombing attacks on escort at different heights
five dive bombing attacks on own ship from different heights and angles of sight
The last attack of each series to be carried out by at least three aircraft in formation attacking in sequence.
(b) Prints of the films of each attack to be joined together as necessary so that one complete reel can show several different or similar attacks.
(c) Targets to be visible between ranges of 300 and at least 3,000 yards.
(d) Changes in bearing and elevation of the target and its range to be accurately recorded while film is taken.

Projection Unit. (Apparatus to be kept as simple as possible).
(a) Projector to be fixed and mirror moved in accordance with the recorded vertical and lateral bearing rates of the target. Scope for training to be as near to 180 degrees and for elevation as near 90 degrees as possible. Datum bearing for projection to be rapidly adjustable by instructor.
(b) The picture is to be projected in a round frame whose perimeter must, so far as possible, be indistinguishable from its immediate surround.
(c) Future position spot to be projected, visible to instructors and onlookers but invisible to trainee manning the sight.

SOUND
(1) Noise of aircraft, aircraft firing, wind and weather to be produced separately, if necessary. Sound to be broadcast inside the Dome for benefit of instructor and onlookers and into trainee's headphone.

(2) Noise of Gunfire - One noise to represent fire for all types of weapons. Sound to be operated by firing trigger on sight unit – the sound at full strength in the trainee's headphones but with reduced strength for loudspeaker in the Dome, and with a control whereby the instructor can reduce this noise if he wants to give instructions to trainees: duration of fire also to be capable of control to represent amount of ammunition on the mounting.

(3) Suitable head phones to be provided for two men manning the sight and speaking set for instructor.

(e) True range of the target to be indicated at selected intervals to instructor and onlookers, but not to men manning the sight.

Mr Bernard Happe was a technical manager for Technicolor. The company produced films until 1935, when they filed for bankruptcy due to financial difficulties caused by the Great Depression. In 1939 came a further threat of closure:

> In my mind the whole Technicolor was in grave danger of being rubbed out. There was after all a period when cinemas were closed, when cinema production was discouraged, when cinema presentation was discouraged. You were not allowed materials or labour. It could easily mean that since film, the cinema wasn't given a particular high rating in the national conscious, let alone the added expense of colour, it could very well have been closed completely. As it was, the maintenance and mechanical precision work was taken over for war work on gyroscopes, gun sights and things like that.
>
> We had a reprieve in finding some worthwhile war work to do. That arose out of a proposal from Lieutenant Stevens [*sic*] in the Royal Navy to improve anti-aircraft gunnery, particularly with hand aimed weapons, the ones which were aimed by eye rather than predictor. And he had the concept that you should build an enormous hemispherical dome the size of the Albert Hall and put on films of aircraft. In the centre of the hall, you would have people being trained in the use of anti-aircraft weapons and their sights, with the appropriate song and dance of sound and battle and the rest of it. That was put up to the Navy people of the gunnery school at HMS Excellent and they said we don't know about this but is this the kind of thing Technicolor might be interested in.

Mr Happe remembered discussions about what might happen. He was enthusiastic about doing something on a much smaller scale but would allow the use of film as a target method, a way of practising on moving targets. As a demonstration he built a small Dome:

> It was only a quarter Dome, built in the men's locker room, two feet across and built of electrical conduit as frame and plaster. The projectionist was also a skilled

plasterer. In the middle of this Dome, we put a projector. A 35mm projector was too damned heavy and immobile and full of inertia to be able to swing it around. We fixed the projector and projected the picture by means of a mirror which could be rapidly moved to project the image of the target up of the surface of the Dome. Close by that we put up a stalk with a suitable gun sight on it. We made several demonstrations to various people from HMS Excellent. People like Admiral Dreyer were concerned with the training for DEMS, (Defence Equipped Merchant Ships).

Mr Happe recalled that Technicolor were chosen for the secret project by Henry Stephens:

Eventually we got a project to build Domes for anti-aircraft gunnery, primarily for the Navy, and associated with that was a major project for instructional films, as to how you should recognise aircraft and by recognising the type, action and direction of flight you could estimate where you should be aiming with the various types of gunsights. That became a very major project, and that took over all our engineering resources. It saved the life of the camera department because we very quickly demonstrated that it was no good going out with a camera, let alone a Technicolor camera, to try and shoot genuine aircraft, even if you could get the appropriate German types, and later Italian and Japanese types. At several thousand yards, they just didn't show up, so we developed the business of producing all our aircraft targets synthetically by animated models.

I had a team of about fifteen girls, because we didn't have computers. They worked out the attitude and the condition of the camera, frame by frame, for each of these runs to produce an aircraft which was making the right sort of manoeuvres and making a dive bomb attack, or a low-level attack, or an attack on the stern and so on. I'm sure it saved our life during the darkest days because we made several hundred Domes. They were initially for the Navy, and they were sent all over the world. Some arrived, like the ones which went to Singapore but too late to be any good. Others went to the States and South Africa.

Mr Happe confirmed the existence of various Dome Trainer sites:

There was one on the Thames at HMS *President*, on the river, and that was particularly useful for merchant seamen coming up the Thames. There were mobile training units sent out on buses [see Plate 16] which could be directed to different ports to meet convoys coming in and to update their crews. As I say, Domes were built, and several hundred target runs were made. It was also taken up subsequently by the RAF regiment for the defence of their air depots. The

Army wanted Bofors and Stiffkey sticks for their training. That gave us quite a lengthy life of activity during the 1941 to 1943 time.

[Author's note: Technicolor used a method of making the required films using models and photographing them frame by frame. They also enhanced equipment design for production. Technicolor became the supplier of films and equipment and received contracts worth approximately £750,000.00].

Henry was posted to the Royal Navy College Greenwich to develop additional enhancements to the Dome Trainer.

From: The Captain, HMS Excellent, Portsmouth,
Date: 19 August 1941.
Ref No I.54\6
To: The Commander-in-chief, Portsmouth.
Copies to: The Director of Gunnery & Anti-Aircraft Warfare HQ, Admiralty London S.W.1.
The Director of Training & Staff Duties Division, Admiralty, London, S.W.1.
The Director of Naval Ordnance, Admiralty, Bath
The President, Royal Naval College, Greenwich

1. With reference to Excellent's X.54/8 of 18 October 1940, Lieutenant Henry Christian Stephens, R.N.V.R. was appointed to HMS Excellent for duty with the A.A. Department in October 1940 to develop the Dome Teacher.
2. The Dome Teacher has been finalised and in production. His work in this direction is now complete.
3. There is, however, a requirement for matching reflector sight for producing deflections for barrage fire and it is possible that Lieutenant Stephens will be able to do some experimental work towards the development of this instrument. It is considered that he would best be able to do this at the Royal Naval College, Greenwich, where he will have the highest scientific assistance. It is therefore proposed that he should be re-appointed to the Royal Naval College Greenwich, as he is not required for further service in the A.A. Department.
   Captain

[Author's note: On 15 August 1942 Henry was promoted to the rank of Lieutenant Commander, RNVR].

In September 1943, the chief instructor, Trials Wing School of A.A. Artillery, requested that the claimant's services be lent to them to consider extending the scope of the Dome Trainers to meet conditions arising from the development of air warfare.

Ref. Tw/BG. 10.
22nd September 1943.
Subject: Dome Trainers.
To: The Captain, Royal Naval College, Greenwich.
From: Lieut. Colonel Tweddell R.A., Chief Instructor, Trials Wing, School of A. A. Artillery, Lydstep Camp, Tenby.
Chief Instructor, Trials Wing, School of A. A. Artillery.

1. I am instructed by the Commandant; School of A. A. Artillery ask if we may have the assistance and advice of Lt-Commander Stephens, R.N.V.R. in investigating various methods adapting the Dome Trainer for our experimental work.
2. It is, at this stage, difficult to detail the amount of assistance which, subject to your approval, we would require from Lt-Commander Stephens. I would therefore suggest that you are agreeable in principle, a meeting between Lt-Commander Stephens and ourselves might be arranged to discuss the matter and that subsequently more concrete proposals should be put before you.

Ref. Tw/G.144
27th May 1944
Subject: Development of Dome Trainer.
To: Major R.M. Fraser, RA (Instructor in Gunnery), Headquarters, 1st A.A. Group, 247 Knightsbridge, London S.W.7.
From: Lieut. Colonel Tweddell R.A., Chief Instructor, Trials Ting, School of A. A. Artillery, Lydstep Camp, Tenby.

Dear Major Fraser,
We are developing several ideas to improve the Dome Teacher in conjunction with Lt-Commander Stephens, RNVR who was the original inventor of the Dome. Unfortunately, he has had a breakdown and is confined to his house in London on light duty.

Could you place the 20' Dome in Hyde Park at his disposal for short periods at times convenient to yourselves so that he may try out various small modifications.

His work should not interfere with the normal use of the Dome, and it is suggested that you communicate directly with Lt-Commander Stephens if you are able to help.

Hope you will come and see us the next time you are in Pembrokeshire.

Ref. Tw/G.144
26th May 1944
Subject: Dome Trainer Trial G.144
To: The Under Secretary of State, The War Office, R.A.3.
From: Lieut. Colonel Tweddell R.A., Chief Instructor, Trials Ting, School of A. A. Artillery, Lydstep Camp, Tenby.

Lt-Commander Stephens RNVR has now returned to duty and work is being continued on the development of the Dome Trainer.

1. May he please be issued with a cam from the projector of a 20' Dome together with the corresponding film for this cam.
2. May permission to write off these stores in the development of modifications also be granted please.
3. The stores should be delivered to Lt-Commander Stephens at the address below.

Copy to Lt-Commander H.C. Stephens, RNVR, 64A Carlisle Mansions. Victoria Street, London S.W.1.

Ref. IG/DO/832
30th May 1944
From: Major R.M. Fraser, RA (Instructor in Gunnery), Headquarters, 1st A.A. Group, 247 Knightsbridge, London S.W.7.
To: Lt-Commander H.C. Stephens, RNVR, 64A Carlisle Mansions. Victoria Street, London S.W.1.

Dear Commander Stephens,
I received yesterday a letter from Lt-Colonel Tweddell, Chief Instructor at Trials, Wing, School of A.A. Artillery, asking me if I would get in touch with you with a view to placing the 20′ Dome Teacher in Hyde Park at your disposal for short periods so that you could try out various small modifications.

As the Dome Trainer in Hyde Park is working to a very heavy training programme – something in the nature of an 80-hour training week – I would be very grateful if you could let me know what your actual requirements are, and I will then make all the necessary arrangements. Should you wish to contact me by telephone my number is Kensington 3411 and my extension is 133 by day and 19 by night.

Yours sincerely,
Michael Fraser, Major, R.A. (Instructor in Gunnery.)

[Author's note: The Dome in Hyde Park was used to build and demonstrate enhancements invented and designed by Henry. These included a Photographic Table, Background Scenic Effects, Future Position Spot, and a Hit Recorder (see Plate 12). The Photographic Table enhanced the accuracy and quality of films as aircraft speed increased and allowed a greater 'aim off' speed. Built with the assistance of Mr Ernest Tapp (who was given a share of Patent with Henry) of Radio Electronics at Norwood Junction, Henry built a Future Position Spot with a gun-mounted photo-electric cell on a gun. Both this and a new Hit Recorder were demonstrated in Hyde Park to the Army, the RAF and to the Navy. HMS Excellent ordered a prototype on 2 May 1945].

Subject: Dome Teacher – Scoring arrangements.
From: The Captain, HMS Excellent, Portsmouth
2nd May 1945 No. T.D. A. / 105/8
To: The Director of Gunnery & A. A. Warfare Division, Admiralty London.
Copy To: The Director of Naval Ordnance, Admiralty, Bath

1. A most promising method of scoring in the Dome Teacher has been devised by Lieutenant Commander H.C. Stephens, R.N. attached to College, Greenwich, and has been demonstrated to my representatives and those of the Army and RAF.
2. The system has the great advantage that the future position spot is positioned independently of the film and therefore can allow for high aim-off speeds. At present it is designed for 400 knot aircraft.
3. The principle of the system is that the future position spot energises a photo-electric cell mounted on the gun.
4. It is considered that this scheme is well worth further investigation in view of the difficulties experienced with the mechanical method under development at HMS Excellent and it is recommended that the following contract be placed with the firm which has collaborated in the designs-
   Messrs. Radio Electronics Ltd., St. George Works, Merton Road, Norwood Junction
   (i) To design and manufacture one prototype Correct Aim Recorder on a photoelectric principal to the technical requirements of the Captain, HMS Excellent.
   (ii) To erect the prototype in a Dome Teacher to be specified.
   (iii) To provide one complete set of production drawings on linen.
5. The estimated cost of the equipment including design and drawings should not exceed £500/- and delivery should be made within four months of the date of contract.
6. The interservice aspect of Dome Teacher modifications is being raised separately.

W.G. Agnew, Captain

A scheme for accurate tracer simulation in the Dome was also put forward and demonstrated as practicable to the Army A.A. Command (Army) and to the Navy. On June 13, 1945, Brigadier R.B. Peters, the Commandant of the School of A.A. Artillery in Bude, Cornwall, recommended adoption. This was British Patent Application No.21511 in 1944. Due to decreased use of tracer the scheme was not required for A.A. Training, although was considered for anti-tank training.

[Author's note: This equipment was built for Henry Stephens by Radio Electronics Ltd. It was a gantry over the gun position on which four Tracer Projector Units were fixed and aligned with the gun. Each unit would project a red spot of light onto the Dome surface, simulating tracer rounds when a gun was fired. The units would be linked to the gun in traverse and have a separate cam to control elevation, allowing the tracer shell to be shown to fall away. Electrical circuits connected to the FP-detecting photo electric cell would momentarily extinguish the light if the shell passed on the far side of the aircraft, therefore indicating that the gun was fired at too great a range. If the shell was fired too short, it would just fall away. If the shell was directly on target and a hit achieved, a separate 'flash' projector would show an explosion on the aircraft. The Army judged this as too expensive and requiring too much modification to a Dome Trainer].

RCAI 7. Particulars of exceptional utility or other special circumstance upon which the claim is based.

The provision of the Dome Trainer effected a complete transformation in anti-aircraft gunnery training, and it has been estimated that, because of such training was improved by no less than 300 per cent. The invention enabled training to be carried on in all weathers as well as in conditions of darkness or blackout. A single aircraft flight can form the basis of innumerable instructional sessions. Indeed, to avoid delay, in the initial stage instruction was carried on with films made up from photographs of models. The saving of life and material loss and damage resulting from the invention are incalculable.

From time to time the claimant applied for permission to seek a patent for the Dome Trainer, but this was withheld.

RCAI 8. Amount suggested as remuneration in respect of alleged use and details of basis on which the amount is computed. If the claimant is correct in thinking that several hundred Domes have been built at a cost of several thousand pounds each, it is clear that even a small percentage on the cost would amount to a very substantial sum. Based on money saved in training the value must also be very substantial, since existing methods of live training involved the use of real aircraft, real guns, real ammunition, as well as entailing delays due to weather conditions and so forth. It has been estimated that one Dome alone trained 40,000 people, and certain Domes were in continual use from 1941 to 1945. Based on money saved by the improvement of A.A. gunnery the value is incalculable. Published figures of Empire and Allied Merchant Shipping lost by aerial attack during the war are 700 ships with a gross tonnage of 2,720,000 tons. While the percentage saved cannot be estimated it is clear that a very small percentage would represent a very large sum of money. The claimant therefore contends that the award should be a substantial one and requests that figures may be supplied, including the extent of the use of his invention by the Admiralty, the RAF Regiment, the Army, and any Allies to whom the invention may have been communicated, to enable an actual sum to be suggested.

RCAI 9. Where a special claim is made for outlay and expenses, brief details should be given.

No special claim is made for outlay and expenses.

RCAI 10. Brief particulars of any contract between the Claimant and any Government Department in connection with the invention, design, drawing or process specifying nature of the contract, e.g., whether for development or production.

There was no contract between the claimant and any Government Department.

RCAI 11. The nature of any technical assistance supplied by any Government Department.

As the claimant was working for the Navy, the Admiralty provided facilities for carrying out his instructions.

RCAI 12. Particulars of payments already received from any Government Department on account of use of the invention, design, drawing or process.

No payment has been received from any Government Department on account of use

RCAI 13. The address of the Government Department to which a copy of this statement has been sent in accordance with the instructions at the head of Page 1.

The Admiralty, C.P. Patents, Foxhill Hutments, Bath. For the attention of Mr. H.D. Law.

I hereby agree to accept as final the recommendation of the Royal Commission under the terms of the said Royal Warrant.

Signature of Claimant. Henry Christian Stephens – dated 28/7/1947

In cases involving large amounts or of a complicated nature, the Claimant may wish to submit more detailed statements. These statements should be included as schedules, carefully numbered to correspond with the headings in the above form. (51731) (3) Wt. 21004-3, 000 8/46 D.L. G. 390

[Author's note: The Admiralty replied to the Royal Commission on Awards to Inventors on 2 October 1947 with a Form 5]:

ROYAL COMMISSION ON AWARDS TO INVENTORS Answer by (name of Department) ADMIRALTY to claim number N/A by HENRY CHRISTIAN

STEPHENS made under Head (3) of the terms of reference of the Royal Commission in respect of THE DOME TRAINER.

Two copies of this answer should be sent to the Secretary, The Royal Commission on Awards to Inventors, Somerset House, Strand, W.C.2, and one copy to the Claimant or his representative.

1. State which of the matters alleged in the Claimant's statement is admitted or disputed.

The Department admits the following matters alleged in the claimant's Statement:

<u>Head of Statement Extent to which it is admitted</u>

1. The whole.
2. The whole.
3. The whole.
4. The whole.
5. The use made of the Claimant's invention is set forth in Head 4 hereof. The Department admits the facts set forth in the last paragraph of this Head of the claimant's Statement.
6. The whole.
7. The whole, except for the last sentence and for the estimated figure of 300 per cent in the first sentence.
8. Paragraph 1. The whole.
   Paragraph 2. The first sentence.
   Paragraph 3. The first sentence.
   Paragraph 4. The figures requested are set forth in Head 4 hereof.
9. The whole
10. The whole.
11. The whole.
12. The whole.

Save as above admitted the Department disputes the matters alleged in the claimant's Statement.

2. State whether the Department admits the validity of the patents or registered designs referred to in paragraph three of the Statement of Claim.
This Head has no relevance to the present Claim.

3. If the validity of any patent or registered design is disputed, give short grounds of objection.
This Head has no relevance to the present Claim.

2. **Statement of the use of the Claimant's invention, design, drawing or process, giving nature, extent and period of such use together with proper account.**

Dome Trainers constructed in accordance with the claimant's invention were supplied to and used by the Crown to the extent particularised in Schedule 4.

3. **Statement of the amount which Department considers should be paid in respect of use, and the basis on which such amount is computed.**
Such sum as the Royal Commission may consider fit, having regard to the matters set forth in Head 4 hereof.

4. **Any objections or further observations upon the Claimant's particulars of claim. If objections are based on prior record by, or trial by or on behalf of any Government Department, sufficient particulars should be supplied.**
The Department admits that the Claimant had conceived of the basic principle of the Dome Trainer prior to the date of his commission in the R.N.V.R. but will contend that after such date he was assisted in the development and perfection of the Dome by the officers of HMS Excellent and the staff of Technicolor.
(i) To the best belief of the Department, Technicolor Ltd. propose to make a claim before the Royal Commission in respect of the contributions made by them to the development of the Dome Trainer. The Department is unable to give particulars of the contributions claimed by Technicolor to until after receipt of their Statement of Claim. The Dome Trainer was the subject of further development and improvement by Lieutenant Commander C. S. Bell, in the substitution in the 'Portobel' Trainer of a portable, inflatable dome for the rigid Dome Trainer previously employed.
(ii) After the said date of his commission, it was the express duty of the Claimant to develop and improve the Dome Trainer.
(iii) The development costs of the Dome Trainer were borne solely by the Department.
(iv) The following claims have been submitted to the Royal Commission in respect of the Dome Trainer in addition to that of the present Claimant.
(a) Col. G. F. Haszard.
(b) Lieutenant Commander C. S. Bell

The Department will make reference at the Hearing to all and any additional and conflicting claims as may be known to them.

* Paragraphs two and three only apply when the claim is made under Head (1) or (2) of the terms of reference of the Royal Commission.

Signed. Deputy Director of Naval Contracts
Date: 29.9.47

[Author's note: Henry responded to the Commission by personal letter dated 5 May 1948. He missed the hearing on 26 April 1948 due to illness].

64a Carlisle Mansions Carlisle Place, S.W.13
To: The Secretary, The Royal Commission, Somerset House, W.C.2

Dear Sir,

In view of an account brought to my notice of statements made by Messrs. Technicolor and witnesses on the last day of their hearing, April 26th, I would like to place before the members of The Royal Commission the following facts for their consideration. As from what I have been told many of the statements made on that day are entirely erroneous.

I was not myself in court owing to illness and I have no knowledge of what had been said by them on their two previous days hearing, but I feel it incumbent upon me to place the true facts to the best of my knowledge before the Commission in respect of what has been brought to my notice. The main points of these statements, as I understand them, are as follows:

A 'That you could not take pictures of real aircraft from 3,000 yards with a two-inch focal length lens from ground to air'.

B 'That you could not take pictures of real aircraft without errors.'

C 'It would be impossible to get the same degree of accuracy from the Photographic Table or from anything else as from films of models.'

D An account given of the differences in accuracy required to suit Army & Navy requirements in the Dome Teacher.

E 'That making films of models was the vital part of the Teacher.'

My answers are contained in the attached sheets which I think are self-explanatory. If, of course it is desired that I should substantiate any points of evidence, I will of course be glad to do so.

I remain, yours faithfully
H.C. Stephens

<u>In answer to A</u>:
'That you could not take pictures of real aircraft from 3,000 yards with a two-inch focal length lens from ground to air'.

The statement that pictures satisfactory for the Dome cannot be so made is just untrue. It is, in fact, done every day and could have been done in 1940 and 1941. I, in fact, did it in 1940. The attached files prove it.

A. Blue film is an actual piece of Technicolor film used in the Dome
B. A piece of RAF film in which you can see it is taken from the ground.

The image of the aircraft in both is indicated by a red circle around them for your convenience. The remainder of the RAF films from which B is cut is also attached as a matter of interest.

I think it is worth noting that the RAF film was taken on Kodak's Normal Plus Stock and not on 'Background X' film, when an even clearer result, owing to finer grain, could be obtained if required.

At HMS 'Excellent' there was in 1940, and still is today, a Mr. P.W.T. Forrow, a Technical Officer in the Royal Naval Scientific Service and a member of the Royal Photographic Society, available for any advice or assistance on photographic work. He oversees Cinematographic work at HMS 'Excellent' and part of his work has consisted of photographing aircraft from ground to air regularly throughout the years. He oversees Cinematographic work at HMS 'Excellent'.

This officer I had in Court on April 7th to give evidence if the Royal Commission were in any doubt as to the practicability and feasibility of photographing real aircraft and he would have stated that photographing aircraft at 5,000 and 6,000 yards (double the range required in the Dome) was quite a common occurrence for him and that he had photographed at 12,000 yards' range. But as I thought that the Royal Commission was satisfied with the Army Report Trial G.144 and did not wish unnecessarily to waste their time and that I had been given to understand by Mr. Aldous that he did not intend to dispute the fact that it was quite possible to photograph real aircraft, Mr Forrow was not called into the witness box.

I enclose letters from Mr. Forrow and copy of 'proof of evidence' of Wing Commander C.J. Craig, C.B.E., who is Kodak's expert (who did not actually give personal evidence for the same reason as Mr Forrow, together with a film taken from ground to air with a two inch focal length lens on a standard 35mm camera, with a covering letter from Mr Sutherland of the Air Ministry, which I should like to be given to the Royal Commission if there should be any doubt in their mind after hearing Technicolor's statements.

In answer to B:

'That you could not take pictures of real aircraft without errors'.

There is no inaccuracy in photographing real aircraft, so it must be as accurate in photographing models.

Technicolor appear to have confined their questions on these matters to their own claimants and to people who were not able to answer correctly owing to lack of knowledge of the subject. The officers working in HMS 'Excellent' who were called to give evidence were not authorities on cinematography – it is not part of their job, and they are not in any way qualified to speak with knowledge on the subject. I am not aware that Messrs.

Technicolor produced any witness with expert photographic knowledge from an outside source to confirm their erroneous statements.

In answer to C:

'It would be impossible to get the same degree of accuracy from the photographic table or anything else as from films of models'.

The recording apparatus at Eastney, HMS 'Excellent', can make most accurate graphs of elevation and training of gun mountings (to which the camera would be fixed). It is used in outdoor 'Non-Firing' trials to determine 'Hits scored' and errors in aim.

As I did not give a very lucid explanation in the witness box of the method I proposed for automatically recording the necessary corrected movement for an 'off centred' mirror while using my Photographic Table, I attack brief diagram to explain the principle upon which the instrument for the Army is being built.

In answer to D:

An account given of the differences in accuracy required to suit Army & Navy requirements in the Dome Teacher.

The most difficult target to hit and the most difficult target to represent accurately on the Dome's surface is obviously a 'Crossing Target', where maximum 'aim off' is required. This was the type of attack most frequently met with and therefore catered for by the Army, because the gun position was usually to one side or other of the target area.

At sea, the primary object of the gunner was to defend his own merchant ship from attack – this, being a direct attack on the gun position, presented the easiest target to hit and the easiest to represent accurately, as only during the very short period whilst the target was passing directly overhead was maximum aim off required; the gunner's main job was to shoot it down before this period was reached, as by then the aircraft had already dropped its bomb. So, accuracy was more essential to the Army in the Dome Teacher. It was under these conditions that the Photographic Table was ordered by the Army, in Trial G.144 Report, to supersede the Synthetic Model attacks.

In answer to E:

'That making films of models was the vital part of the Teacher'.

The Dome Trainer was not an aircraft recognition Teacher. It was a device to teach how to HIT a target and at the same time give psychological training. Aircraft recognition was taught by other devices altogether in all three Services. In the teaching that I saw carried out in both the Naval and Army Domes the instructor would call out to trainee and class what type of plane was carrying out the attack.

With reference to the use of models, I agree

(1) That it was more convenient to use models instead of painting our own planes or using captured enemy planes stationed at Farnborough Experimental Station at that time,

if it was considered desirable to give accurate representations of enemy targets. I think it was better for targets to be representative of German aircraft, but not essential. For example, we were still practising with German aircraft target runs in the Japanese war.

(2) That the Naval officers in charge of the Development of the Dome, on Messrs. Technicolor's advice, decided that they preferred models. This was a matter for them to decide.

But in view of the foregoing evidence and the evidence I put forward in Court, I wish to state that the use of Synthetic Model attacks was in no way a vital part of the Dome Teacher.

LETTER FROM THE AIR MINISTRY

AIR MINISTRY, WHITEHALL, LONDON, S.W.1.
3rd May 1948,

Dear Stephens,

As you say, the last bit of film I sent you was taken air to air, but I now enclose a further section taken ground to air using a two lens and at a range of 4,000 yards. Given reasonable conditions there is nothing new in obtaining clear pictures either air to air or ground to air at this range, and I cannot imagine why, what is a perfectly normal, everyday procedure should give you or anybody else a headache. The picture was shot on normal Plus X stock but of course if required you could expect clearer results if using 'Background X'.

Yours sincerely,
Mr Sutherland

Chapter 15

The Private Journal of Henry Stephens

[Author's note: In evidence to the Royal Commission on Awards to Inventors, Henry compiled a private journal to prove he was the sole inventor of the Dome Trainer. His evidence was concise].

Henry Christian Stephens, of 64a, Carlisle Mansions, Carlisle Place, London, S.W.1. will prove:

In the World War of 1914–1918 I served as midshipman and Sub-Lieutenant in the Royal Navy, and for a time during this period was a shipmate of Commander Phelips, R.N., who was then a Sub-Lieutenant. Between the wars I was, amongst other things, in business as a consultant in photographic matters, and since the last war I have been similarly engaged.

Early in the last war, late in 1939 or early in 1940, I conceived the broad idea of projecting a cinematograph film of an aircraft on the inner surface of a dome using camera and projection lenses of the same focal length and running the projector at the same speed as the camera. By causing the projector to reproduce the movements made by the camera in taking the film, the representation of the aircraft on the dome surface would appear to be of the correct size and in the correct attitude, and to move exactly as a real aircraft when seen by the naked eye located at the same position. By causing the projector to reproduce the movements made by the camera in taking the film, the representation of the aircraft on the dome surface would appear to be of the correct size and in the correct attitude, and to move exactly as the camera which took the film.

I thought that if an anti-aircraft gun were located at the centre of the dome the crew would be able to aim the gun to the moving image of the aircraft and so obtain useful training without real aircraft having to be used. I gave considerable thought to various aspects of the scheme and devised several additional features and refinements. These included projecting a spot of light on to the dome surface to indicate the correct point of aim at the aircraft and projecting a spot of light on to the dome surface which would indicate the actual point of aim as set by the gun crew, so that mistakes in aiming would be at once apparent and so capable of immediate correction.

I appreciated that since the future course of the aircraft could readily be obtained from the film and the speed of the projectile and the range of the aircraft were known, the correct point of aim could be determined. I also thought that sound effects such as the noise of the aircraft engines, falling bombs, etc., could be incorporated to increase the realism of the training. I had read in various reports in the newspapers about the demoralising effects caused by dive bombing, and I considered that if the training were carried out with all the sound effects taking place, then at the time of real attack the men who had been trained would be quite used to the noise and would not be likely to lose their heads for those few vital seconds by meeting something to which they were unaccustomed.

When my ideas had been developed to this extent, I decided that it was time to put my invention up to the authorities. I approached my friend Commander Phelips, then in charge of the Royal Naval Photography School, Tipnor, and sought his advice in this connection. This was sometime early in 1940. Commander Phelips advised me that the best method of getting the scheme adopted would be to re-join the Navy, and as I was too old to re-join in the normal way, Commander Phelips wrote to a friend at the Admiralty about me, which I gather assisted my recall. Shortly after this I was commissioned a Sub-Lieutenant in the R.N.V.R. [see plates 1 & 2] and was posted on 8th July 1940 to the Royal Naval college, Greenwich.

Shortly after my arrival at Greenwich, on 15th July 1940, I put forward a short statement of my proposals (Enclosure 63 of my claim) to the President, Captain Davis, and explained the details to him verbally. Captain Davis required to be convinced that my suggestions were practicable, and so he attached me to Lieutenant Commander Pigou, R.N., and instructed us to visit various photographic and cinematographic experts to discuss the matter. We were instructed for security reasons not to divulge the whole of my proposals to these experts, but merely to seek their confirmation of the practicability of specific features. Among the experts we visited was Mr. Warmisham of Messrs. Taylor, Taylor & Camp Hobson Limited, a well-known authority on cinematographic lenses, whom we saw on 2nd August 1940 and who confirmed certain of the optical aspects of my scheme. Mr. Warmisham suggested that we should have a further interview and should discuss the matter with representatives of Messrs. Technicolor limited who were stated to be capable of working to the degree of accuracy which was thought to be necessary.

On the 6th of August 1940, Lieutenant Commander Pigou and I visited HMS Excellent at Whale Island, Portsmouth and explained the plan to Commander Campbell of the A.A. Department, who expressed the opinion that the scheme would be of the greatest value. Commander Campbell took us to the A.A. School at Eastney, where we were shown various apparatus for recording the movement of guns which it was suggested might be employed for recording the movements of cameras photographing aircraft. I had already suggested to Lieutenant Commander Pigou, Commander Phelips and Captain Davis that I should work out details of mechanism for recording the camera movements and reproducing these movements in the projector, but they all had told me that there was no need do this, since the Navy already had apparatus which could be adapted for this purpose without much difficulty.

The next day, which is 7th August 1940, Lieutenant Commander Pigou and I went to see Mr. Warmisham again, who on this occasion was in company with Mr. Oliver of Technicolor Limited. Further details of the proposal were discussed at this meeting. A few days after this, on 12th August 1940, Mr. Oliver and I visited the Royal Naval Gunnery School, Chatham, and inspected certain naval machinery, and Mr. Oliver expressed the view that good use could be made of this machinery to move projectors and to take pictures. Shortly after this, on 14th August 1940, I submitted a fuller report on my scheme to the President of the Royal Naval college, Captain Davis. Commander Phelips was subsequently shown this letter and had indicated thereon the points which I suggested to him before I joined the Navy at his recommendation.

My letter of 14th August 1949 is divided into two parts, namely for long-range and short-range training. This division was not part of my original suggestion but was made on the advice of Lieutenant Commander Pigou, who had indicated to me that differences in the shooting technique at long and short range necessitate different kinds of training in the Dome. This letter also refers to my suggestion to include an indication of the range of the aircraft. On 21st August 1940 we had a big meeting at HMS Excellent with Captain Brind, Commander Campbell, Lieutenant Commander Hamilton and Lieutenant Commander Clarke, of HMS Excellent, Commander Phelips and Lieutenant Commander Pigou, Mr. Oliver and Mr. Gunn of Technicolor Limited and me, at which various aspects of the project were discussed.

Mr. Oliver and Mr. Gunn visited Eastney and saw certain machinery from which they obtained useful information for transferring the movement of filming cameras to projectors.

On 24th August 1940, Captain Brind submitted a report on the scheme to the Commander-in-Chief, Portsmouth, in which he recommended that while the scheme had been proposed for both long and short-range training, the short-range aspect should be studied first. The Commander-in-Chief, Portsmouth passed this report on to the Admiralty and recommended that the project should be got on with at once.

On 29th August, Mr Oliver of Technicolor Limited sent me a letter setting out the schemes then envisaged, involving the filming of real aircraft, and making an estimate for carrying out this filming and for erecting a pilot Dome with hired equipment.

On 8th October 1940 I was posted from Greenwich to HMS Excellent. At HMS Excellent I was engaged on work in connection with the production of a prototype Dome, and numerous discussions were held on all practical aspects. During this period, certain practical improvements were embodied in the apparatus, among them the use of a mirror in the Dome to which movements were imparted while keeping the projector stationary. This improvement was, I believe, suggested by Mr. Gunn. Various methods of moving the mirror were discussed, among them methods of moving it in accordance with a sound track on the film. Eventually, a system of moving it by means of cams was adopted, but I cannot say where the suggestion to use cams originated.

I suggested that the Dome should be constructed of plaster segments and that blue background light [see Plate 9] would be employed to create the illusion of distance. I demonstrated the latter feature to the authorities at HMS Excellent, because of which the suggestion was adopted. In October 1940, I built a model Dome and experimented with miniature reflected projections, trying out various positions of the projector in relation to the mirror in the Dome.

It was apparent to me that if the film was to be projected using a mirror it would be desirable to take the films through a mirror, and accordingly in November 1940 I devised an apparatus which I termed a 'Photographic Table' for taking photographs of real aircraft using a stationary camera and a movable mirror. I was assisted in this by Mr P.W.T. Forrow, a civilian on the staff of HMS Excellent. The apparatus included means for recording the movements of the mirror and for moving it by a series of wires and pulleys in a manner like that subsequently adopted in the Dome Teacher itself. I showed this apparatus to various people, including Mr. Oliver of Technicolor, and took some films of real aircraft with it. I believe that the films produced by Messrs. Technicolor Limited were made with models instead of real aircraft, owing to the difficulty of obtaining enemy types of aircraft, and the fact that films made up from models were quite satisfactory.

While at HMS Excellent I was given facilities for carrying out my experiments, and the staff of HMS Excellent assisted in the development of the Dome Teacher by formulating requirements for the training films, and by devising the form of gun sight to be employed. HMS Excellent bore the expense of the development work on which I was engaged. The relationship between the other officers of HMS Excellent, Messrs. Technicolor and myself may be illustrated by considering the future position (FP) spot. As already explained, I had the original idea of providing a future position spot and suggested a way in which its correct position could be determined. I conducted some experiments, using equipment provided by HMS Excellent, to determine the most favourable colour for the spot, and demonstrated this. As a result of this demonstration, Mr Oliver recommended to HMS Excellent that a yellow spot should be adopted, and HMS Excellent made the final decision based on this recommendation.

I am not sure whether it was first I who suggested providing a filter to an eyepiece so that the aimer could not see the future position spot, although it would be visible to the instructor and the class, since detail proposals of this nature often arose in general discussions at which other officers of HMS Excellent, representatives of Technicolor Limited and myself were present. I demonstrated that to achieve this object it would be necessary for the future position spot to be put on the film. This is because the future position spot is projected from another projector and constitutes additional light on the Done surface, and a filter will not render it invisible.

It was also suggested that my original proposal of projecting a spot of light on to the Dome surface to indicate the actual point of aim should be modified by projecting an image of the gunsight graticule. At first it was suggested that a filter in the gunsight piece would render this projected graticule invisible to the aimer. I disputed this, pointing out that it constituted additional light on the screen and that a filter could therefore not render it invisible. My opinion was ignored until I gave a demonstration to prove it, and it was thereafter agreed that the projected image of the gunsight graticule should be obscured by the real graticule. I also suggested other improvements, and HMS Excellent decided whether these were worth including in view of the need for producing as many working Dome Trainers as possible in a short time. For instance, HMS Excellent decided that a suggestion I made for projecting a scenic background on to the Dome, or painting a background, should not be pursued at that time.

During this period work was progressing on a prototype Dome Trainer at the Old Racquets Courts, Whale Island. This was completed in early 1941, and a demonstration was given to Admiral Sir Frederic Dreyer, who was Inspector of Merchant Navy Gunnery. After this demonstration Admiral Dreyer asked who had invented the Dome Trainer, and I was then introduced to him as the inventor. He thereupon commended me upon it. I believe that shortly afterwards he gave instructions for work on several Dome Teachers to be pushed ahead with all possible speed.

My development work on the Dome Teacher at HMS Excellent was now substantially completed, since details of the production models had been settled, and in August 1941 I was posted back to the Royal Naval College, Greenwich, to carry out development work on another device known as a Matching Sight.

In the meantime, the Dome Teacher had proved a success and the Army had become interested in it and were considering making various modifications to it for their own purposes.

In September 1943 the Chief Instructor, Trials Wing, School of A.A. Artillery, asked the Navy if I could be lent to them to assist and to create new developments for increasing the scope of training in the Dome to meet further requirements they formulated.

I found that the Army wished to make films of real aircraft and to speed up the period between formulating a requirement for a film and having the finished film available for projection in the Dome Teacher. This period they considered lengthy with the existing model technique. I accordingly built a 'mock up' and made proposals for an apparatus based on the principles I had demonstrated at HMS Excellent on my Photographic Table. The Army authorities, however, decided to take the photographs directly instead of through mirror, although I pointed out that this would not be satisfactory. An apparatus was devised, based on my Photographic Table proposals, for taking pictures of aircraft directly, which automatically scribed the cams as the camera was moved. Tests of the apparatus that the idea of taking films of real aircraft and simultaneously scribing the cans was practicable, but it was admitted by the authorities that the films should have been taken through a mirror in accordance with my original proposals.

In the latest editions of the apparatus which are now being built by Admiralty Research Laboratories, under Mr. Dixon, for the Admiralty and the Army real aircraft will be photographed using apparatus based on my original Photographic Table, incorporating a mirror. This apparatus is a development of that tested in Army Trial G. 144. I acted in a consultative capacity in connection with the new apparatus up until the time I was demobilised.

[Author's note: Henry then outlined the broad principle of the Dome Trainer].

Broadly the purpose of the Dome is to give practice in short range anti-aircraft shooting. The normal method of training by shooting at targets towed behind real aircraft have disadvantages referred to under the note on Utility.

The Dome utilises cinematography, projecting an image of the aircraft on to a screen in the field of a gun sight through which the pupil can practice following the target. The image on the screen has the same apparent speed, appears the same size and assumes the same attitude as an actual aircraft. To accommodate the wide variations of angle through which a gun of a camera would have to move in following an actual aircraft, the screen is in the form of a hemispherical dome (or a half hemispherical) and the projected beam is caused to move through angles corresponding to those through which the camera would have to move when photographing the aircraft.

Since one of the purposes of the Dome Teacher (as set out in the notes on utility) is to accustom the pupil to the psychological background of an actual attack, sounds representing those of an attack are reproduced in the Dome.

These sound effects are of three types: (a) the sound of the aircraft itself, (b) the sound of the aimers' own gun which is controlled by a trigger on the gun sight like that on the actual gun, and (c) the sound of other guns, bombs and so forth.

To enable the instructor and the remainder of the class to judge the aim of the pupil at the gun sight, a small torch projector is mounted on the sight and projects an image of the graticule on to the screen. In the case of the cartwheel sight this takes the form of several radial lines and circles. This projected image is visible to the instructor and other members of the class who can see exactly where the man at the gun is aiming but is hidden from the aimer by the actual graticule. A skilled instructor would know the correct direction and amount of aim-off and would therefore know which part of the graticule should coincide with the target to allow for the moment of the target during the time taken for a shot to reach it, and so secure a hit.

To provide a check on this and demonstrate to other pupils the correct point of aim, a yellow 'future position spot' is projected on to the Dome, indicating at each moment the correct point of aim, namely the point with which the centre of the graticule ought to coincide if the correct aim-off is being applied. The gun sight is provided with a colour filter which renders this spot invisible to the aimer although it is clearly visible to the instructor and to the rest of the class. In certain circumstances it may be desirable to remove the filter so that the aimer can see for himself the mistakes he is making.

The background light in the Dome is coloured blue since this give an illusion of distance.

[Author's note: Henry described the apparatus of the Dome Trainer].

The Dome A.A. Teacher comprises a quarter spherical screen, together with the floor and a flat back wall, forms a room in which are accommodated the gun sight, the projection and sound equipment and the instructors and class. The quarter spherical screen represents the field of fire which can be covered by a gun aimer stationed at one side of a ship. The Domes constructed for the Army employ a complete hemisphere.

The Screen. The curved screen of the Dome is built up from a few preformed plaster segments mounted on wooden formers.

The Gunsight. The gunsight is located so that the line of sight passes as through the geometrical centre of the curvature of the Dome. The sight is mounted on a pedestal arranged so that the various sights corresponding with those of different actual guns can be placed in position. In some cases, the sight is operated only by one man whilst in other cases it employs two men, one to control the position in azimuth and the other controlling the elevation. In the Domes constructed for the Army there are three men: one man to control the position in azimuth, another controlling the elevation and a third operating a part of the apparatus known as a 'Stiffkey Stick'.

The Projector. To avoid the necessity for moving a comparatively bulky projector, a mirror is employed, the projector kept stationary, and the direction of the projector beam being varied by the movement of the mirror. Thus, the projector is mounted on the floor of the Dome and points towards the back wall. The beam is intercepted by the mirror located close to the mounting of the gun sight and carried in gimbals so that it can move both in azimuth and elevation. The mirror is caused to move in the desired manner as follows. For each film, two cams are provided on a shaft which is driven through reduction gearing from the film advancing motor in the projector. Both the film and the cams are started at a given point and once they have been properly set in relation to one another they cannot get out of step. The movement of the cams is transmitted to the mirror by rollers which bear against the cams and are carried by pivoted arms connected to the mirror by wires running over pulleys. One cam controls the azimuth of the mirror whilst the other controls its elevation.

Projected image of graticule. A small torch projector is provided on the gun sight to project on the surface of the Dome an image of the graticule of the sight, for example, a cartwheel. The torch projector moves with the gun sight and is arranged to coincide with it to indicate the exact point of aim to the instructor and onlookers. The image is invisible to the aimer since it is obscured by the actual graticule of the sight.

Future position spot. A yellow spot is projected on to the Dome to indicate the correct point of aim, allowing the necessary aim-off to ensure the aircraft will be hit. The eye-piece of the gun sight is provided with a coloured filter which prevents the gunner from seeing the future position spot, although this is clearly visible to the instructor and the rest of the class. In most of the equipment, the future position spot is marked on the actual film. In some recent equipment intended for high-speed aircraft with which the future position spot is a considerable distance ahead of the aircraft and therefore outside the field of the film, a separate projector and mirror are employed.

Sound effects. Sound effects representing the noise of the aircraft, and some bombs and other guns, are reproduced through normal loudspeaker apparatus from a normal sound track on the film. The noise of the aimer's own gun is represented by means of another loudspeaker from a special amplifier and timing device which produces and times sound synthetically. This gun noise is initiated when the aimer operates the trigger or other firing control on the gun sight. By moving a switch, the instructor can select either the noise of a Lewis gun or similar small weapon, or the slower noise of a heavier gun, for example, a Pom-Pom or Oerlikon. The total firing time is restricted to represent exhaustion of ammunition. In the case of the Lewis gun the total firing time will be 5 seconds to represent the firing period with a small pan, whereas with the noise of the heavier type of gun the total firing period is 15 seconds. In either case the operation of a re-cocking switch 'reloads' the gun and allows a further period of gun noise to be initiated. The gun noise amplifier may also include apparatus for representing the noise of additional bombs which can be dropped at will by the instructor pressing a switch.

Range indication. A range indicator is mounted above the gun sight in a position where the instructor and the class, but not the aimer, can see it clearly. The range Indicator is caused to light up and give an indication when the range of attacking aircraft is 200, 500, 1,700, 1,000, and 400 yards. The range indicator is operated automatically from suitable contacts provided on the cam unit. The object of the range indicator is to enable the instructor to ascertain whether the aimer is opening fire at the proper time. Another form of range indicator is employed in the Dome constructed for the Army, which indicates the range continuously on a dial. This form of range indicator is also worked from the cam unit.

Lighting. Two sets of lighting are provided; a white light for illuminating the Dome when an attack is not being projected, and a uniform blue light of low intensity for use when an attack is being projected. The low intensity enables the projected image to be seen sufficiently clearly by the aimer while the blue colour creates the illusion of distance.

[Author's note: Henry described the method of use of the Dome Trainer].

The problems of providing practice in short range anti-aircraft shooting in a modern war is an extremely serious one, bearing in mind the numbers of men that must be trained and the difficulties involved in normal methods of training by shooting at targets towed behind real aircraft.

For instance, if live ammunition is used, the expense is serious and the areas in which training is possible are limited. A single pupil requires an enormous area of ground, a weapon and a target, so that the number of pupils that can be trained with reasonable resources is very small. Conversely the number of actual engagements that each pupil can rehearse is extremely limited. If live ammunition is not used there is no immediate check on the accuracy of aiming. Apart from the expense of operating real aircraft, training cannot be carried out at all in bad visibility or in weather which is bad enough to keep aircraft grounded. In wartime, enemy interference may prevent this form of training. The speed at which target towing aircraft can fly is limited, the realism of aiming at an actual aircraft or even a specific portion of an aircraft is lacking, and much time may be wasted between runs. In contrast to this the Dome can be operated day and night in all weather conditions and with little risk of enemy interference, and no fear of infringing blackout conditions.

A film of a single run of an aircraft, once made, can be multiplied to any desired extent and put through the projector thousands of times. Accordingly, the need for real aircraft is enormously reduced. Indeed, a method of photographing models was employed by Messrs Technicolor, and this eliminated the need for real aircraft. By this means the speed represented can be chosen irrespectively of the type of aircraft available. There is no necessity to use either an actual gun or live ammunition to obtain a check on the accuracy of the shooting. In fact, the Dome provides a better check on accuracy than live ammunition since the instructor can see immediately just how far the aim diverges from its proper direction and in what manner, whereas with actual ammunition, even using tracer, considerable skill is required to determine this. Moreover, in the Dome the errors are obvious to the reminder of the class and in addition the projection of the graticule enables them to appreciate what the aimer sees and to envisage the correct point of aim in relation to this.

At the time when the Dome came into service the training of short-range anti-aircraft gunners was of special importance in relation to merchant shipping. Losses of merchant shipping due to enemy air attack were extremely heavy. It was essential to find some means of training in a very short time the large number of merchant seamen required to handle the anti-aircraft weapons with which merchant ships were being equipped. The expense which would have been involved in training these men, not to mention those required for the Navy and Air Force, with live ammunition would have been astronomical. Admiralty and Ministry of Supply orders show 407 Domes (active and spares) in all were constructed, including 90 Portobel Domes.

In a single Dome on HMS President, approximately 70,000 to 80,000 men were trained. 88 Domes were provided for the Royal Navy, with 119 Domes for the Army and

112 for the RAF. 35mm systems were used by the Navy, Army and RAF. Both the Army and RAF deployed 16mm systems.

Expenditure and deployment of the 407 Dome Trainer and later Portobel units:

1 x Prototype at Whale Island

Equipment	£6,289 and 13 shillings, 5 pence
Structure	£910 and 12 shillings, 0 pence
	£7,200 and 5 shillings, 5 pence

44 x For Home use

Equipment	£61,061 and 14 shillings, 0 pence
Structure	£40,764 and 18 shillings, 4 pence
Installation and Electrical	£7,339 and 4 shillings, 4 pence
Transport	£2,625 and 1 shilling, 7 pence
Filter and Resistance Units	£317 and 14 shillings, 11 pence
	£1,12,108 and 13 shillings, 2 pence

41 x for Overseas Use

Equipment	£58,882, 19 shillings, 10 pence
Transport	£2,193, 5 shillings, 6 pence
	£61,076 and 5 shillings, 4 pence

30 x for RAF use

Equipment	£21,340, 2 shillings, 6 pence
Installation	£1,182, 0 shillings, 5 pence
	£22,522 and 2 shillings, 11 pence

Cancellation charges	£4,345, 19 shillings, 10 pence
	£4,345, 19 shillings, 10 pence

Projectors and Amplifiers supplied by Admiralty

	£29,366, 2 shillings, 8 pence
	£29,366, two shillings, 8 pence

Portobel equipment

2 x Experimental	£7,250
88 x Production	£100 ,915
Annual Spares	£8,750
Maintenance	£3,750
	£120,665

<u>Ministry of Supply Contracts:</u>

119 x for Army use	£232,610
82 x for RAF use	£110,439
	£343,049

[Author's note: Henry recorded Domes set up for training].

(a) In the United Kingdom
Ainsdale-on-Sea (HMS Queen Charlotte, Belfast)
Bristol
Cardiff
Chatham (Gunnery School, Royal Marines)
(Coastal Forces Gunnery School)
Devonport (Gunnery School, Royal Marines)
Dover
Fort William (HMS St Christopher)
Glasgow
Greenock
Grimsby
Harwich
Hull
Leith
Liverpool
London (HMS President)
Londonderry
Lowestoft 1 & 2
Middlesbrough
Newcastle
Newhaven
Portsmouth (HMS Excellent)
Portsmouth (Eastney Royal Marines)
Pwllheli (HMS Glendower)
Scapa Flow – Lyness
Scapa Flow – Flotta
Sheerness (Dockyard: A.A. Range)
Southampton (HMS Safeguard)
Swansea and Weymouth

(b) Abroad
- Colombo
- Trincomalee
- Durban
- Kilindini
- Simonstown
- Bombay
- Calcutta
- Karachi
- Aden
- Alexandria
- Port Said
- Sydney, N.S.W. 1 & 2
- Auckland
- Wellington
- Bermuda
- Curaçao (Royal Dutch Navy)
- Freetown
- Gibraltar
- Trinidad
- Esquimalt
- Halifax 1 & 2
- Montreal (in summer)
- St John, New Brunswick (in winter)
- St John's Newfoundland

Chapter 16

Evidence and Award

Henry's claim for an award was supported by senior colleagues in all the services. His return to the Royal Navy Volunteer Reserve to develop the Dome Trainer was due to the personal intervention of Commander Guy Phelips. Guy and Henry served together in the First World War, with Guy as a Sub-Lieutenant and Henry as a midshipman. In charge of the Royal Navy Photographic School, Phelips immediately appreciated the value of Henry's ideas, even as Henry was by then a civilian photographer.

Educated at King's School, Canterbury and joining the Royal Navy in 1908, Guy Phelips served in various posts, including on HMS *Africa* in 1916 and HMS *Tiger* in 1919. After a gunnery course at HMS *Excellent* in 1920 he honed his specific skills as a gunner with the Royal Australian Navy in 1922, running the gunnery school at HMAS *Cerberus*. By 1922 he was Assistant Gunnery Officer on the battleship HMS *Malaya* in the Mediterranean. In 1927 Phelips served as Gunnery Officer on HMS *Mackay*, part of the 5th Destroyer Flotilla of the Atlantic Fleet. In 1931 he served as Gunnery Officer on the aircraft carrier HMS *Furious*. His connection with the skills of Henry Stephens started in 1932 with specialist training at the RAF School of Photography. In 1934 Phelips was the Fleet Photographic Officer for the Mediterranean Fleet, moving in 1936 to serve as Photographic Officer for the Home Fleet with the battleship HMS *Nelson*.

When approached by Henry in 1940, Commander Phelips was in charge of the Royal Navy Photographic School, based alongside the gunnery school of HMS *Excellent* in Portsmouth. He was critically involved in sponsoring Henry's ideas to the Royal Navy. By 1946 Phelips had been promoted to run the Royal Navy Film team at HMS *Excellent*., and he wrote to Henry:

24th November. 1946
170 Park Avenue, Purbrook, Hampshire

Dear Stephens,
I have read your letter dated 22nd November 1946 addressed to the Director of Admiralty Contracts stating your claim as inventor of the Dome Trainer. I would like to take this opportunity of substantiating that the information as set out on page two down to the penultimate paragraph was disclosed to me by you before you re-joined the Navy in

July 1940. Similarly, the information I have marked and initialled in the copy of your letter dated 14th August 1940 to Captain Davies was also disclosed to me prior to your re-joining the Navy.

In fact, I will affirm here that it was as a direct result of your disclosing this information to me and realising the importance of it to the war effort, that I counselled you to re-join the Navy forthwith, as being the quickest way of bringing your proposals to the attention of the interested authorities.

If you recall I then and there wrote a personal letter to Commander Weekes, which I believe was largely responsible for your initial interview. I wish you the very best success in your efforts to get an award for your invention, you certainly deserve it.

Yours sincerely,
G.M. Phelips.
Comdr. (Ret)

During the assessment by the Cohen Commission, Pheips wrote to Henry's wife:

7th April 1948
170 Park Avenue, Purbrook, Hampshire.

Dear Mrs Stephens,
I managed to get a seat on the two o'clock coach OK and I had a very comfortable journey down.

Many, many thanks for a most enjoyable stay and a grand time all round. My wife said I was very naughty to have brought anything back, but I know she much appreciated it all the same. I was particularly instructed to thank Eve for the chocolates from her, may I add mine.

Here is wishing you all the very best of luck on your final day in court, and confusion to the opposition and a particular form of nastiness to that arch B—Captain Campbell. May he rot!

Kindest regards to yourself and husband and love to your unmarried daughter.

Yours ever,
Guy Phelips

Rear Admiral Sir William Agnew, KVCO, CB, DSO, the Deputy Chief of Naval Personnel in November 1947, wrote in support of Henry's claim to Messrs Kilburn and Strode, solicitors, acting for Henry Stephens as inventor of the Dome Trainer:

During the last war I had experience of the Dome Trainer whilst I was at sea in command of the cruiser HMS Aurora from 1941 to 1943, and later when I was in command of HMS Excellent, the Portsmouth Naval Gunnery School, from February 1944 to September 1945.

In 1940 HMS Aurora had only very few short-range anti-aircraft weapons. In 1941, whilst at Scapa, the ship was fitted with Oerlikons, and it became necessary to train the crews as quickly as possible in handling and aiming these weapons. A Dome Trainer was available at Scapa, and I sent my men ashore to be trained in it. In my opinion this training improved the accuracy of the short-range anti-aircraft shooting, and good results were obtained later when the ship was subjected to air attacks in the Mediterranean.

Before the Dome Trainer became available there were three methods for training anti-aircraft shooting.

(a) Verifying sights. These were auxiliary sights fitted to the weapon which enabled the instructor to see where the pupil was aiming. The instructor, relying on his own skill and experience, could then correct the pupil's mistakes. This method had the disadvantage that it could only be used in gunnery schools where the equipment was available, and in addition expert instructors were essential. It could not be used in bad visibility or in weather which prevented target aircraft from flying.

(b) Recorders and analysers. These recorded the movements of the target and the gun, and by examining the plot the accuracy of the gunners' aim could be determined. This method had the disadvantage that the apparatus was only available at the three Navy gunnery schools, and the gunners' mistakes were not immediately apparent. It could not be used in bad visibility or in weather which prevented target aircraft from flying.

(c) Towed targets. These were cloth-covered sleeves towed behind aircraft and fired at with live ammunition. This method had the disadvantage that the target speed did not usually exceed about 80 knots, and a pupil trained to judge the correct aim off at this speed would find difficulty in judging the correct aim off when he encountered aircraft moving at about 200 knots. This method of teaching was available at more centres than (a) or (b) but was similarly impractical in bad weather.

The Dome Trainer was of great value to the aimers of close-range anti-aircraft weapons from ships for the following reasons:

(a) It provided a means of indicating to the aimer where he was at fault whilst practising his aim. This could not be done with 'live' targets simulating attacks on the ship since no verifying sights were provided.

(b) Whenever my aimers were sent ashore for practice in a Dome Trainer they came back to the ship with added keenness on their job and their shooting was improved.

The Dome Trainer was also of great value to the men in the Gunnery Schools all over the country who were learning to be aimers of close-range anti-aircraft weapons. Only for principal Gunnery Schools verifying sights were provided as well as Recorders and Analysers for the main gunnery schools. A Dome Trainer was available for use in bad weather when aircraft could not fly and acted as a welcome change from the only other method of training, namely aiming at aircraft or firing at towed targets. Time to train correct target aiming was considerably shortened.

The Dome Trainer was produced at a useful time, since it coincided with the extensive provision of short-range anti-aircraft armament on ships, for which it was necessary to train hundreds of crews in a short time. I doubt whether this could have been done at the same time with the other training methods. The training in the Dome Teacher gave the men confidence, and I am convinced that it saved many casualties.

On 11 April 1948 Henry received a letter from Mrs Nora Donaldson, wife of Admiral Donaldson, who was the son of the Victorian painter Andrew Donaldson and his wife Agnes Twining. Admiral Leonard Donaldson CB, CMG served as Director of Torpedoes and Mining from 1922 to 1924, and as Admiral-Superintendent of Portsmouth dockyard from 1927 to 1931:

My Dear Mr Stephens,
I am so delighted to hear about the Dome. Someone read it out from our Portsmouth evening paper and said, 'this is something that you will be glad to hear' and indeed it was.

I do hope that you will get a proper award. (Captain) Phelips was telling me all about these disgusting people who are preventing the claim. It was all most thrillingly interesting. It must have been most nerve-wracking for you all. I do hope you are rested and that they will be quick to settle the whole thing. With love to Mrs Stephens and Eve, and again I am so glad.

With love from Leonard and myself.

Yours very sincerely,
Nora Donaldson

Another letter supporting Henry against a claim by Technicolor came from Captain Davis (RN College, Greenwich):

24th June 1942
To: The Secretary of the Admiralty.

Lieutenant Stephens originated this idea early in 1940 and re-joined the R.N.V.R, with the intention of being able to bring it to official notice, on the advice of Commander Guy Phelips, R.N. Photographic School, Tipnor.

He was appointed Sub-Lieutenant, R.N.V.R on 8th July 1940, and joined The RN College, Greenwich for training on that date. During the first week of the course, he interested the commander of the College in the idea, and the latter brought it to my notice. Realising the value of the idea, I removed Mr Stephens from his class work and attached him to Lieutenant Commander G.C. Pigou, R.N. with instructions to go further into the matter and place it in concrete form.

Having produced a specification of the idea, Lieutenant Commander Pigou and Sub-Lieutenant Stephens visited Professor A. Warmisham of Messrs. Taylor, Taylor and Hobson, Ltd., to confirm the practical optical aspect of the apparatus proposed.

This report was favourable, and Commander Pigou arranged an interview with Mr. Oliver of Messrs. Technicolor Ltd, as they were the only firm capable of working with films within the fine limits of accuracy required. Proof of this sequence is available in the R.N. College, Greenwich and in Sub-Lieutenant Stephens' possession.

Following this, Lieutenant Stephens was sent to 'Excellent' to work in conjunction with the staff of the Gunnery school to produce the apparatus which is now known as the Dome Teacher.

It is obvious, therefore, that Messrs Technicolor have no claim to patent rights in connection with the Dome Teacher as a whole. They merely acted as manufacturers of apparatus in accordance with requirements formulated in HMS 'Excellent'..

The inventor of the Dome Teacher is undoubtedly Lieutenant H.C. Stephens RNVR, who, being a serving officer, placed his invention at the disposal of the Lords Commissioners of the Admiralty in accordance with service practice.

Captain, Davis R.N.,
R.N. College, Greenwich.

Admiral Dreyer wrote:

8th April 1948

My Dear Stephens,
I was very happy to and give a hand on your behalf about the 'Dome'. I hope that the Committee will realise how important it was. I think they do. Glad they have seen me. I said what I did for different targets to try to make it clear you were the only one with the celestial concave. Everything true to life. People might run about in a room with a model aeroplane on a stick or string, but nothing gave the true enemy attack except the Dome. I remembered in the train why I was enquiring about Domes or the miniature Portobel in February 1943. It was from the Marine guard on each of the Fleet Air Arm aerodromes and from 'air to air' practice, i.e., aeroplanes fighting enemy aeroplanes. It was a pity that I got angry when I could not remember the above and said, 'I am over 70 and forget some things.'

That referred to Portobel which never came into supply while I was Inspector of Merchant Navy Gunnery. The President realised that and said so, so it cannot have spoilt my evidence for the Dome. Take care of yourself, Stephens and sit back and put your heels on the mantelpiece. It was fun meeting a lot of chaps, including Agnew, Davis, Pile, etc. Thank you very much for the succulent lunch.

I hope the Committee will give you a really good award. You have done great work for the country. So go easy. Don't wear yourself out.

Yours sincerely,
Fred Dreyer

Admiral Dreyer wrote again:

8th November 1948

My Dear Stephens,
Your letter of 4th November reached me yesterday in a letter from Kilburn and Strode. I was very glad to hear from you and am writing to K + S a brief statement of the great value of the Dome Trainer and telling them I shall be glad to arrange to come to London to give evidence as to the originality and great merit of the Dome Trainer. (I always refer to it as the Dome Teacher but doubtless you have it right). What happened to the Matching Sight? That too was very ingenious but not so outstanding as the Dome Trainer.

I am glad to see from Kilburn and Strode that the Admiralty and other Departments do not dispute that you were responsible for the D.T. invention. I well remember congratulating you publicly at Whale Island after the first demonstration – as the inventor of this most valuable invention. Can you please send me a list of the Domes at the end of the war? My data in 1942 gives Merchant Navy 26 at Home Fleet & 25 abroad and I believe R.N. had more than 50, i.e., 100 in all. The cost about £9,000 apiece, including the Dome itself, I think.

I hope they will give you a good award. You deserve it.

My wife and I lived at 5 Morpeth Mansions in 1930 to 1933 so I know where Carlisle Mansions is.

Yours sincerely
Fred Dreyer

Briefing from Admiral Dreyer, Inspector of Merchant Navy Gunnery
PHEASANT SHOOTING AT SEA:

ADMIRAL DREYER
The Dome Trainer:
SIR FREDERIC DREYER, GBE, KCB, RN., of Freeelands, Winchester, will prove:

Before the last world war, I was a Naval Officer, and held, among others, the following commands and positions.

1904–7

Gunnery Lieutenant of HMS Exmouth, 1904–7, flagship of Channel Fleet; during this period HMS Exmouth was the outstanding ship in the Navy in gunnery, first in gun layers test and battle practice.

1907–9

Assistant to Director of Naval Ordnance.

1909–10

Commander of new Dreadnought, HMS Vanguard.

1910–12

Flag Commander to Admiral Sir John Jellicoe in the Atlantic Fleet and afterwards in 2nd Division Home Fleet.

1913

Captain, HMS Amphion; in this year HMS Amphion was first in gun layers test and battle practice.

1913–15

Captain, HMS Orion (a Dreadnought).

1915

Made a C.B. in birthday honours, for services in gunnery.

1915–16

Flag Captain to Admiral Sir John Jellicoe in the Fleet Flagship of the Grand Fleet, HMS Iron Duke, including Jutland Battle.

1916–17

Assistant Director, Anti-submarine Division, Admiralty Naval Staff.

1917–18

Director of Naval Ordnance.

1919–20

Commodore and Chief of Staff to Admiral of the Fleet, Viscount Jellicoe, on Naval Mission to India and the Dominions.

1920–22

Director, Gunnery Division, Admiralty Naval Staff.

1922–23

Commanded Battle-cruiser HMS Repulse.

1924–27

A Lord Commissioner of Admiralty and Assistant Chief of Naval staff.

1927–29

Commanded Battle-Cruiser squadron, consisting of HMS Hood, HMS Repulse and HMS Renown.

1930–33

A Lord Commissioner of Admiralty and Deputy Chief of Naval staff
1932
Promoted Admiral
1933–36
Commander in Chief, China Station

Therefore, I have some standing in the Service in regards of gunnery. In his book, 'The Grand Fleet 1914–1916', Lord Jellicoe referred to my 'great gunnery knowledge and experience', to the excellent gunnery organisation of the flagship 'Iron Duke' at the Battle of Jutland, which I commanded, and to the new and successful armoured-piercing projectile which was designed under my immediate direction when I was Director of Naval Ordnance.

In his book 'The Crisis of the Naval War', he paid a special tribute to the work of the anti-submarine Division, of which I had been appointed Assistant Director on Lord Jellicoe's recommendation. He also referred to the rapid progress of the defensive arming of merchant ships in 1917, for which I was responsible when Director of Naval Ordnance.

I was placed on the retired list in 1939 but was soon recalled to my full rank to take part in the Second World War. I became Chief of Naval Air Services (CNAS) in July 1942.

Lieutenant-Commander H.C. Stephens invented the Dome Trainer at a very critical moment in the Second World War.

At the end of February 1941, the then First Sea Lord, Admiral of the Fleet Sir Dudley Pound, rang me up at Winchester on the telephone and asked if I would come and help. Of course, I would. So, he sent his car for me.

When I reached the Admiralty, he told me that we were losing merchant ships at a quite intolerable rate of three and a half million tons per annum due to low level bombing attacks by enemy 4-engined long range aircraft operating from France. He wanted me to put a stop to this. I was to be appointed 'Inspector of Merchant Navy Gunnery' at once.

Before that I had held the following appointments (I retired in May 1939):

(a) Commodore of ocean convoys from October 1939 to May 1940.

(b) On staff of General Officer Commanding Home Front (GOCHF) from May 1940 to September 1940 for anti-invasion duties.

(c) Chairman of Admiralty Committee to assess number of U-boats sunk. (Important to know what results our A/S (Anti-Submarine) measures were achieving)

In the posts (b) and (c) I served in my proper rank of full Admiral and continued to do so as Inspector of Merchant Navy Gunnery (IMNG). I had an office at Admiralty and got going at once and teach the Merchant Navy what I called 'Pheasant Shooting at Sea'. The 4-engined Focke-Wulf aircraft made low masthead bombing attacks (low to make a good percentage of hits and near misses. They usually attacked from ahead and dropped the bombs (mostly 500 lb) about 400 feet ahead of the ship attacked.

What we had to do was:

(X) If possible, shoot him down before he got to 400 feet and before he dropped bombs

(Y) If not, then anyhow shoot him down as he went over.

We increased the HA equipment of merchant ships. The problem was how to teach them to shoot well enough to achieve (X above). At this moment I heard of Stephens and his Dome suggestion, and went at once to HMS Excellent, our principal Gunnery School where I got full details. I realised at once that Stephens had in effect thrown us a lifebuoy in our time of greatest distress.

I went to the Admiralty and 3rd Sea Lord (now 2nd Sea Lord Fraser) and told him of the Dome Trainer and that I felt certain this would be of enormous help. He approved my getting on at full speed and getting one made so I telephoned to the captain of 'Excellent' and next day Lieutenant Commander G. Hamilton R.N. arrived in London with full information about the Dome. I drove out along Great West Road with him to 'Technicolor' and put them in touch with Stephens and gave them full authority to on at the highest priority with the manufacture of the first Dome and erect it in HMS 'Excellent'.

I remember attending a demonstration of the first Dome Teacher at HMS 'Excellent', probably in early March 1941. I commended Lieutenant Commander Stephens for his invention. Shortly after this, on 25th March 1941, I received an official report from HMS 'Excellent'. The next day I placed an order for 14 Dome Trainers to be constructed.

On 31st March, an Admiralty message was sent to out to the DEMS centres in various parts of the United Kingdom and to Halifax, Nova Scotia, Bermuda, Gibraltar, Freetown, Simonstown and Port Said. Arrangements were being made to provide them with Dome Teachers. I recall that this message said, 'The device provides the most realistic instruction yet produced of any Teacher, and by its use DEMS personnel can be given invaluable training.'.

This turned out to be invaluable. I was never attacked by a German bomber when afloat, but there was no doubt that here was a true to life simulation of such an attack. It included the noise of the airplane's engines.

One saw on the film thrown on the inner surface of the Dome – the enemy roaring in to the attack and a coloured disk showed where the gunner under instruction was aiming his machine gun. A differently coloured disc showed where he ought to be aiming. (A coloured filter on this signed prevented the Gun-layer seeing this disk). The instructor and the rest of the class could see what mistake in laying the Gun-layer made. The instructor could tell the Gun-layer of his error and teach him how to correct them.

It was in truth a marvellous instrument and a real stroke of genius.

To men who had been instructed in the Dome, the German aircraft low bombing attack had been robbed of the element of surprise. They knew exactly how to shoot him down and did large number of practice 'runs' in the Domes. I questioned Army generals in March 1941 about the effect of low bombing runs on troops. They said the first attack was terrifying but if they survived it troops faced up to it well the next time. The Dome Teacher sent our own gun layers to sea as veterans even if they had never experienced live bombing.

The result was very quickly apparent at sea. The German planes were shot down and were compelled to find the game not worth the candle.

The Focke-Wulf's continued to carry out reconnaissance duties at sea for their U-Boats, but practically gave up their devastating low-level attacks on our merchant shipping. A large measure of this success was due to the Dome Trainer, i.e., to Lieutenant Commander Stephens' invention. The Focke-Wulf's encountered veterans not trainees in the art of shooting them down at their first encounters with our merchant shipping.

The 'Horror of the Blitz' attacks at sea had been dispelled by Stephens.

In 1942 we lost more than 6 and a half million tons of shipping by submarine attack, which nearly brought us to ruin. If on top of this the air attacks had continued the heavy scale of the early part of 1941, I am of the opinion that we should have been completely ruined.

The value of the shipping and cargoes saved by the improved standard of shooting resulting from the training which the Merchant Navy gunners, and the Navy and Army gunners on board the ships, received in the Dome Teacher was immense. All the improvements we made in teaching shooting and putting in place by August 1941 saved some £350,000,000 per annum.

It is difficult to give a figure to the Dome Trainer. I shall guess about £100,000,000 per year from mid-1941 onwards.

Fred Dreyer, Admiral

A third letter from Admiral Dreyer came in June:

Freelands, Winchester,
Date: 5 June 1948

Mr Dear Stephens,
It was very good of you to write. I had hoped that you would get much more – but I am afraid there is no appeal.

We had to stop the Hun bombers from sinking our merchant ships by low level (to hit) bombing. The situation was desperate. Some 8 to 10 months later I took Pound [Admiral of the Fleet Sir Alfred Pound] to the 'Dome' of the 'President'. He understood its immense value at once.

It is nice of you to ask me to a small cocktail party, but alas! I cannot come so have to ask to be excused. But in a few weeks, I must come up to see my dentist and will try and come up and see you, old chap and your family.

With every good wish,

Yours very sincerely,
Frederic Dreyer

General Pile, Commander-in-Chief, UK Anti-Aircraft Command, wrote:

GENERAL SIR FREDERICK ALFRED PILE, Bart., GCB, DSO, MC.
Stuart Advertising Agency Limited, 37 Park Street, W.1. (Tel: Mayfair 9255)
To: Royal Commission on Awards to Inventors
12th November 1947
To Messrs Kilburn & Strode, 31-33 High Holborn, W.C.1,

Dear Sirs,
I am in receipt of your letter of the 4th November re the Dome Trainer.

I have also received a letter from Lieutenant Commander Stephens in connection with this matter. In this letter he points out that the Navy were primarily responsible for using this invention. I shall be only too glad to give evidence before the Lord Justice on the matter, although I feel that evidence from Naval officers would be much more fruitful.

The evidence that I would give would be that the Dome Teacher did fulfil a very useful function at the time when low flying attacks were a great peril and when there was no outstanding method for training the troops to combat these attacks. I was so impressed with the Teacher that I asked for many of them, but the Admiralty got in first, we only obtained two, one of which was erected in Hyde Park and gave most useful service, and one at the practice camp at Manorbier.

I would have no hesitation in saying that the device does merit an award to its inventor.

Yours faithfully,
F. A. Pile

Briefing from General Pile

GENERAL SIR FREDERICK ALFRED PILE, Bart., G.C.B., D.S.O., M.C.
Pale Farm House, Chipperfield, King's Langley, Hertfordshire

I was General Officer Commanding-in-Chief of Anti-Aircraft Command during the whole of the last world war from 1939 to 1945, and I was directly responsible for the anti-aircraft defence of the whole of the United Kingdom.

In the early part of the war the enemy air attacks were delivered by aircraft flying high, with only spasmodic attacks by low flying aircraft. Later, I think in about 1943 the enemy launched heavy low-flying air attacks.

These attacks took place with great rapidity, the time which elapsed from the gunner of a close-range weapon sighting an approaching aircraft until it passed out of range being very short. The technique of engaging these low-flying aircraft with close range weapons was different from that required for engaging high-flying aircraft with long-range weapons, and it was necessary to give many troops suitable training in a comparative short time to combat these low-flying attacks. The Dome Teacher proved to be a very suitable device for such training, and indeed it was the best training device we had.

In my opinion it improved the standard of close-range shooting, enabled many men to be trained in a short time, and enabled training to be carried out indoors in bad weather which would have prevented outdoor training. The greater realism of the training in the Dome Teacher was also an advantage.

I first heard of the Dome Teacher from a senior Naval Officer, I think it was Admiral Lord Fraser. I asked for a large number but since the Admiralty had got in first, I only managed to obtain two for my Command. One was erected in Hyde Park and the other at Manorbier. These Dome Teachers gave most useful service. I believe another one came into use later in Liverpool. I know that several Dome Teachers were sent abroad for the use of our forces overseas.

General Pile wrote again:

GENERAL SIR FREDERICK ALFRED PILE, Bart., G.C.B., D.S.O., M.C.
Pale Farm House, Chipperfield, King's Langley, Hertfordshire
1st August 1947

Dear Commander Stephens,
It was very kind of you to write. I was only too glad to give evidence on your invention which of course was a great contribution to the war effort.

I was so sorry to hear of your heart attack. The strain of the hearing must have been great, but I hope when it is over you will be well again.

With best wishes to you and your family and may you get a very substantial award.

Yours very sincerely,
F.A Pile

Barrister Pat Graham wrote:
3 Essex Court, Temple E.C.4.

Dear Stephens, Eve and Mrs Stephens,
Many thanks for your kind letter. It is very nice to know that one is appreciated when one has tried. I found the only real satisfaction in life is to do the best one can whether it be arguing in court or making a bookcase!

I am so sorry to hear that the old heart problem returned. I was afraid that it might but now it is over you can take it easy. You can at any rate take the largest measure of credit for yourself. There is no doubt whatsoever that you greatly impressed the Commission when you were in the witness box and in my experience of these things the impression given by the Claimant has more effect than anything on the award.

I hope they won't keep you waiting too long. Unfortunately, Technicolor did not finish by Friday and is appearing again on the 26th. I doubt if they will make any award before hearing Technicolor's case.

I hope to see you again soon,

Yours sincerely,
Pat Graham

In his journal, Henry was particular in recording private letters from shipmates Chief Petty Officer Harris and Chief ERA Mason:

F.A. Harris, Addison Ward, Guys Hospital, London S.E.1.
2nd April 1948

Dear Commander Stephens,
I was indeed very pleased to see in the evening paper of yesterday your intended claim before the Royal Commission.

I take this opportunity in wishing you every success. I have not seen your assistant, Chief E.R.A. Waller since we demobbed from the College.

Yours sincerely,
F.A. Harris C.P.O. (Retired)
Late Seamanship Instructor

January 26th, 1949
Chief E.R.A. P. Mason
59 Jenkins Grove, Portsmouth

Dear Sir,
It was with great pleasure I heard broadcast the news of your award for the 'Dome'. Little did I think at the time when you asked me to demonstrate a movement from a shaving mirror (if my memory's correct) that it would be such a great success.

Why I feel I must congratulate you is because of the opposition you met with at Whale Island, and the 'A.A.' school Eastney, although I think we did our best to help at the school at Eastney, which didn't meet with the best of approval. Still, success was achieved and rewarded, and so again, congratulations.

From Mr P Mason

***

In April 1948, good news arrived for Henry Stephens:

The Secretary of the Admiralty, Bath.
29th April 1948
Quoting: C.P. Patents 4674/48
TO: Lt. Cdr. H.C. Stephens, RNVR,
64A Carlisle Mansions, Carlisle Place,
London, S.W.1.

Sir,

1. I am commanded by My Lords Commissioners of the Admiralty to refer to your application to the Royal Commission on Awards to Inventors in connection with the Dome Aiming Teacher.

2. The Admiralty are advised that the Royal Commission have recommended an immediate payment to you of £1,000 pending the final assessment of their award, which must be deferred until another application in the same field has been considered, and The Lords Commissioners of H.M. Treasury having been pleased to accept this recommendation, a Navy Bill of £1,000 will be forwarded to you at an early date.

I am, Sir,
Your obedient Servant,

ROYAL COMMISSION ON AWARDS TO INVENTORS
28th May 1948
HEAD (3)
CLAIM BY MR H.C. STEPHENS
In respect of THE DOME ANTI-AIRCRAFT TRAINER (C.44)
RECOMMENDATION

The Commission have enquired under Head (3) of the Royal Warrant into the circumstances of the claim by Mr Henry Christian Stephens dated 28th February 1947 in respect of the Dome Anti-Aircraft Trainer. In view of the special merit and utility of the invention, the basic idea of which was conceived by the claimant before he re-joined the Navy in July 1940, the Commission recommended that an ex-gratia payment of £5,000 pounds be made to Mr Stephens.

The Royal Commission on Awards to Inventors ruled that Lieutenant Colonel Haszard had no claim for contribution to the Dome Aiming Trainer. Technicolor was awarded £1,500 for assistance with the Dome Anti-Aircraft Trainer and Tracer Attachment.

PART IV

Post War

Chapter 17

Newspaper Reports

[Author's note: Henry's journal noted that the Dome Teacher was on the Secret List from its inception in 1940. No locations, names or detailed description or account could be in the press].

THE TIMES, 6 December 1941 (describing general A.A. training and mobile bus units only) (see Plate 16).

A.A. GUNNERY IN THE MERCHANT NAVY INGENIOUS TRAINING
From Our Naval Correspondent

From the outbreak of war, the enemy has made his chief effort at sea in direct attack on merchant shipping, devoting all his ingenuity to devising fresh methods. U-boats have proved disappointing to him, except during the period in which we suffered from a grave deficiency of escort craft. The magnetic and acoustic mines have been mastered. Surface raiders have either met the fate of the *Bismarck*, *Scharnhorst*, or *Kormoran*, or if they have evaded it, have done little destruction. But air attack proved more promising, and last April the merchant ship losses by that agency rose to a figure that was disquieting. But that threat too has now been mastered, and the average losses of the last five months caused by bombing have been no more than one-twelfth of those in April. This successful result has been brought about chiefly by the advanced training of merchant seamen in A.A. defence – an expression which includes not only the actual shooting, but also look-out, control of fire, and maintenance of A.A. weapons. Merchant Navy A.A. schools have been set up at all British ports and at a great number abroad, and 7,000 merchant seamen have taken a training course in one or other of them. But it is not always easy to find time in a merchant seamen's life – he amongst others needs periods of leave between voyages, so in addition to these schools where actual shooting can be practiced, a number of two-decked motor buses have been fitted up as mobile A.A. schools. Each has two classrooms, above and below, and run down to the docks alongside the ships.

THE TIMES, 8 May 1942

R.A. GUNNERS AT SEA PROTECTING CONVOYS FROM BOMBERS SUCCESSFUL EXPERIMENT

From our special correspondent with the Army

It is a singular happening that, with all it the perfections of modern war, the wheel in several instances should have turned full cycle to the early days of the British Army. The Commandos are a case in point, and another link with the past may be found in the Maritime Regiments of the Royal Artillery, which were raised at the time of Dunkirk as anti-aircraft gunners for the Merchant Navy. The traditions of these sea-going soldiers go back to Cromwell's 'sea-fencibles'. Several British regiments of glorious fame were formed three centuries ago as Marines. There could not be a more encouraging example of unity between the Royal Navy and the Army than is to be found in the camp of one of the Maritime Regiments in Scotland, which is typical of similar organisations in other parts of the country. Most merchant ships, from ocean-going liners to the humblest of coastal tramps, now carry a complement of R.A. gunners who could carry their own weapons or man permanently mounted guns. Already they have accounted for many German aircraft, or equally important, scared away scores of raiders. The intensity of fire-power of a convoy nowadays is such that pilots in German broadcasts speak of the courage needed to thrust home an attack.

SURPRISE WEAPONS

At a range by the sea, one was able to watch the Maritime Regiment practise with some of the surprise weapons, including rockets and grenade-projectors. One saw, for instance, what a terror the Oerlikon gun can be in the hands of a trained marksman who, with his second burst, could hit a toy balloon as it soared in the wind. After each spell at sea the gunners return to camp for 14 days and take further courses of training in the R.N. gunnery school alongside naval ratings and merchant seamen. Most of them have remarkable tales of adventure to relate, and not a few are survivors from torpedoed ships. Some helped in the evacuation of women and children from Singapore, and one young gunner, now looking the picture of health, described how his ship had been torpedoed and shelled off West Africa. His boat for was machine-gunned as it pulled away and, incredible though it sounds, he and his companions spent 31 days in it before being picked up by a Dutch ship, having subsisted on half a biscuit and a tiny measure of water a day. At the start, when the scarcity of naval gunners was acute, the Maritime Regiments were composed of volunteers from every regiment in the Army. The experiment was so successful, the relations established so happy, that the batteries were incorporated in the Royal Artillery – not without regret at the break with old regimental ties – and made a permanent part of an organisation known as Defensively Equipped Merchant Ships.

TRAINING BY FILMS

By the side of a secluded loch members of the regiment were at their lessons in sea lore. Under the eye of the Navy, they sailed a cutter, went through the motions of life-saving, tied knots, or tried their hand at semaphore- or anything that could be of value to them during their stay at sea. But the core of their training is proficiency with their weapons. Some batteries are equipped with a variety of machine-guns from the Lewis to the Oerlikon, of Swiss origin, but one has nothing but a Bofors (see Plate 10). The essence of gunnery instruction is that a dive-bombing attack is over in a matter of seconds, and everything depends on the action taken by the gunner in that time. Here the first essential is an unfailing system of look-outs. Students go through a recognition course; they learn how to judge the speed and approach angles of aircraft – a far more complex business than it sounds – and become swift masters of their weapons through a method known as 'eye-shooting'. Films are playing an increasingly useful part in instruction. An apparatus called the Dome Trainer is now being taken up extensively by the gunnery establishment of the Navy, and it is the ideal means of teaching men how to deal with low-flying attacks. Broadly speaking, films of a variety of attacks, taken specially for the purpose, are projected within a large quarter-sphere, which resembles the sky in the dim light, and the gunner merely trains his sight on to the aircraft. The noise of the machine is reproduced, ranges are precisely gauged, and altogether it is as near the real thing as possible.

THE TIMES, 7 April 1947

SNIPERS TRAINED IN DOME OF 'PRESIDENT'

The Thames, near Blackfriars bridge, will look empty and unfamiliar when HMS President is towed away shortly for a dockyard refit. This, the mother ship of the London division of the RNVR, will return looking more like a ship without the grotesque-looking superstructure, the 'Dome' Teacher – which was such a hush-hush affair during the war. It can now be revealed that this lofty dome of corrugated iron, now being dismantled, was an ingenious affair for teaching Ack-Ack gunners, with the help of a cine-camera, to hit a fast-moving plane. Pupils had to wait for the split second in which to pull the trigger on the plane, and there were impressive sound effects. Between 70,000 and 80,000 men were trained in the Dome, which has been described as one of the best wit-sharpeners in the Royal Navy. The British Merchant Navy, Naval DEMS (men in defensively-equipped merchant ships) and personnel from all the allied countries did courses in the ship. HMS President, which has been in the Thames since 1922, has only been shifted from her moorings on three occasions - 1926, 1931 and 1939. Her 'overflow' or sister ship, HMS Chrysanthemum, will remain moored near Blackfriars Bridge, and her job during the war was the training of men in signalling.

EVENING NEWS, 7 April 1948

INVENTION SAVED US £100 MILLION
War Chief's Disclosures

Admiral Sir Frederic Dreyer, Inspector of Merchant Navy Gunnery in 1941–1942 said at the Royal Commission on Awards to inventors in London today that the Dome teacher anti-aircraft training invention had saved Britain £100 million worth of merchant shipping and cargoes. Disclosing British merchant shipping losses from dive-bombing attacks, Sir Frederic, called as a witness by the Dome teacher inventor, Lieutenant Commander H. C. Stephens said: 'In 1941 we were losing merchant shipping at the rate of £350 million per annum, or 3 ½ million tons a year. We reduced this figure of 3 ½ million tons to 1/14th, which is a quarter of a million tons.'

DAILY EXPRESS, April 8, 1948

GENERAL PILE PRAISES THE 'TALKIE' GUN

GENERAL SIR FREDERICK PILE, wartime GOC-in-C. Anti-Aircraft Command, said yesterday that the Dome training device turned out skilled gun teams 'as quickly as a sausage machine'. It uses sound-film effects to teach gunners how to beat attacks from the air. Lieutenant Commander Henry Christian Stephens is claiming an award for the Dome before the Royal Commission on Inventions. He says he got the idea at a news theatre in Charing Cross Road in 1939. And he joined the Navy to develop it. Admiral Sir Frederic Dreyer, former Inspector of Merchant Navy gunnery, said yesterday: 'It was a stroke of genius . . . a lifebuoy . . . which saved £100,000,000 a year.' The Commission adjourned until today.

Chapter 18

RAF Langham (1940–1958) with RAF Weybourne

With German rearmament from 1933 and delays won by political appeasement, in 1934 the British government put into place the RAF Expansion Scheme. This including the specifications for and orders of aircraft in large quantities, alongside 'Shadow Factories', where motor car companies set up new plants to produce aircraft. If war was declared they could act as backup facilities in case main aircraft factories were destroyed. The Expansion Scheme also ordered the compulsory building of new airfields and upgrading of existing facilities.

An airfield at RAF Bircham Newton in Norfolk was constructed in the First World War and opened in 1916 as a fighter training station with No.3 Fighter School. In the spring of 1918, it became a long-range heavy bomber station. This remained as the only operational RAF airfield in Norfolk for the inter-war period.

Bircham Newton was upgraded and developed as part of the Expansion Scheme. In 1936 it was transferred from being a bomber airfield to 16 Group, RAF Coastal Command, responsible for maritime reconnaissance and anti-submarine and shipping warfare in the southern North Sea and the Channel.

As Bircham Newton required satellite airfields, farmland owned by the Allen family of Langham in Norfolk was requisitioned to build a new base. Langham was a small village of around 250 souls where employment had revolved around agriculture. New Army and RAF personnel were billeted with local residents until the airfield was built. From 1941 to late 1943 the grass airfield was expanded and permanent concrete runways and hangars were added. The population of the village rose to over 2,000 people.

The newly created RAF Langham was initially used as training airfield for crews to practise emergency landings. Accommodation was basic Nissen huts or village billets. Early protection for the aircraft and men working on them took the form of engine tents. These were just a metal frame covered with canvas and placed over the nose of the aircraft. A flameless heater was placed in tents against frost, but the tents were often blown away. The bitterly cold conditions of a North Norfolk winter were well remembered by many of the airmen who were based at Langham!

Night operations were facilitated by a Gooseneck flare path and a single Chance floodlight, whereas Bircham Newton had no illumination. Fatal accidents were inevitable. In early 1941 a detachment of Blenheim aircraft from 248 Squadron arrived to carry out coastal patrols. On 14 February 1941 a Blenheim, piloted by Squadron Leader Joseph

Chamberlain of 235 Squadron, attempted a night landing at Langham when the flare path was suddenly extinguished due to enemy activity. The plane crashed at Croxton, near Fulmodeston. Pilot officer E. R. Phillips was killed and is buried in St Mary's Church, Great Bircham.

Due to close proximity to the anti-aircraft gunnery ranges at Stiffkey and Weybourne, Anti-Aircraft Co-Operation Units arrived to fly target-towing aircraft, such as the Hawker Henley. In December 1941, 'K' and 'M' Flights with 200 staff as No. 1 AACU (Anti-Aircraft Co-Operation Unit) arrived from Bircham Newton with twelve Hawker Henleys, two Tiger Moths and a Lysander. In Hawkers three flag targets could be carried in the internal bomb bay. These were 30 feet long when unfurled and 5½ feet wide. Seven pounds of lead weights held red fabric steady. Deployment was via a wind-driven winch mounted outside below the rear cockpit. The drum held 7,000 feet of cable, operated by an RAF rigger in the rear cockpit. Target-towing (TT) operations were flown with the rear cockpit cover left off, and it was often destroyed by the wind velocity.

Target practice at Langham was linked to the nearby Royal Artillery anti-aircraft camp at RAF Weybourne. From 1933, novel radio-controlled aircraft called 'Queen Bee' were launched by catapult for use as targets by R.A. Territorial Regiments during annual summer camps. The Queen Bee was an adapted Tiger Moth, a two-seat single-engine biplane training aircraft specially adapted to be flown by radio control without a pilot. Twin floats were added for sea landings. Revealing the requirement for Dome Trainers, a demonstration of Queen Bee rocket target practice for Winston Churchill was held in June 1941. V4797 Queen Bee was flown at 400 feet. 160 missiles were fired and all missed. A few days later, further trials took place when V4755 Queen Bee flew at 5,000 and 9,000 feet for two hours. Ninety rockets were fired and all missed. During the next visit, L5894 was launched. After 45 minutes all rockets missed. The Army used 40mm Bofors to down the Queen Bee.

Reflecting the paucity of modern aircraft at the time, on 17 July 1942 six Swordfish 'string bag' biplanes (serial numbers W5641/M, W5914/G, W5915/F, W5916/A, DK698/B and DK760/C, a design which first flew in 1933) arrived at Langham from 819 Squadron, Fleet Air Arm in Scotland. Painted black for night operations, the two crew gave up a third seat to an extra fuel tank, allowing minelaying sorties along the Dutch coast.

In late July 1942, Langham was upgraded to an independent RAF airfield with a grass field. No. 2820 Squadron RAF Regiment became responsible for the airfield defence. The RAF Regiment honed anti-aircraft skills within a new anti-aircraft gunnery Dome Trainer on the fringe of the airfield. Details of servicemen who experienced the Dome Trainer are provided in Chapter 7, including Tom Wright, No. 222 RAF fighter squadron, based at Hornchurch, who came to Langham for a week's A.A. course in 1943. Alan Eade was a Dome Trainer instructor whilst serving as a Lieutenant in the Norfolk Yeomanry (TA) at Langham Dome (see Plate 14).

The Langham Dome was designed by the Trussed Concrete Steel Co. Limited. It was made from sixteen pre-formed vertical curved steel lattice ribs with six horizontal steel lattice ring ribs of diminishing diameter welded to them. Wired to this framework was an inner and outer 'skin' of metal mesh (Hy-Rib), between which was poured concrete. The inner surface was then lined with pre-formed curved fibrous plaster sheets (to form the projection surface) which were attached to wooden blocks. These blocks had been attached to the inner metal mesh before the concrete was poured. However, attacks on Langham were limited. In May 1941 a Heinkel 111 dropped four 250 kg bombs which failed to explode. In March 1945 anti-personnel bombs were dropped, killing cattle in fields between Langham and Binham.

In November 1942 the airfield was closed for construction of concrete runways and large T2 Type hangars, resuming operations in March 1944 as part of No. 16 Coastal Command and commanded by Group Captain A. E. Clouston DSO, DFC, AFC. New squadrons in April 1944 were 455 Squadron, Royal Australian Air Force and 489 Squadron, Royal New Zealand Air Force. Flying Beaufighters, units spent seven months on anti-shipping operations along the coasts of Norway, Denmark, Germany, Holland and France. Casualties were high in these squadrons; 489 Squadron lost twenty-two aircrew.

280 Squadron arrived with Warwick air-sea-rescue aircraft. These flew with lifeboats that could be sent by parachute to aircrew in the sea. This Squadron was heavily involved in the failed Allied airborne operation at Arnhem, rescuing ditched gliders and aircrew.

In October 1944 Wellingtons with 524 Squadron were posted to Langham, also flying anti-shipping patrols. They were replaced by Wellingtons with 612 Squadron in December 1944, also flying anti-submarine patrols with newly developed radar. A very bright new radar-guided searchlight called the Leigh Light proved decisive for 407 Squadron Royal Canadian Air Force at Langham, revealing both ships and U-Boats at night. Previously in command of No 224 (Leigh Light) B-24 Liberator squadrons, Group Captain Clouston was a Leigh Light pioneer and had completed early flight testing

Also in October 1944, the 521 Meteorological Squadron was posted to Langham to provide critical weather reports with a variety of aircraft, including Flying Fortresses, Gladiators and Venturas. By November 1945 this role had passed to 1402 Flight (meteorological) with Hurricanes and 1561/1562 Flight with Spitfires.

Trevor Morgan witnessed the dangers of flying from Langham in 1945:

> On 11th May 1945 we had just returned from our usual visit to the flicks in Holt and were back in the billet where I was engaged in one of my frequent arguments with LAC Batey. Suddenly we heard a Wimpy flying overhead. You could always tell a Wimpy, they made a distinctive whistling sound. Batey said, 'That aircraft is in trouble' and I said, 'No, it's just an old OTU training aircraft with de-rated

> engines.' They flew on 87 octane petrol and so sounded different. As we argued about that, the lights in the billet flickered, we all rushed outside in time to see the Wimpy with its landing lights on coming down on the village. We jumped on our bikes and set out to look for it.
>
> The plane had hit the wireless mast and the Church tower, then demolished one side of the barn on the other side of the road. The fuselage slid along to the WAAF site and came to rest with its tail against a tree. The captain was dazed and joined the others in the ambulance which left. He realised the rear gunner was missing so he insisted on returning to the crash. Chiefy Tyson took charge, telling everyone to douse their fags and search for the missing gunner. In an outhouse at the end of the barn we found the turret jammed up in the roof beams. Chiefy and a couple of lads climbed up and got the gunner out but he was dead on arrival at sick bay.

The rear gunner was Flying Officer (Air Gunner) Glen James Hayfrom Loon Lake, Saskatchewan, Canada. He is buried in the Brookwood Military Cemetery, near Woking, Surrey.

Leading Aircraftwomen Ivy Cross was awarded of the British Empire Medal for her bravery.

> On the night of 25th March 1945, a heavily-loaded Wellington aircraft crashed and burst into flames near the airfield shortly after taking off for operations. Leading Aircraftwomen Cross drove her van across several fields to reach the scene of the crash. She helped to drag clear several of the crew who had been thrown out of the aircraft although ammunition and explosives were detonating at very close quarters. Owing to the intense heat she was unable to approach the aircraft again in order to try to rescue other trapped airmen. She returned to her station of duty at Flying Control and shortly after arriving there another Wellington aircraft crashed on the edge of the airfield. Leading Aircraftwomen Cross was also first on the scene with her van. Most of the crew members were able to get clear of the wreckage, but the rear gunner was trapped. She assisted in smashing the rear turret and in helping the rear gunner to safety. Leading Aircraftwomen Cross has attended fourteen crashes and on twelve occasions has helped members of the aircrew from crashed and burning aircraft. She has shown outstanding courage and complete disregard for her own safety.

After the end of the war in Europe in May 1945, Langham continued to provide meteorological flights until June 1946. At the end of the war it was not possible to organise training for a Netherlands Air Force in Holland, so a new technical training school with 700 Dutch servicemen opened at the airfield, rebuilding the wartime Dutch air force with aircraft maintenance and electronic skills. Many men trained at Langham went on to join the new KLM civilian air service. However, the winter of 1946/47 was one of the coldest on record. The village was snowed in for days at a time. Provided with little suitable clothing and limited fuel for their Nissen hut accommodation, the Dutch were very reliant on local support until the arrival of a very welcome spring!

These aircrew suffered less than their countrymen in the Netherlands. At the liberation of the south of the Netherlands in the autumn of 1944, the Dutch government in exile in London ordered a total railway strike to support Operation Market Garden on 17 September 1944, and 30,000 railway workers went on strike. In revenge, the Nazis blocked food transports to the provinces of North and South Holland. Once the rivers and canals froze, nothing moved by water. People ate everything from tulip bulbs and sugar beets to dogs and cats. About 20,000 people died because of the extreme winter. Breakfast was hot water and a slice of bread, made from brown beans. Lunch was a small potato, and there was no milk, sugar or cereals. Many in Holland (including the later film star Audrey Hepburn), working for the Dutch Resistance, suffered from severe edema, due to lack of nourishment.

Beyond the airfield and incorporating the Dome Trainer, 43 Light Anti-Aircraft/ Search Light Regiment, (Royal Artillery) were posted to Langham in 1947 and merged with the 84th Searchlight Regiment. With 40mm Bofors guns and training in the Dome, gunners moved on to the Stiffkey live firing range on the coast, remaining at Langham until 1951.

In 1952 the airfield was taken over by Marshall of Cambridge, who had been awarded the contract to take over the Civilian Anti-Aircraft Co-operation Unit, flying target-towing aircraft for the Heavy Anti-aircraft range at Weybourne and the Light Anti-aircraft range at Stiffkey, using Beaufighters and Mosquitoes. Marshall would continue in this role until October 1958.

Between 1951 and 1957 Langham was host to various American units, including the 50th Radio Controlled Target Aircraft Detachment equipped with large radio-controlled model aircraft known as RCATs. They would launch these aircraft from a circular roadway commonly referred to as the 'whirlygig'. In 1953 a battalion of the 32nd Anti-Aircraft Artillery Brigade arrived. They were equipped with the Skysweeper 75mm automatic radar-operated anti-aircraft gun. A meteorological section deployed hydrogen-filled balloons from Weybourne. These balloons measured the wind speed at high altitudes, as well as the humidity and temperatures, all of which could affect the flight of the shells from the Skysweeper guns.

With radar-operated gunnery, there was little use for the Dome Trainer facility, using now outdated technology. Anti-aircraft missiles made the ranges at Stiffkey and Weybourne redundant.

In 1958 RAF Langham was closed, and the land was sold in 1961. Bernard Matthews used the land for turkey production, and the rest of the airfield reverted to agriculture.

In January 2010, the local community set up the Friends of Langham Dome (see Plates 23 to 26) to work with the North Norfolk Historic Buildings Trust, who had been donated the Dome by Bernard Matthews PLC. On 11 July 2014, after grants of over £350,000 and assistance from both the author and the Imperial War Museum with Henry's private journal, the Langham Dome re-opened to the public as a unique working museum and a memorial to those who flew from Langham. The author attended on behalf of the family, and Evelyn Ward-Thomas, the daughter of Henry Stephens, wrote:

> I am very sorry, due to a family commitment, not to be with you all today. This memorial to my beloved father Lieutenant Commander Henry Christian Stephens and his achievement means more to me than I can say. His invention of the Dome Trainer saved thousands of lives and over 100,000 tons of Allied shipping during the Battle of the Atlantic. My heartfelt thanks to Patrick Allen and his colleagues for their marvellous achievement in restoring this historic Dome. I am so glad my son Ewan is here to represent us. He has worked tirelessly to bring this about. My father died in 1953, 100% disabled and partly blind due to the stress of his war service. He would be so proud and grateful to you all. Have a great day and God bless you.
>
> Eve Ward-Thomas

Appendix A

Summary History of the Dome Trainer

1939–early 1940

Henry Christian Stephens conceives idea of Dome Anti-Aircraft Gunnery Trainer (Dome Trainer) for instruction in the use of light anti-aircraft guns (up to 40mm calibre).

8 July 1940

Stephens rejoins Royal Navy at Greenwich as a Sub-Lieutenant to help get his idea adopted (having served in the RN in the First World War).

15 Jul 1940

Stephens suggests Dome Trainer idea to Captain J. C. Davis at Greenwich.

6 Aug 1940

Stephens and Lieutenant Commander Pigou visit RN Gunnery School HMS *Excellent* at Whale Island, Portsmouth. Head of anti-aircraft (A.A.) section Commander Campbell reports to his superiors about the Dome Trainer. He is told to start development immediately.

August 1940

Discussions between Stephens, HMS *Excellent* and Technicolor Ltd.

8 October 1940

Stephens posted to HMS *Excellent* as a Lieutenant

15 November 1940

Meeting between RN (Stephens and Campbell) and Technicolor to agree a specification for the Dome Trainer.

November 1940

Technicolor and Henry Stephens develop a photographic table to photograph a model at various angles in a stop frame film process to produce a film of an attacking aircraft.

January 1941

Stephens, Technicolor (Messrs Oliver, Happe and Gunn) and HMS *Excellent* develop the Dome Trainer (at first officially known as a 'Dome Teacher').

March 1941
Technicolor build a 20ft (6.1m) diameter free-standing wooden dome at their premises in Harmondsworth. They suggest that an initial 40ft (12.2m) diameter half dome at HMS *Excellent* be a steel structure with an inner screen surface of fibrous plaster (see plates 7 & 11).

April 1941
Admiral Sir Frederic Dreyer, Inspector of Merchant Navy Gunnery, (merchant ships equipped with A.A. guns were called 'Defensively Equipped Merchant Ships' or DEMS) sees Dome Trainer at Technicolor (HMS *Excellent*) and orders fourteen systems before development is complete.

19 August 1941
40ft (12m) diameter half-Dome Trainer complete and housed in the Old Racquet Court, Whale Island for HMS *Excellent*.

December 1941
Technicolor finish development work and manufacturing standard Dome Trainer systems.

February 1942
Lieutenant Charles Bell (A.A. training officer on the staff of Admiral Dreyer) visits the Dome Trainer at HMS *Excellent*. Merchant Navy gunners at locations within ports show a need for a portable Dome Trainer system. Lieutenant Bell and Caxton Metal Company Ltd reduce internal equipment within a portable structure. RFD Company Ltd produce a 20ft (6.1m) diameter Inflatable Dome made of barrage balloon fabric.

May 1942
Bell forms a company called CB Projections (Engineering) Ltd to supply the now named 'Portobel Domes'. CB Projections sub-contract the inflatable dome to RFD and internal equipment to Caxton Metal Co.

6 May 1942
Inflatable 20ft (6.1m) diameter Dome building made of barrage balloon fabric demonstrated at RFD Godalming.

12 May 1942
Contract for two 'Portobel' inflatable Domes placed, one for HMS *Excellent*.

27 September 1942
'Portobel' Dome Trainer and equipment tested at HMS *Excellent*.

14 October 1942
Bell files patent for 'Portobel' Dome.

10 May 1943
Contract placed for 110 'Portobel' Dome Trainers. Eighty-eight supplied by the end of the war (see plates 20 & 21).

August 1944–June 1945
Henry Stephens at Lydstop Camp, Tenby with Royal Artillery. A.A. section improves Dome Trainer with separate infra-red future position spot and scenic/sky projector proposals. Similar improvements not adopted until early 1953 by RFD.

By 1945
Total of 407 Dome Trainer systems supplied:
88 Technicolor for the Royal Navy
88 CB Projections 'Portobel' Domes for the Royal Navy
119 Technicolor Domes for the British Army
122 Technicolor Domes for the Royal Air Force.

1945
Technicolor cease supply of Dome Trainer systems.

1946–47
RFD buy the production licence from CB Projections for target projection system inside the 'Portobel' inflatable Dome and supply the 'Portobel' Dome Trainer system. Caxton Metal Company supply the target projection system.

1948
Ministry of Supply (for British Army) require RFD to supply additional Dome Trainers with more sophisticated equipment and an expansion in the range of weapons.

1948
Royal Commission on Awards to Inventors grants Henry Christian Stephens £5,000 for his invention of the Dome Trainer.

1948–54
RFD sells 300 Dome Trainer systems in the UK and overseas, including to Royal Navy, Ministry of Supply (for British Army), Sweden, Finland, Iceland and US Forces in Europe. 35mm film projectors as standard.

1950

British Army evaluates and orders the 30ft (9.1m) diameter 'Portobel' Dome Trainer, designated as 'Apparatus, Dome, A.A., Training No.4 Mk.I'.

1951

Separate Future Position (FP) Spot projector and Double Mirror Column developed. With increased speed of aircraft on new films, the future position spot can no longer be accommodated in the film frame of the target aircraft. A new and separate FP projector is fitted to the top of the film projector. This projects a pulsed yellow FP spot onto a new separate small moving mirror above the existing target mirror. It is controlled by two additional cams for traverse and elevation. Dome Trainer systems are converted to the new double mirror column and FP spot projector specification. The pulsed yellow spot of the new separate FP spot projector is picked up by a photo-electric cell mounted on the Anti-Aircraft training gun (or replica gun) and aligned to the centre of a gun sight. When the gunner is correctly aiming at the FP and presses the trigger, it will register hits at the firing rate.

1951

Mechanical rolling platform to simulate firing A.A. guns at sea for naval gun mounts (see Plate 22).

1953

RAF supplied with 30ft (9.1m) diameter 'Portobel' Dome Trainers.

1954

Ministry of Supply orders thirty smaller (16mm projector) 'Portobel' Dome Trainers from RFD. Larger 'Portobel' Dome envelopes are replaced by prefabricated 30ft (9m) diameter wooden domes.

1955

Ministry of Supply request RFD develop a Dome Trainer for use with Bristol Bofors 40L70 anti-aircraft guns.

1956

RFD acquires all rights to manufacture and sell Dome Trainers.

Early 1960

RFD produces its own films (and associated cams) to represent more up-to-date and faster aircraft. 40ft (12.2m) diameter wooden prefabricated Dome built (see plates 37 & 38). In some Dome Trainers actual AA guns replace dummy or replica gun mounts.

Barrel of the gun would be removed, and a counterweight added. A 40ft (12.2m) diameter Dome with two guns fired simultaneously.

1962– 65

RFD assists British Aircraft Corporation in the development of a simulator for the Vigilant and its successor Swing Fire anti-tank wire-guided missile systems. Contract awarded to RFD by Ministry of Defence (MoD) for twenty-eight new Dome Trainers.

1965

RFD develop Dome Trainer for Royal Navy Short Sea Cat optically-tracked AA missile system.

October 1965

Army's LAA wing at Manorbier using 'Portobel' and static Dome Trainers for instruction of gunners in how, if necessary, to take over manual operation of radar-equipped guns.

1969

RFD introduce a 60ft (18.3m) diameter wooden pre-fabricated Dome Trainer for three AA guns.

1970

Hydraulically-operated rolling platform system for the Dome Trainer to simulate pitch and roll for training AA gunners on ships.

1974

RFD develop a Dome Trainer system designed for shoulder-launched heat-seeking Redeye missile system training for West Germany.

1975

RFD produce Dome Trainer systems for General Electric Vulcan multi-barrel air defence system for Saudi Arabia.

1982

RFD develop a Dome Trainer for training with Russian SA-7 'Grail' shoulder-launched anti-aircraft missile for Nigeria.

1984

RFD win contract (against BAE) to develop the ADT3 (Air Defence Tactical Training Theatre) with totally new target presentation equipment, projecting aircraft images through a rotating prism system controlled by a computer programme. New 56ft (17m)

Dome Trainer of sectional wood developed. Five Domes produced for British Army and RAF Regiment for training on Rapier AA missile. RFD now known as GQ Defence Equipment Limited.

1986
RFD Group taken over and GQ Defence Equipment Limited sold to Ferranti.

2014
ADT3 Dome Trainer rights eventually owned by BAE Systems.

Appendix B

Dome Trainer Army Instruction Manual - extract

Part A

1. General description:
   (a) There are two main types of Dome trainers: Apparatus, Dome, A.A. Training, No. 1, Mk. I, which has a 20-feet radius dome, and Apparatus, Dome, A.A. Training, No. 2, Mk. I and No. 3, Mk. I, which have 10-feet radius domes. This handbook deals with the 20-ft. Dome Trainer.
   (b) The main difference between Dome Trainers Nos. two and three is that the latter are specifically designed for use in tropical climates. There is no operational difference.
2. Objects:
   The objects of the Dome Trainer are:
   (a) To provide practical laying instruction for the detachment of the No.3 Predictor or alternatively instruction for a 40-mm AA gun detachment in laying and sight setting with the correctional sight.
   (b) To provide realistic practice in engaging fast enemy aircraft.
   (c) To accustom personnel to the general conditions of dive-bombing attacks in so far as noise and psychological reaction are concerned, so that they will be mentally prepared to meet this form of attack.
   (d) To make personnel aware of the extremely short time during which a fast-attacking aircraft can be engaged by the 40-mm. gun at gun control or with the No.3 Predictor.
3. Film:
   Films of aircraft attacks are projected on to a screen which takes the form of a quarter sphere (the dome). This Domed screen surface represents the arc of sky seen from the gun or predictor. By making use of such a large screen area the image of an aircraft can be placed anywhere in the sky, within the limits of '0 degrees' to '180 degrees' in azimuth and from zero angle of sight to the zenith.
4. The Principle:
   The underlying principle by which the attacks are reproduced on the dome surface is as follows. During an aircraft attack a cine-camera could be sighted continuously on the target and, while the camera was running, an accurate record could be taken of

its movements in bearing and elevation. If the film thus photographed were put into a projector mounted at the centre of the dome, and if the projector, while running, were moved precisely in accordance with the recorded movements of the camera, an exact representation of the attack would be reproduced on the dome surface.

5. Application of the Principle:
To avoid complicated and bulky laying and traversing gear for a 35mm. projector the application of this principle is affected by keeping the projector fixed and making it project on to a reflecting mirror to which the required movement is imparted. The movement of the mirror is controlled by two cams, one for elevation and one for bearing. Since the vertical and lateral rates which obtained during any one attack will be peculiar to that attack alone, each attack has its own pair of cams. The cams are connected to the projector motor by direct mechanical drive, through reduction gearing. They therefore run with synchronisation to the film. Movements are imparted to the mirror by means of the cam arms and connecting wires. Provision is made for ensuing that the cams and the film start together in exact synchronisation. Once started, they cannot get out of step [see Plate 11].
6. Owing to other equipment the mirror cannot be placed at the exact centre of the dome. A conversion factor is introduced in the design of the cams to allow for this.
7. To allow German aircraft to be used at the high speeds required, the set of films issued are not made by photography of actual attacks but are reproduced by a special process of model photography, the vertical and lateral rates being deduced by calculation. This in no way affects the accurate representation of the attack, the image on the screen always appearing the same size as the real aircraft would at any range.
8. Associated with the projector is ordinary sound-reproducing equipment consisting of an amplifier and a loud speaker. The noise of the aircraft, bombs and other incidental noises are recorded on the sound track of the film and broadcast with the film in the normal manner. The speaker which does this is termed the projector amplifier and the dome attack speaker.
9. The Sight Unit. A steel platform mounted on casters can be pushed into position immediately in rear of the mirror columns and accurately located by screwed bolts which run down into holes in the concrete floor. On this platform are mounted the sight unit consisting of the essential gearing and hand wheels that are used by the layers on a 40-mm A.A. mounting. On either side are the two layers adjustable seats. At the rear centre of the sight unit is a small platform on which the Stiffkey stick operator stands to operate the correctional sight. This sight is carried on two arms geared to the elevation hand wheel and can be deviated from 0 degrees angle of sight up to 85 degrees while the whole unit can be rotated through 180 degrees in azimuth, upon a racer plate mounted on the main platform, by movement of the line layers hand wheel.

In order that the two sights and sighting head shall be located as close as possible to the centre of the dome, the sighting head is mounted between and above the two sights, the Stiffkey stick operator standing between and behind the layers.

The sights are slightly inset to conform to the radius of the dome and within the limits required by the films supplied can both be lined up on the target. The sighting head and clicker gear are designed to move the sights in exact simulation of the movements effected by the service correctional sight. To enable the Stiffkey stick operator to know when his clicker gear is in the central position the indicating pointer and the zero position are painted with luminous paint.

This unit represents the 40-mm. A.A. mounting with correctional site, but a suitable sighting arrangement can, of course, be designed and installed to represent any other type of gun. In fact, simple unit (Sights Training L.A. Personnel, Mk 1) comprising a Cartwheel Sight and Sight bar, mounted on a pillar mounting and popularly known as the 'one man sighting unit' is supplied to simulate any form of AA Light Machine Gun.

It is to be noted that the sights may jam at maximum elevation when following a fast target when flying overhead. This is due to the screw thread along which a stop nut runs having such a fine pitch that the nut jams when brought up against the maximum elevation stop. The design of suitable limiting stops is being cleared by the manufacturers. It may be that the jam can be cleared by a sharp blow with the palm of the hand on the elevating handwheel in the direction of depression. If the jam occurs at maximum depression the reverse procedure should be tried. Before the fitting of the stops referred to, if the procedure outlined does not clear the jam the defect should be reported to R.E.M.E.

10. Predictor. When using the No.3 Predictor for laying instruction in the dome its necessary to mount the predictor on Stand Instrument, No. 48, which differs from the Stand, Instrument. No. 38 only in height. This is necessary because the predictor mounted on the latter stand is too high for comfortable laying when the base of the stand is not 'dug in'.

Owing to the short distance between predictor and the target image (20 feet) it is also necessary to use special anti-parallax telescope attachments. These are mounted on the predictor telescopes by simple clamps and consist of extension tubes containing short focus lens and each carrying a mirror mounted at an angle of degrees to the line of sight through the telescope.

The effect of these attachment is that the layer for elevation views the target through his telescope in the normal way while the lay for bearing has his line of vision deflected by the two mirrors is such a way that the line of sight from the telescopes converge at the target on the dome surface.

The mirror of the elevation telescope is adjustable for lining up and suitable counterweights are fitted to both telescopes. Locating pads are provided in the floor to receive the feet of the Stand, Instrument No. 48, to ensure the accurate positioning of the instrument within the dome.

11. Verification. A small, still projector, termed the gun sight projector, can be fitted to the sight unit or the predictor, whichever is in use. This projects on to the surface of the dome an image of cross wires, cartwheel or other type of graticule. Provision to be made for converging this projected sight on to the layer's line of sight at the surface of the dome, so that it shows the exact aim taken by the layers; suitable fine adjustments are provided for lining up. It can be seen clearly by the instructor and the rest of the class but is invisible to the layers. The sights or telescopes are converged on to a laying mark on the surface of the dome and the gun sight projector is lined up to this point.
12. The correct aim which the layers should be taking is shown on the film by a yellow FP spot which moves ahead of the aircraft indicating its future position. At predictor control the projected sight should be coincident with the target and not with the future positions spot. The layers and the Stiffkey stick operator cannot see this spot, since they are provided with yellow goggles. If the lay is correct and the handling of the correctional sight is accurate the centre of the projected sight should always be on the future positions spot. The projected sight, which shows the point of aim, and the future position spot enable the instructor to carry out instant and continuous verification during the attack. Meanwhile the rest of the class will benefit from comparing the point of aim with the yellow future position spot and noting the general tendencies. The future position spot appears on the film when the range is 2,000 yards and remains on for the rest of the run.
13. Opening Fire. When the range setter or Stiffkey stick operator decides that the target is in range, he orders 'Fire' and the instructor will press the gun noise switch. This is attached to a wandering lead and can be carried by the instructor during runs. This switch operates a special gun noise amplifier which produces a sound simulating a 40-mm gun firing at either auto or single shot.
14. Range Indication. Suspended in a position where it can readily be seen by the instructor is a range indicator. This consists of a suitably graduated voltmeter and is operated automatically through a variate resistance as the cams rotate. This gives continuous indication of the slant range to the target enabling the instructor to check the range at which fire is opened.
15. Lighting. The general lighting in the dome is provided by two fluorescent tubes fixed to the back wall. These flood the whole done with an even white light. When projecting attacks, however, the general lighting must be switched off and blue lighting, consisting of one florescent tube, switched on. This floods the whole dome with blue light of an intensity low enough for the light from the projector to overcome it. It also creates the illusion of distance, as when looking into the blue void of the sky.
    (a) Night or Dark Conditions. Varying conditions of darkness or low visibility can be simulated in the dome by means of placing suitable filters in front of the

projector. These filters are all incorporated in a simple filter which can be fitted in the lens adapter tube in the front of the projector. This unit, which is very easy to fix, allows any required filter being place in front of the projector lens. The suggested variations are as follows:

(i) With blue lights on in the dome and the light neutral filter in use, the picture is so dimmed down that the aircraft can be heard approaching but cannot be seen until it has closed to 1,000 yards. Then it gradually shows up and can be seen dimly until overhead, or, in the case of a crossing run, until the range has opened again. With the permanent neutral filter only in use the aircraft will be seen at a longer range. Nothing can be seen when the dark or medium filters are used

(ii) With no lighting in the dome and one of the neutral filters in use the aircraft will be picked up at different ranges to para. (i) above.

(b) When using either (i) or (ii) above, the projected sight from the gunsight projector must be dimed, since its brightness is normally required to overcome the bright light on the picture. With the darker picture obtained by using filters it is much too bright, and a lamp resistance is accordingly introduced in the circuit of the gunsight projector lamp.

The resistance is fitted with a dimming switch for varying the intensity of light and is mounted on the switch panel. Having decided which filter to use on the main projector, the instructor must set the dimming switch so that the projected gunsight can only *just* be discerned by himself when it is directed at the picture. It must be kept as dim as possible so that the gunner looking through yellow goggles cannot see it at all.

(c) In these conditions the light which escapes from the projector, particularly through the threading slot, will have a blinding effect on the gunner. To avoid this, some form of light excluder should be made locally to fit over the top of the projector, and a black screen should be fitted underneath the arc attachment (without touching it) to shade from the gunner the light reflected by the floor.

(d) It is essential that the picture be correctly focussed before the filter unit is fitted.

16. Dome Attacks. The cams, which control the movement of the mirror, are geared down to make one complete revolution in a minute. From the point of view of an engagement, no close-range attack lasts as long as a minute. It is therefore possible for two attacks to be put on to one cam. It would be undesirable and would waste too much instructional time to have to change cams and re-lace film every minute, this is to say after every two attacks. Rolls of film, therefore, have been made up to last for five complete cycles of the cam. Thus, if a cam contains two attacks those attacks will be repeated in rotation five times each, making ten attacks for one loading of the projector. If the attack were a long one and occupied the whole of a cam, then

that one attack would be repeated five times in one roll of film. During the few feet of blank time between attacks the projector can be stopped for as long is required. When started again, the film and cam will be in synchronism.

17. Details of dome attacks (i.e., films and cams) supplied with the Teacher are given in Appendix II.
18. Instructional Films. In order that the projector in the dome may be used for showing instructional films, it has been mounted on a rotating pedestal which enables it to be rotated through 90 degrees. This takes the projected beam clear of the mirror and makes full use of the dome surface direct for showing the film.
19. When this is done another loud speaker is brought into use. This Instructional Film Speaker is positioned on the floor, just below that part of the dome which is used for the picture. It broadcasts the commentary recorded on the sound-track of the film in the normal manner. A changeover switch is provided to enable the instructor to use the appropriate loud speaker.

Part B
TRAINING

20. The primary use of the dome is to give verified laying and aiming practice.
21. The purpose of the dome is not to take the place of air co-operation but to fill the gap between towed target practice or silent practice and action against the enemy. It should not, therefore, be used for elementary training if air co-operation is available. It is a waste of its special facilities to teach and practice detachments in an early stage of training, the basic lessons which can be taught as well with co-operating aircraft. Detachments should be trained to a reasonable standard of laying and fire control and learn the basic principles against such elementary targets. They should then learn to apply those principles, and to improve their performance, in the dome on targets which represent in speed and difficulty those against which they will be shooting in action. Every type of enemy aircraft is represented in the dome attacks, from the slow heavy bomber to the fast ground strafing fighter, and there is a wide range of difficulty in the targets represented. Even the simplest of these targets is more difficult than a towed sleeve, and the instructor should not try to teach a detachment to run before it can walk. Training should be progressive and should begin with simple level flying attacks as in Rolls 215, 216 & 201, and simple diving attacks in Roll 203, and should lead gradually to the fast targets at high maximum angles of sight, as in Roll 203, the more difficult diving attacks in Roll 208, and fast fighter attacks as in Roll 210. To introduce these difficult targets too soon will only lead to discouragement. A suggested sequence which this progressive training might follow is given in paragraph 34.
22. The instructor should remember that the dome will enable him to point out and demonstrate during attacks many points that he will have discussed in the classroom.

For example, he can illustrate with the moving aircraft in the dome, the way in which direction of aim-off changes which he will have already explained on a blackboard. He can stress the way in which the gunner must apply this knowledge and demonstrate what happens when he does not do so correctly. There is almost no end to the value which a good instructor can obtain from using the dome intelligently in this way and driving home points which no amount of lecturing will succeed in making so clear as the illustrations provided by a detachment engaging an aircraft in the dome. No instructor should be content to use the dome solely to practice detachments in their drills in action.

23. The dome may be used to demonstrate change of direction and amount of aim-off to a class in the following manner. Using the lens in the gunsight projector which throws a cartwheel on to the dome surface, a skilled layer or pair of layers, not using the yellow filter, lays with the centre of his sight continuously on the future position spot. The class can then see how the aircraft, always flying towards the centre, occupies constantly changing position in the sight, and how the layer must bring it further and further from the centre as the approach angle increases.
24. Although the 35-mm projector can be used to show training films in the dome, this is a waste of the special equipment provided and of the time available for using the dome for its proper function. 35-mm. training films should be shown in a cinema or hut on a flat screen.
25. It is an uneconomical use of time to regard instruction in aircraft recognition in the dome as being anything other than incidental. Instruction in eyes-shooting and sights correctional always assumes that the gunner knows the speed of the target. To do this in real warfare he must not only recognise a machine as hostile but be able to identify its type to know its speed. For this purpose, putting on dome attacks without reference to the type of attacking machine will provide valuable practice in recognition, although its primary object will be to give realistic instruction,
26. The Instructor's Duties: General
    (a) The instructor should stand where he can best see both the detachment and the aircraft. Standing to the right rear will be close to the volume cut-out switch, the gun noise switch and the range indicator, which are fixed to the rail in the right-hand corner. In runs with targets at high maximum angle of sight, he should stand chose behind the gun, where he gets a less distorted view of the attack
    (b) It is recommended that until the instructor is completely accustomed to the dome, he should make up his mind beforehand what point he is going to look out for during an attack. Experience is required before an instructor can spot and correct all errors in the very short duration of the future attack and is better at first to concentrate on one fault at a time.
    (c) The instructor must remember that he must coach the detachments by pointing out and correcting errors while they are being made. He will be unable to cover

all points and will need to amplify what he has said at the end of an attack, but a 'post mortem' alone is of no value. The gunner has forgotten how and when and why he made the mistake; it must be pointed out to him while he is making it, and he must be told then how to correct it.

(d) The layers and fire controller are provided with yellow filter spectacles so that they cannot see the future position spot. If a consistent error is being made, the gunner may benefit from being allowed to see his own error during one attack. An exceptionally bad beginner, for example, who always puts on aim off speed with the wrong hand, can best be made to realise the fault by seeing for himself the result it produces. The danger of allowing him to do this, however, is that he will cease to think for himself and rarely follow the future position spot. This method should, therefore, be very sparingly used.

(e) Although concentrating on the men manning a gun or predictor, the instructor should not forget the training value of the dome for the remainder of the class. They should be encouraged to make their own estimates of aim off speed, and to watch the general tendencies of the errors, and their attention should be kept by being asked to give their opinions and criticisms at the end of an attack

(f) All personnel, whether they are manning the sight or not, should automatically appreciate the time factor while attacks are being made. The instructor must draw their attention to it at the start of their instruction and he should point out to them that the part of the attack which really concerns them is that during which the aircraft is within effective range of their weapons. In order, therefore, to get a true measure of the time available for engagement they must be taught not to regard the duration of the attack as the total length of the run (and this is short enough) but to watch for when the aircraft comes within effective range and see how small a time there is after this before the target has passed out of range.

(g) The instructor can at any time operate the volume cut-out switch which reduces the volume of sound in the dome, so that he can criticise and coach the detachment during an attack without his voice being drowned. The switch is self-returning and has simply to be released to give play once more to the full sound effects. It is important, however, particularly in the dive bombing attacks, to allow full sound effects to continue throughout some runs because there is no doubt that the noise of the aircraft attack has a numbing effect on a man's brain. The object is to accustom men to this noise, and to the sensation of being dived on, that when it occurs in action, they will be ready for it and their minds trained to ignore it.

(h) The detachment commander should be included in the training and should give the orders 'Plane' or 'Engage', and indicate the target in the proper way. The instructor may find it useful to allow some men of the detachment to use the firing button. He can then be free through the motion to concentrate on the rest of the detachment, and the firing number can go through the motions of the normal drill and become accustomed to the correct rate of single shot firing. Troop officers should play a large a part as possible in the training of their detachments.

27. Predictor Control.

(a) The projected cross-wire indicates the point of lay only. The future position spot is of no significance with the predictor.

(b) With the predictor the dome provides laying practice only. The aircraft is at a much greater range than that recorded on the range indicator. No attempt should be made, therefore, to train range setters in the dome in range estimation. The range-setter should set a range after the target is picked up and make alterations to that range for drill purposes only. The instructor should see that the ranges set are not wildly incorrect, but no attempt must be made to verify the range accurately against the range indicator. While ensuring that the range-setter does not set absurd ranges, the instructor should devote their attention to coaching and practising the detachment in pick-up and laying.

(c) The instructor should concentrate at first solely on steady laying, correcting the unsteady layer and showing him how he should move his hand wheel. The cross of light will indicate clearly which layer is at fault and the error he is making. He should not expect the layer at first to be able to get steady in a very short time, but should work up to quickness in getting steady by degrees.

(d) At this stage the range setter can be practised in quick pick-up but changing targets should not be practised in the early stages.

(e) When the layers can lay steadily, practice can be given to them and to the range setter in the 'Fresh target' drill. Attacks can be run in quick succession and the detachment trained in quick pick-up and quick changing from one target to another.

(f) Experienced detachments can be told to take post and be prepared to pick up any aircraft that attacks. Such detachments can be given practice in engaging war speed targets, which is not available against co-operating aircraft.

(g) In the blue lighting of the dome it is not possible to see the deflection indicators. It is essential therefore that rates are zeroed correctly, and hand wheels are left at 12 o'clock before the main lighting is switched off. Thereafter detachments gain useful training in zeroing rates by returning the hand wheels to 12 o'clock without reference to the deflection indicators, as is necessary in action at night.

28. Sights, Correctional (Stiffkey Stick).

(a) A considerable portion of the training, particularly at first should be devoted to the layers alone. The Stiffkey stick operator should be in his position in action and should match the straight edge with the fuselage of the aircraft. He should not, however, apply any aim-off speed. Thus, the projected cross of light will indicate the point of lay and should be continuously on the aircraft. When the layers can lay accurately with no aim-off speed applied, they should be trained to react correctly and instantly when aim-off speed is put in and their sights move with each click applied by the instructor or Stiffkey stick operator.

(b) When the layers have reached a satisfactory standard, the Stiffkey stick operator can be trained to apply the correct aim-off speed. With aim-off speed applied, the projected cross of light presents the point of aim. When the aim is correct, the cross will be on the future position spot. The instructor can tell from the position of this cross in relation to future position spot, whether the rounds are high or low or on the line of sight. The detachment cannot see the future position spot, since they wear yellow spectacles. The instructor must use his experience to distinguish whether errors are the result of the Stiffkey stick operator's error in matching or in amount of aim-off speed, or of a layer's error in lay.

(c) The instructor should in later stages give observations (high, low, left, right, plus, minus, hit), He may, if he wishes, delegate this to a member of his class. He should explain to the class how it is possible to tell from the projected cross of light where the round would be.

(d) In early training the instructor should tell his class the type of aircraft and its target speed.

(e) The instructor, using the range indicator as a guide, should watch to see that the Stiffkey stick operator does not order 'Fire' when the target is out of range. He should remember, however, that the range is greater than it really is (see para. 27 (b)).

(f) With experienced detachments, the elementary training can be omitted. The instructor should tell the detachment to take post and be prepared to engage any hostile aircraft that attack. He should not tell the target speed or type of aircraft. The value of this is to provide training against war speed targets, which is not possible with co-operation aircraft.

29. Eye-shooting.

(a) All the layers must be taught to use the one-man sight competently before any attempt is made to start training them on the two-man sight.

(b) The lens fitted to the projector for eye-shooting [see Plate 32] projects a cartwheel on the dome surface, the centre of which represents the point of aim and should coincide with the future position spot. The instructor can thus see at once errors in both directions and amount of aim-off and can trace them to the two-man lying to the layer concerned.

(c) The instructor should at first tell the detachment the type of aircraft and its target speed.

(d) With experienced detachments, the more elementary training can be omitted. They should be told to take post and be prepared to engage any hostile aircraft that attack. The instructor should not tell them the type of aircraft or the target speed.

(e) To provide aiming practice in the dome for as many gunners as possible at a time, the Hand Aiming Sights Pattern No 10666 can be used by six members of the class from a position in rear of the central sight. Not more than six hand aiming sight should be used, as otherwise the gunners on the extreme left or right will get a distorted view of the attack.

(f) The hand aiming sights must be correctly lined up with the projected sight before the attacks are started.

30. Procedure for using the Trainer

(a) Before the trainer is used, the operator should have carried out the daily routine inspection and tests, see chapters three and four. Their purpose is to ensure that the apparatus is perfect running order and that all lenses and reflecting surfaces are clean.

(b) The instructor should issue his orders whether the predictor, or a one-man or two-man gun unit is to be mounted. Having mounted the required equipment, the operator must mount and line-up correctly the gunsight projector. On the two-man sight, in addition to lining up the gunsight projector, the bearing sight should be lined up to the elevation sight for both line and elevation. (See para. 35) This should be done every time the sight is fitted to make sure that the sights are correctly converged and the that the gunsight projector is truly indicating the aim taken by the gunner. The lining up should be checked at intervals during the instruction.

(c) After the operator has carried out the daily tasks and mounted the required equipment, the dome is ready for the class to commence training. The daily maintenance and testing routine should be done before the class are due to arrive.

(d) When the class arrive in the dome, nobody should be allowed inside the railing except the instructor, the operator and the men manning the equipment. All other members of the class should be placed beyond the railing immediately behind. The closer they keep to the centre, the better will be their view of the attack.

(e) The instructor should order what attacks he wishes to put on. The operator will see that the appropriate camera roll and cam are fitted and will set the apparatus ready for running. Since this operation involves the control of several switches and the inspection of a number of points, it is essential that the operator should work in a definite routine sequence of operation. See paragraph 47. By rigidly adhering to this sequence the chances of an accident resulting from neglect of some small point will be obviated.

31. Blue Lighting.
It is important that the instructor should switch off the general lighting and switch on the blue lighting some minutes before calling on the class to man the equipment and engage an aircraft. This is because unless the gunner's eye has had an opportunity of accommodating itself to the dimmer lighting, he will not be able to see clearly when viewing the aircraft attack through the yellow filter. Once the cam has been fitted and lined up to the 'Start' mark, the operator no longer requires the general lighting. This, therefore, is the moment when the instructor should switch on the blue lighting.

32. Stopping between runs.
After any attack the projector can be stopped for as long as is required, thus enabling the instructor to point out mistakes, etc. to the class and to change the equipment. The projector can be started again at a moment's notice as the cam and the film will still be synchronised. It should not be necessary when changing round or when pointing out mistakes, to switch on the general lighting. This need only be done at the end of the series of ten attacks when it is necessity to reload the projector and change cams. The same roll of film can, of course, be run again, but this will entail a longer interval since it will have to be rewound before lacing into the projector

33. Ventilation and Heating.
The dome is ventilated by two extraction fans high in the back wall, ducts being cut through the plaster at floor level close to the doors to allow for the free entry of fresh air. The arc lamp generates considerable heat, and since the dome, when operating is an enclosed space, it is necessary to run the extraction fans when a class is under instruction. At the end of each roll when the film is being changed, both doors should be opened and the class should go outside.

34. Suggested order in which rolls should be taken in progressive training: -
1. Roll 215 Heinkel 111, low distant crosser.
2. Roll 216 Dornier 215, low distant crosser.
3. Roll 201 Heinkel 111 and Dornier 215, both direct approach.
4. Roll 213 Heinkel 111 low distant crosser.
5. Roll 214 Dornier 215 low distant crosser.
6. Roll 202 Heinkel 111 low crosser and direct approach.
7. Roll 204 Junkers 87 and 88 diving.
8. Roll 211 Junkers 52 crossing.
9. Roll 207 Junkers 88 diving.
10. Roll 205 Dornier 217 direct approach and low crosser.
11. Roll 212 Junkers 52 landing.
12. Roll 209 Junkers 88 low level crosser and Junkers 87 diving.
13. Roll 203 Dornier 215 high crosser.

14. Roll 206 Messersmith 110 low level crosser.
15. Roll 208 3 Junkers 88 diving in succession
16. Roll 210 Messerschmitt 109 ground strafing in succession.

Part C
TESTS

35. Lining up and checking line up.
   (a) Correctional sights.
   Set the aim of speed indicator to zero and insert the pins in the sight bar. Lay the elevation sight on the check mark on the dome surface. Adjust the bearing sight until it is similarly laid on the check mark. Switch on the gun sight projector and adjust by means of the three knurled screws until the projected point of lay is coincident with the check mark for bearing and elevation.
   (b) Predictor.
   Lay the elevation telescope on the check mark on the dome surface. Switch on the gunsight predictor on the elevation telescope and adjust as in sub-para. (a) above to bring the projected image on to the check mark for bearing and elevation. One operator looking into the bearing telescope and without touching the bearing hand wheel, directs the other operator to adjust the mirror on the elevation telescope until the check mark and projected image of the gun sight projector are seen to be coincident with the centre of the bearing telescope.
36. Mirror Alignment and Tracking Test.
   (a) Object. The purpose of this test is to ensure that the alignment of the apparatus is correct and is working smoothly so that the projected picture will give an accurate representation of attacks and that illumination is satisfactory.
   (b) For this test an alignment aperture plate is provided. This reduces the aperture of the projector to a small spot of light in the centre of the beam. Two check marks are positioned on the surface of the dome at 10 degrees elevation, at dome azimuth 10 degrees and dome azimuth 170 degrees. An alignment cam is provided.

[Author's note: The 1942 Naval Dome Trainer manual superseded a previous 'Preliminary Pamphlet'. The 1942 manual shows dummy guns for a 6-pounder quick firing gun as fitted to Royal Navy ships and DEMS. Loading a new shell each time it was fired as an AA gun, it compares poorly with other AA guns fed with continuous ammunition together with tracer rounds. An Amendment to the manual dated 1944 notes two new films showing radio-controlled glider bomb attacks with a parent aircraft releasing the bomb outside gun range. After the initial drop from the aircraft the glider bomb fired rockets, travelling up to 325 knots or 370 miles per hour].

[Author's note: The Gunnery Pocket Book (Royal Navy 1945) in Appendix F refers to training close-range gun crews under section 568. 'There are numerous methods of training close-range guns' crews. At all anti-aircraft schools, non-firing practices are carried out against aircraft. These can then be analysed immediately, so that the gun layers and trainers can at once see the mistakes that they have made in their aim. Dome Teachers are also used for exercising close-range guns' crews. In these, realistic photographs of attacking aircraft are thrown on to the inside of the roof of a dome-shaped building. The gun layer aims a sight at the aircraft and the instructor can at once tell whether he is aiming correctly or not.']

[Author's note: For security, the corresponding Royal Navy Handbook (example with serial no 585, dated 1942) has a specific instruction: 'This book is invariably to be kept locked up when not in use and is not to be taken outside the ship or establishment for which it is issued without the express permission of the Commanding Officer.']

Appendix C

Second World War Dome Trainer Sites

Concrete RAF 40ft Diameter Anti-Aircraft Dome Trainers

The Dome at RAF Langham (see plates 14, 23 to 26 and 31) is one of forty-four Dome Trainers built of reinforced concrete in 1942. A second Dome survives at the RAF/USAF base at RAF Mildenhall (see Plate 27), Suffolk, and is used as an Officers' Mess. The Dome at RAF Wyton has been stripped of all equipment. Domes at RAF Pembrey (see Plate 30), Carmarthenshire, RAF Shoreham Airport and RAF Limavady, Co. Londonderry are derelict.

Alness (two)
Andover
Bovington
Burtonwood
Carew
Chariton
Castle Bromwich
Chipping Warden
Church Fenton
Detling
Douglas (Villa Marina)
Dumfries
Errol
Fairford
Felixstowe
Filey (Butlin's)
Hook
Horsham St Faith
Hornchurch
Kidlington
Langham
Lee-on-Solent
Limavady
Locking

Long Kesh
Longman Lulsgate
Mildenhall
Montrose
Penrhos
Pembrey
Portreath
Shoreham
Squires Gate
Tangmere
Tatenhill
Tempsford
Towyn
Watchet
Warmwell
Wellesbourne Mountford
West Raynham
Westwood
Wyton

Appendix D

Technicolor Dome Trainer Films Worldwide

Technicolor had already used stop frame animation process in the 1930s for feature films and early military aviation instructional films. Technicolor Ltd worked with Lieutenant Commander Stephens to produce a prototype Dome Trainer and confirmed initial cinematographic limitations. The original idea of filming real aircraft to be projected in the Dome was not feasible as it was not possible to establish the exact position in the sky of an aircraft being filmed. However, with stop-frame animation that photographed models frame by frame, with a cine camera, the precise location of the aircraft was established by a manual flight plan script. The films were produced by Technicolor, who manually calculated the complicated film flight plans and also determined the profile of the cams for each film to be manufactured. Film of German, Italian and Japanese aircraft were produced during the war using models.

The target aircraft on the various attack films were produced on a circular film frame rather than the usual rectangular film frame. The idea of this was to make it easier to merge the light circular background of the target image into the blue-sky lighting. However, the edge of circular film frame still appeared brilliant and sharp, and to make it merge more effectively with the new scene projection, a 'vignette' was fitted to the target projector to diffuse the sharp edge.

The aircraft image was projected by a 35mm or 16mm projector onto a gimbal-mounted mirror (thus allowing it to traverse and elevate), which reflected the image onto the projection surface of the Dome. The movements of the mirror were controlled by cams driven from the projector motor, via a reduction gearbox, this being used so that the cams moved in synchronisation with the film in the projector.

There were three cams: one for mirror elevation, one for mirror traverse and one for indicating the range of the target either by the cam follower operating a potentiometer which showed the range on a voltmeter or by a mechanical pointer which indicated the range on a graduated sheet of metal. The method of moving the mirror from the cam follower arms was by steel wire routed over pulleys to the mirror mounting column. As only one cable was used for each, return springs were attached to the mirror.

To show the correct aim-off point (Future Position, or FP), a yellow spot (on some types a yellow line) was printed ahead of the aircraft on each frame of the film. To fit the spot on the same frame of film as the aircraft, both spot and aircraft image were pushed to opposite edges of the frame. This FP spot would be made invisible to the gun aimer by his wearing yellow-tinted spectacles.

The FP position varied depending upon the course and speed of the target aircraft and the velocity of the shell. There would be differing films and cams to match a rifle calibre gun or a 40mm weapon. To allow instructors to see where the gun was being aimed, an image of the gun sight was projected from a gun sight projector on the gun. This also could not be seen by the gunner as the actual gun sight would be aligned so that it coincided exactly with the projected gun sight image. When the centre of the image from the gun sight projector coincided with the yellow FP spot, the instructor knew that the gunner was scoring hits as long as the target was within range.

At the end of the Second World War the increased aircraft speeds required the Future Position aiming point to be much further in front of the aircraft. However, it was not possible to accommodate this increased distance within the film frame. The solution was a new separate yellow FP spot projector mounted on top of the main projector. This projected the yellow FP spot onto a new secondary smaller mirror above the main mirror, which was controlled by an additional set of cams which were attached to the cams operating the main mirror.

These additional cams allowed the yellow FP spot to vary in distance away from the front of the aircraft according to its line of flight in relation to the AA gun position. The maximum FP Spot distance ahead of the aircraft would be required for a flight directly across the front of the AA gun (left to right, or vice versa). For an attack approaching the AA gun at 45 degrees the aiming point would be roughly half the above distance.

With the later separate FP spot projector, Henry Stephens investigated how to vary the diameter of the yellow FP spot according to the range of the target. At greater distances the spot would be small, and as the aircraft flew nearer to the gun position the diameter would increase. The size of the spot would be changed by having a variable aperture iris fitted to the front of the FP spot projector which would be driven by the range cam/contacts. However, the new function was not adopted as it was seen as an unnecessary complication and extra cost.

With the later separate FP spot projector, Henry Stephens proposed using a pulsed invisible Infra-Red Future Position spot instead of the yellow FP spot. With a photo-electric cell mounted on the gun directly in line with the centre of the graticule sight, it would automatically record when the gunner was on target and scoring hits. However, this was too expensive and the yellow FP spot remained. In post-war RFD Dome Trainers with a separate FP spot projector, the yellow FP spot itself was pulsed with a gun-mounted photo-electric cell recording the number of target hits.

The trainee(s) used simple simulated guns which had the same controls as the real weapons, but a real two/three-man 40mm Bofors gun (see Plate 10) could be used with gun barrels removed. To show the actual aiming point of the gun, a gun sight projector (graticule projector) was attached to the dummy/real gun aligned directly with the gun sight and projected the gunsight graticule onto the Dome wall. This represented the gunner's actual point of aiming. The projected graticule would be unseen by the gunner as it was covered exactly by the gun sight graticule itself. When this graticule coincided with the future position (FP) spot the instructor would see hits on the target. In early stages of training the spectacles/filter would sometimes not be used so that the trainees could familiarise themselves with the principle of aim-off by seeing a future position spot to aim at. Only half of the Dome would be used for projection as the mirror was limited to 180° in traverse and 90° in elevation.

The films were made by photographing models frame by frame, and the movement over the Dome surface would be calculated and converted into the contours of the cams. Mirror movements for each attack would vary, and so a different set of cams would be used with each film. Each film would show one or two attacks, but these could be repeated by an extended length of five films spliced, with the cam rotating five times.

The initial Stephens Dome Trainers were all solid structures. The first was a 40ft diameter half dome (a quarter sphere) of a metal or wooden external rib framework with a plaster inner curved projection screen. The whole construction was housed within an existing building such as a hanger. The 40ft Domes were designed to use 35mm projectors and could accommodate 40mm AA gun mountings.

A second type was of a 20ft diameter Dome that formed a free-standing building in its own right. Constructed of wooden framework sections with plywood sheet outer and inner surfaces, plaster-finished inner screen and bitumen outer weatherproof covering. The 20ft domes were designed to use 16mm projectors and to house single-man type AA gun mountings.

A third type was a 40ft diameter free-standing Dome constructed of reinforced concrete as at Langham. Used exclusively by the RAF, forty-four were built on RAF airfields in the UK only. The six surviving 40ft concrete domes in varying conditions are all of this RAF variety.

A fourth type was a 20ft diameter free-standing inflatable dome constructed in barrage balloon material and capable of being portable with a miniaturised 16mm projection system (see plates 20 to 22).

The 40ft diameter domes with 35mm projector systems were used by the Navy, Army and RAF, but only the Army and the RAF used the 20ft diameter wooden domes with 16mm projector systems.

A total of 319 systems of the Technicolor-type dome equipment were produced, 88 for the Royal Navy, 119 for the Army and 112 for the RAF.

On later post-war Domes manufactured by RFD (see plates 37 & 38), four or five scenic projectors were placed on the Dome floor around and a few feet away from the radius of the screen, with each projecting part of a 180° panoramic scene. A cloud/sky projection system designed by Henry Stephens consisted of an inverted glass goldfish-type bowl (see Plate 9) with two cloud/sky scenes painted on its internal surface (Patent No. GB707877). This was on a tall pole behind the gun position in the dome with a light placed within. A commercial cloud projector consisting of a clear cloud-painted disc rotating in front of a projected light was available in later RFD domes.

Technicolor made target films for all the Domes they supplied. The range of films available was:

35mm Admiralty Dome Trainer	31 Aircraft films 10 E-boat films
35mm Army Dome Trainer	52 Aircraft films 4 Tank films
35mm Army Dome Trainer (Special for Small Arms School Bisley)	4 Aircraft films 1 Motor Transport film
16mm Army Dome Trainer	19 Aircraft films 4 Tank films
35mm R.A.F. Dome Trainer	13 Aircraft films
16mm R.A.F. Dome Trainer	15 Aircraft films
TOTAL	153 films

German aircraft depicted on these films included Messerschmitt 109, Messerschmitt 110, Junkers 52, Junkers 87, Junkers 88, Dornier 215, Dornier 217, Heinkel 111, Focke-Wulf 190 and Focke-Wulf 200. The British aircraft was a Hawker Henley. Japanese targets were Mitsubishi A6M/Type 0, Mitsubishi Type 99, Nakajima B5N2 'Kate' Type 97/3, Type 96 and Type 97/1. The Italian target was a Savoia-Marchetti SM.84.

The position of the future position 'spot' varied on some films as the ballistic data for the guns to be used was different, i.e., from a machine gun to a 40mm Bofors. Altogether, 34,696 films were supplied by Technicolor for use in Dome Trainers.

Technicolor also made and supplied films for the 'Portobel' inflatable Dome trainers, air-to-air gunnery trainers, Army Arc trainers (forty-one tank target films) and Navy Arc trainers (twenty-four ship and land target films). Both the Arc trainers used a basic cylindrical-type screen.

Typical films from Technicolor required both accurate target identification and accurate shooting. Some examples were:

Film No 207

1st Attack: Dive-bombing attack on own position by German Junkers 88. Speed 300mph in the dive. Initial height 8,000ft, initial range 3,250yds. The aircraft dives to 5,000ft and flattens out before turning into aiming dive. This dive is directed towards a point 130yds. short of own gun position. The aircraft starts to pull out at a height of 1,300ft for bomb release at 700ft and passes overhead at this height. Target sighted on Dome Azimuth bearing 135°.

2nd Attack: Dive-bombing attack on own position by German Junkers 88. Speed in dive 300 knots. Aircraft sighted at range 2,000yds, height 4,150ft. Diving towards a point slightly behind and to the flank of gun position. Target sighted on Dome Azimuth bearing 115°.'

Navy Roll No. 1, Army Roll No. 201

1st Attack: Low-level bombing run by German Heinkel 111 of speed 200 knots in level flight at a height of 2,000ft passing over own position. Target first sighted at 3,000yds.

2ndAttack: Low level bombing attack by German Dornier 215 of speed 250 knots in level flight passing over own position at a height of 1,000ft. Target first sighted at 3,200yds.

Navy Roll No. 2, Army Roll No. 202

1st Attack: Low-level bombing attack by German Heinkel III speed 200 knots in level flight at a height of 500ft passing over own position. Target first sighted at a range of 3,000yds.

2nd Attack: Low-level bombing attack by the same aircraft in level flight, height 500ft. Target is sighted at a range of 3,000yds.

Navy Roll No. 8, Army Roll No. 208

A series of three dive-bombing attacks. The aircraft are German Junker 88 of speed 300 knots in the dive, first sighted in formation at a height of 8,000ft and they turn into the dive attack at approximately six-second intervals. The first two machines are diving towards the gun position and the third machine slightly over.

Navy Roll No. 12

1st Attack: (Japanese) Torpedo attack by Japanese Navy Mitsubishi Kajima B5N2 'Kate' Type 97/1 of speed 170 knots on own ship. Aircraft sighted at range of 3,700yds, height 4,250ft on bearing D.A. (Directly Ahead) of 70°, losing height. It dives until at a height of 320ft. Torpedo is dropped at a range of 1,000yds, after which the plane banks away to its starboard and climbs. Closest range 700yds.

2nd Attack: (Japanese) Machine-gunning attack by Mitsubishi A6M / Navy Type 0 fighter of speed 300 knots on own ship. Aircraft sighted at range of 3,000yds. on bearing 75°, coming into a 20° dive directed at own position, and opens fire at a range of 800yds. It starts to pull out at a range of 300yds and is last seen at a range of 80yds.

Navy Roll No. 13

1st Attack: (Italian) Torpedo attack by Italian bomber Savoia-Marchetti SM.84 astern at speed 150 knots. Aircraft sighted at range of 2,600yds. on bearing 105° dropping from 550ft to a height of 100ft for aiming run and banking in a wide curve on to aiming course. Torpedo is dropped at range of 500yds. Aircraft last seen at a range of 480yds.

2nd Attack: (German) Double machine-gun attack by two German Focke-Wulf 190 fighters of speed 330 knots in dive on own ship. First plane seen at range of 3,000yds bearing 135°, coming into a 20° dive directed at own ship, and opens fire at a range of 800yds, to range 300yds, when it starts to pull out, being lost about range 100yds. Second aircraft which is seen from range 3,700yds on bearing 124° turning in a sharp bank, comes into a similar dive on bearing 139°. Pulls out as for first aircraft but is followed to range 160ft.

Navy Roll No. 22. (German E-Boat)

Attack by fast German Torpedo boat (E-Boat) at speed 20 knots to starboard of own ship, which turns towards target. Target remains on course, still to own ship's starboard, finally crossing own ship's earlier course, swinging round and starting back on parallel course to own ship.

Appendix E

The Portobel Dome Trainer Operation - extract

WORKING INSTRUCTIONS FOR APPARATUS DOME TRAINING
No. 4 Mark 1 (PORTOBEL) 1950
CROWN COPYRIGHT RESERVED
These Instructions are complementary to, and should be read in conjunction with the Provisional User Handbook for the 'Portobel' Dome Training Apparatus No.4 Mk

Part 1 - General and detailed description
Part 2 - Erecting and striking instructions
Extract - Drill manual for setting up Portobel on site
Part 3 - Setting up and operation

THE PORTOBEL DOME TRAINER
PART 1

1. The Apparatus Dome Trainer No.4 Mk.1 is an AA training device which acts as a substitute for aircraft co-operation when training the layers and the operators of the sights correctional Mk.5 on the 40mm LAA gun. It provides, synthetically, practice conditions closely resembling those experienced in actual warfare, without the necessity of full firing practice. It may also be used to project the 35-mm films for instructional purposes.
2. The Dome Trainer can be readily packed up and moved. One such Trainer may, therefore, be used to train several units.
3. The uses of the trainer are:
    (a) To provide practical laying instruction for the detachment of a 40-mm gun in laying and sight setting of the Sights Correctional Mark 5.
    (b) To provide practical laying instruction for the layers of a 40mm gun in eye-shooting.
    (c) To provide realistic practice in engaging fast moving targets.
    (d) To provide training in fire discipline and tactical control.
    (e) To accustom personnel to the general conditions of dive-bombing attacks, in so far as noise and psychological reaction are concerned, so that they will be mentally prepared to meet this form of attack.

(f) To make personnel aware of the extremely short time during which a fast-attacking aircraft can be engaged by a 40mm gun.

4. The working principles of the Dome Trainer. Films of aircraft attacks are projected on to the inside of the dome which acts as a screen. The image of the aircraft moves across the screen in the same way as if it were flying; a sound track is provided on each film to reproduce the sound effects which would be experienced in actual warfare. The students under training man a dummy gun and operate it in the same way as they would in action. When the image of the attacking aircraft projected on the screen is being engaged the instructor can, by putting on a switch, project the future aim-off point, in the form of a cross and circle, onto the screen. He is then able to see if the correct aim off is being applied. On pressing another switch, the present position of lay is shown on the screen by a cross surrounded by two circles. He can thus see if there are any irregularities in the lay of the gun. A button is pressed on the order of 'Fire' which produces a noise like that of the gun firing. The number of rounds fired is automatically recorded. When the instructor considers that a hit has been made, he presses a button. These hits are also automatically recorded.

5. The projection of the target on the dome is done by keeping the 35-mm projector fixed and causing it to project on to a mirror to which the required movements are imparted. The movements of the mirror are controlled by two cams, one for elevation and the other for bearing. Since the vertical and lateral path of a target during an attack are peculiar to that attacks each film has its own pair of cams. The cams are connected to the projector so that they are run in synchronism with the film. Movements are passed to the mirror by means of cam arms and connecting wires. The mirror of the projector is placed at the exact centre the dome.

6. Associated with the projector is a sound reproducing equipment consisting of an amplifier and a loudspeaker. The sounds of the aircraft, bombs and other incidental noises are on the film and are reproduced in the normal way.

7. The Dome Trainer No.4 Mk, 1 consists of the following units:

The envelope with its valise.

The air blower with its cover.

Two air relief valves with their transit container.

The airlock.

The base ring (sixteen segments of concrete).

The floor covering (six coconut mats).

The mirror mechanism.

The projector unit.

Three fluorescent lamps with their transit container.

A loading ramp.

A cable drum stand.
Maintenance and spare parts cabinets.
A ground sheet with its valise.
An inner sheet with its valise.
A 40-mm instructional mounting.
A circular net with guy ropes.
Three sectional frame supports.
The sandbag bases.

8. The envelope. The screen of the Dome Trainer, or the envelope as it is more generally known, is made of rubber-proofed plied cotton fabric, with a white surface facing inwards. As well as forming the curved surface, this fabric covers the circular floor, the whole being made. When inflated the envelope is 30 feet in diameter and is 20 feet high.
9. The air blower. The flow of air necessary to inflate the envelope and to maintain the correct pressure is obtained from a low-pressure air blower driven by an electric motor. The power supply for this motor is 220–230 Volts AC 50 cycles. The motor is fitted with a starting switch, a fuse box and a waterproof socket to which the wire to the internal equipment is connected. The delivery or orifice of the blower is coupled to the intake orifice of the envelope by a short length of hose. An earth pin is provided.
10. The two air relief valves. To maintain the correct internal pressure blower is kept running the whole time that the apparatus in use. The excess air is allowed to escape through two air relief valves. A constant flow of air is therefore provided for ventilation purposes. The valves are modified 8-inch diameter balloon gas relief valves. The pressure is equivalent of a barometric pressure of .25 inches of water atmospheric pressure.
11. The air lock. Access to the inflated envelope is allowed for through the air-lock, which takes the form of a corridor 6 feet long, 6 feet wide and 7 feet high, formed by a steel framework covered in rubber proofed fabric. At each end of the air lock, doors are provided, giving access into the envelope at one end and opening to the outside at the other. Each door comprises two portions, the main door or frame which is bolted to the air-lock frame and the smaller inset door. The whole of the main doors together with their inset doors are removed to take the large equipment into the envelope. The inset doors are primarily intended to give personnel easy access.
12. The base ring. To render the envelope stable when inflated and to prevent it lifting, a base ring of ferro-concrete is supplied. This is in the form of sixteen segments, constructed to the radius of the circular floor, which are bolted together. To this base ring the air-lock base and sand-bag bases are bolted. The rubber proofed fabric envelope is laced with tethering cords to the base ring at six-inch intervals.

At the point where the air-lock is situated there is a wooden platform 6 feet by 6 feet.

13. The floor covering. A ground sheet is provided and is first put down under the base ring to protect the envelope which lies on top of it. A circular under sheet of jute or fabric matting is supplied with the equipment. This covering is put inside the envelope and serves the dual purpose of protecting the proofed fabric floor and improving the acoustic properties of the envelope. Six pieces of coconut matting are fitted around the base of the projector and in the airlock to reduce wear on the floors.
14. The internal apparatus. The main internal apparatus consists of a steel chassis carrying the 35-mm cinema projector and mirror mechanism and the 40mm Bofors synthetic gun mounting. The projector chassis houses all the amplifier equipment for film and gun noise and loudspeakers, the mains transformer and motors and the projector control panel. The other main items of the internal equipment are the fluorescent lighting equipment for general illumination of the inside of the envelope, and the maintenance and spare parts cabinets.
15. The mirror mechanism. The mirror mechanism consists of a pedestal carrying a mirror frame, which is rotated, elevated and depressed by a wire linkage driven from levers, the movements of which are controlled by a double cam. A loose coupling with a universal joint connects the cam drive with the synchronising gear box on the projector.
16. The projector unit. The projector issued is a Kalee S.P. 35-mm cinema projector using a 1,000-watt projector lamp. It is based on a standard design but is specially adapted for this purpose. The projector is modified by the provision of an aperture plate with a circular hole instead of the usual rectangular one. A two-inch (50.8mm) projector lens is used. It is equipped with a pair of specially modified 500 ft. magazines which bolt on to the projector. There is a coupling which links by a chain and sprocket the synchronising gearbox to the shaft driving the cams controlling the mirror movements. A standard 35mm rectangular aperture plate is also provided for use when ordinary films are displayed. A Pyrene automatic carbon dioxide (CO_2) fire extinguishing apparatus is fitted to the projector.
17. Internal lighting. Three 5ft, 80-watt fluorescent tubes, carried on metal stands are provided to give an internal daylight effect. Mounted at the highest point of the envelope is a 150-watt lamp to give normal light during the assembly of the apparatus, changing films and cams etc.
18. Gunshot amplifier. By depressing the shot recorder switch on the instructor's control box, noise of a gunshot is made by the 18-inch loudspeaker. The loudspeaker unit is mounted in the chassis of the projector stand. The gunshot speed is adjustable inside the amplifier unit. This unit is bolted to the base of the projector stand. On the control panel is fitted a switch which can select any of the

following shot noises (a) Machine gun (b) 20-mm (c) Bofors (120 rpm) (d) Single shot.

NOTE: The amplifier must NOT be switched on until the valves have heated up for at least 30 minutes. The heaters are connected as soon as the mains switch on the projector unit is switched ON.

19. 40mm instructional mounting. The mounting is the reproduction of the essential controls and equipment required by the Sights Correctional Mark 5 operator and the two layers on actual 40-mm guns [see Plate 10]. The gearing speed of traverse and elevation are identical with the actual weapon. The unit is mounted on a steel trolley which is moveable on three castors. It is fitted with four levelling jacks. The sights may be elevated from 0 degrees to 85 degrees, and the whole mounting traversed through 180 degrees. In order that the two sights and the sights correctional may be located as near as possible to the centre of the dome, the sighting head is mounted between and above the two sights. The operator stands on the platform behind and between the two layers. The sights are inset to reduce difficulties in parallax which would otherwise be experienced.

Two electrical graticule projectors, coupled to (a flexible wired) wandering instructors control box are fixed to the mounting so that the point of lay and point of aim may be shown. The projector attached to the mounting shows the axis of the gun, i.e., the point of aim. The projector attached to the sight bar projects the smaller graticule showing the point of lay, i.e., the present position. The instructor can switch either or both lights on from his control box. The gun mounting is 5 foot 6 inches high and with Sights Correctional Mark 5 it is 8 feet 6 inches. The base of it is 4 feet by three feet and 6 inches.

20. Gun sights and films. The films used with this apparatus incorporate a special yellow target mark, which enables the instructor, to tell at a glance if the pupil under instruction is aiming correctly. This is done by providing on the film, in the correct position, a yellow dot at the point where the gun should be aimed.

21. Range indicator. A range indicator is fitted to the projector and consists of a cam-driven lever coupled by a rack and pinion to the shaft of a potentiometer. The potentiometer is supplied with a constant voltage, and the voltage tapped off by the slider is fed to a voltmeter which is calibrated in yards.

22. Electrical supply and circuits. The power supply required is 200/250 volts 50 cycles AC single phase, a current of 25 to 30 amps being required. IP DC supply only is available a rotary converter is required.

23. Fuses. The fuses on the apparatus have the following values and can be fitted with standard fuse wire. Fuses mounted on the projector lamp, motor control panel and blower motor are 15 amp. Other fuses mounted on the control panel are 5 amp. Projector sound amplifier fuses are two amp and 500 milliamps.

PART 2
GENERAL ERECTING AND STRIKING INSTRUCTIONS

24. It is assumed that a Portobel Dome Trainer will have a travelling team of an instructor and a projectionist. The drill for the erection and dismantling of it has been written for a team of six. Of these six men, two are expected to have a full understanding of the equipment whilst the remaining four need have no previous experience at all. The detachment will therefore consist of one in command and (probably) the instructor, the projectionist and four personnel who need no previous experience with the equipment.
25. Throughout this working instruction the term 'rear' of the Dome Trainer refers to the airlock end of the trainer.
26. For erecting and striking the Trainer the detachment MUST wear gym shoes. On no account may any person wearing ordinary boots or shoes be permitted to walk on the deflated envelope.
27. The Trainer is designed for erection either in the open or in a suitable building. It can be unpacked from its valises and containers and erected ready for running by a team of six men in two hours. It can be struck by the same team in one and a half hours.
28. Choice of site. A level site, sheltered, if possible, must be chosen for the erection of the equipment. The site must be at least 40 feet by 35 feet with a height clearance of 21 feet. The surface of the site must be firm, preferably rolled gravel, tarmac or concrete. If the Dome Trainer is to be erected in the open it is advisable to dig a small ditch around it to prevent rain collecting near the apparatus. Free access by road to the position must be available as the equipment is heavy.
29. Availability of power. The position selected must not be too far from the source of electrical current as loss in voltage and amperage may give poor results. 25 yards of mains connecting cable are supplied with the equipment. The supply should be kept constant.

EXTRACT FROM DRILL MANUAL FOR SETTING UP PORTOBEL ON SITE
(Instructor and 5 men)

(Instructions 1–34 omitted)

35. 3 and 4, directed by 1, unfold the wooden air-lock base and place it in position so that the curved edge is facing the groundsheet.
36. 2, 5 and 6 undo the securing strings of the envelope and inner sheet valises.
37. 2, 4, 5 and 6 lay out the base ring segments bolted together, as directed by 1 in a clockwise direction. 2 aligns two segments against the base of the air-lock ensuring that the red arrows on the base and on the segments coincide. He then bolts the

segments to the air-lock base. When all the sixteen segments are positioned, and not before, they are bolted together by three, 4, 5 and 6. NOTE: These segments must be carefully handled as they are liable to break if roughly treated.

38. 2, 3, 4, 5 and 6, directed by 1, remove the envelope from its valise and carry it to the centre of the base ring. It is then unrolled so that the airlock canopy portion is towards the airlock base and the indicating marks on the envelope are coincident with the indicating marks on the base ring segment brackets.
39. 2, 5 and 6 secure the tethering cords to the base ring, using the lacing hooks provided.
40. 3, 4 and 5, if necessary, fit the sandbar bases as directed by one. They will only be fitted if the equipment is put up in the open. They will then be bolted at intervals to the base ring segments in the area from which the prevailing wind blows.
41. 1, 3 and 4 erect the airlock frame. The bottom of the frames is in the holes in the air-lock base. The frame is locked in position by using the Allen key provided and erected in the design. When the frame is erected, the mains lead which is secured to the inner door frame will be connected to the blower motor by 3. 4 will connect the inspection lamp to the socket in the inner door frame. He will then switch on the mains supply and ensure that the inspection light lights. It will be left on and hanging from the middle of the airlock frame.
42. 1, 3 and 4 will draw the air-lock canopy over the air-lock, securing it to the inner and outer door frames by the 27-winged nuts.
43. 1 will ensure that the reinforced rubber portion of the envelope lies over the edge of the floor of the airlock.
44. 3 and 4 will unpack the two air relief valves. They will undo the winged nuts on the valves so that the two parts are separate. The inner part is then placed inside the envelope so that the screws pass through the holes in the envelope, the winged nuts are then tightened up again. 1 inspects the air-relief valves to ensure that they are correctly fitted and that they are shut, ready for operation.
45. 1 fits the envelope light bulb and guard and the envelope connecting sleeve to blower motor. If erecting out of doors, 1, 3 and 4 spread the net over the envelope.
46. 2, 5 and 6 secure the inner door to the frame by three bolts.
47. 1 ensures the baffle plate of the lower blower outlet is fully open and then starts the motor. To lessen the initial torque on the motor, the switch should only be put on first all for a few seconds and then switched off. This must be repeated at short intervals until the motor is running at full speed. The switch is then left on.
48. 2 and 3 will ensure that the envelope inflates correctly. They will, if necessary, pull on the toggle ropes. If the envelope is being inflated out of doors, all numbers, directed by 1, will steady the envelope by means of the toggle ropes and net.

<u>BREAKING DOWN THE PORTOBEL (extracts 1-110 omitted)</u>

111. 2, 4, 5 and 6 place the gun seats, matting ramps and inner sheet valise inside the airlock.
112. 5 and 6 brush the floor of the envelope, removing any dirt from the inside. It is most important to remove all grit before the envelope is deflated.
113. 2 and 3 remove the two air relief valves from their apertures and return them to their transit container.
114. 1 removes the inspection light.
115. The outer door is opened, the ramps placed in position and 2, 3, 4, 5 and 6, under the direction of 1, wheel the gun mounting away.
116. 2 removes the inner door.
117. 1 switches off the blower motor and disconnects the main lead from the motor. He winds it on the bracket provided on the inner door frame, He disconnects the extension sleeve from the blower motor.
118. 6 disconnects the detachable handle from the gun mounting and attaches it to the projector mounting.
119. 2, 3, 4, 5 and 6, under the direction of 1, wheel the projector mounting from the airlock.
120. 3 and 4 disconnect the airlock canopy from the air-lock frame by undoing the turn buckles.
121. 2 and 3 put away all surplus stores.
122. 5 disconnects the inspection light and winds it up.
123. 3 and 4, under the direction of 1, dismantle the airlock frame using the Allen key provided.
124. 3, 4 and 5, if necessary, remove the sandbag bases.
125. 2, 5 and 6 undo all the tethering cords.
126. 3, 4, 5 and 6 undo the bolts connecting the base ring segments.
127. 3, 4.5 and 6 remove the base ring segments, stacking them well clear of the Trainer.
128. 3 and 4 fold up the wooden airlock base and carry it clear.
129. The envelope must not be folded up if it is wet.
130. 1 must thoroughly inspect the envelope for holes and should patch them before folding up. French chalk should be liberally sprinkled on the envelope before it is folded.

PART 3

SETTING UP AND OPERATION

GUN MOUNTING AND SIGHTS (extracts 131-9 omitted)

140. The following procedure is necessary so that the Sights Correctional Mark 5 are correctly aligned:
(a) There is no aim-off speed set on the Sights Correctional Mark 5.

(b) No 2 directs No 3 and lays his sights on the aiming point marked on the envelope opposite the air lock.
(c) No 3 sight is adjusted, if necessary, to aim at the aiming point.
(d) The present position graticule light is switched on and is adjusted so that it is on the aiming point.

141. The lining up should be checked at intervals during the instruction.

SECTION 9 - TO SET UP THE GUN NOISE GENERATOR

142. 2 operates the mains switch (bottom centre control panel) and leaves it on for 30 minutes. Premature operation of the gun noise switch on the Instructors Control Box will cause serious damage to the generator.
143. 3 operates the switch marked Gun noise 'ON/OFF', top left centre of control panel.
144. 2 rotates adjacent switch to '20-mm' position.
145. 2 sets screwdriver adjustments in end of gun generator chassis fully anti-clockwise,
146. 2 operates the spring-loaded toggle switch marked 'shot recorder' on Instructors Control Box.
147. 2 slowly rotates the slot control between valves until gun noise is heard. This should be rotated until approximately 480 shots per minute are heard.
148. 2 switches to 'LMG' on control panel. A faster rate of fire should be heard. In the event of the device not operating on 'LMG', i.e., just giving one single 'bang', 2 releases control box switch instantly and switches to 20mm again and turns the slot control between valves slightly anti-clockwise, thus reducing the speed. 2 switches back to 'LMG'. This will only occur when the 20mm setting is too fast.
149. 2 switches to 'Bofors' and rotates the slot control beside terminal strip until rate of shots is 120 per minute. The control between valves must not be altered while at 'Bofors'.
150. 2 switches to single. The firing rate will then be approximately one round every second if toggle switch is held or as desired by the instructor by releasing and operating the toggle switch on his control box.
151. 2 re-checks the operation on all four positions.

Appendix F

The Gunnery Pocket Book (Royal Navy 1945) - extract

The Gunnery Pocket Book (B.R.224/1945) was created near the end of the Second World War and therefore represents the peak of British gunnery at the time. This limited and condensed example starts at section 446 with a selection of images and helps to show the complexity and sophistication of gunnery in 1945, and how the Stephens Dome Trainer's functional scope evolved.

EXTRACT FROM CHAPTER VIII - AIR DEFENCE OF THE SHIP

446. Members of the high angle control team may be widely separated from each other, so that very good co-operation is necessary if quick and accurate fire is to be opened, especially against enemy attacks, which may come in from different directions at once and may give very little warning of their approach. The Air Defence Officer receives all the available information from the Action Information Centre, when hostile aircraft are reported, and he can then get the H.A. directors on to the best possible look-out bearings. When a formation is sighted, he immediately trains his sight on to it, sending elevation and training by Evershed to whichever H.A. director he decides. As soon as the H.A. director has picked up the aircraft, the angle of sight cut lamp in the air defence position lights. The Air Defence Officer then closes the 'open fire' switch, situated in the air defence position, which burns a light in the H.A. director. This gives the Control Officer permission to open fire.

At night or in thick weather neither the Air Defence Officer nor the H.A. Directors will be able to see the enemy aircraft, so the responsibility for the Air Defence of the Ship rests with the Target Indication Officer. This officer is stationed in the Aircraft Direction Room situated below decks and part of the Action Information Centre. He is assisted in his task by an instrument called the Target Indication Unit (T.I.U.), worked by four operators. This unit is linked with a Long-Range Warning Radar and gives a picture of all targets within range of the set. The T.I.U. has a number of hand wheels (depending on the type of ship) for transmitting Relative Bearing to the appropriate H.A. Director or Close-Range Group and can also transmit range by Range Transmission Units on either side of the Radar Display. There are switches for controlling Call-up Gongs in the Air Defence Position and H.A. Directors, and the Check Fire Bells at the guns.

447. *Barrage Firing.* We consider 'predicted firing' against high-level bombing attacks, when each fuze is calculated to burst at the future position of the aircraft. When the enemy aircraft dive to attack, it is necessary to fire a barrage ahead of the aircraft. This barrage is fired at a fixed range, and therefore with a fixed fuze setting such that the aircraft must fly through the barrage to complete an attack.

448. *A.B.U. Firing.* An instrument called the Auto Barrage Unit is fitted in the H.A. Calculating Position for firing the guns. Its function is to measure the rate of change of range of the aircraft by radar and, having previously been set with a barrage range, it will fire the guns at the correct moment so that the shell and aircraft arrive at the same instant. The A.B.U. operator, by pressing a foot pedal on the instrument, will automatically fire the guns at the correct time. A change-over switch, which decides whether the A.B.U. or the director layer will fire the guns, is in the H.A. director. The great advantage of this form of barrage firing is that the shell is definitely fired to hit the enemy aircraft and not only to deter them from pressing home an attack.

DRILL AT HIGH ANGLE GUNS

449. The object of the H.A. control system is to burst a shell at the aircraft's future position at the moment when the aircraft reaches it. To achieve this, two things, apart from accurate pointer following, are necessary at the gun: (i) The shell must be fired with the correct fuze accurately set. (ii) The shell must be fired at the right moment.

So far as (i) is concerned, a heavy responsibility for the accuracy of the gunfire against aircraft rests on the fuze-setter (if setting fuzes by hand) or on the fuze follower when using a fuze-setting machine. In either case the fuze must be set immediately the 'load' lamp lights. A round fired with a badly set fuze is a round wasted. It will be appreciated that so far as the second condition is concerned, this can only be achieved by the closest attention being paid to the time of the drill by the captain of the gun and the tray worker, who must not allow the gun to be loaded with an out-of-date or 'stale' fuze.

When the target gets within a certain range of the ship, 'barrage' procedure may be used. Rounds with a previously ordered 'barrage' fuze setting are loaded as quickly as possible, whenever the gun fires. The gun may also be required to engage a target in 'local barrage', in which case the gun is aimed by the gun layer and trainer, using eye-shooting sights or their equivalent, and rounds set to the barrage fuze are loaded and fired, locally, as quickly as possible.

In H.A. as well as L.A. fire it is important to understand that what has to be learnt by the gun's crew is the action required of them on receiving any given order, and not a set sequence of orders, which may vary in action.

EXTRACT OF CHAPTER IX - CLOSE RANGE A.A. GUNNERY

455. *Necessity for simple control.* Close range weapons are used against low flying or diving aircraft, moving at very high speeds at close ranges (3,000 yards and below). The time during which the enemy is within range is very short, so that it is important for the control of these weapons to be simple and, if possible, under the direction of one man. The guns are in all cases designed to fire very rapidly, with a high muzzle velocity, and are capable of being swung quickly when following an aircraft or for picking up a fresh attacker.

CLOSE RANGE GUNS' CREWS

456. The crews of the close-range weapons are the 'commando troops' of the ship. They have got to be tough, well disciplined and capable of withstanding hardship. They are not protected from the weather or splinters and have got to be able to keep cool and collected, and shoot accurately in spite of all that is going on around them. Strict discipline at close-range weapons is essential, otherwise, in action, you may easily become distracted or be caught napping by a surprise attack. The following are the usual faults apparent in air battles and must be guarded against:

(i) When excited, men are apt to forget to aim accurately and usually miss astern.
(ii) In the excitement, men are apt to forget the fact that our own fighters are in the vicinity.
(iii) When excited, men are apt to look at events happening which have nothing to do with them and, as a result, they are caught napping by an enemy aircraft which suddenly dives at them from some other direction. You must always anticipate the next attack.

It is essential for all lose-range weapon crews to keep a look-out. Do not rely on the Air Defence Position to see the enemy or to communicate with you, or the bridge to tell you when to open fire. You must be ready to open fire on your own at the correct target as soon as it is within range. Close-range weapons are usually to be found in the most exposed positions in the ship so that they can have the best arcs of fire. This is all the more reason why they and their ammunition must be scrupulously clean.

CLOSE RANGE GUNSIGHTS

458. The latest method of sighting close range weapons is by using gyro gunsights. All that need be said about them in this book is that steady aiming and constant practice are essential. The other method, which is the 'stand-by' method, is 'Eye-shooting'.

EYE-SHOOTING

459. 'The Eye-shooting Pocket Book' (B.R. 254) contains full information regarding the principles and application of eye-shooting sights on close-range weapons and should be thoroughly understood by all crews. You can buy a copy of it for a few pence, or borrow it from the Gunnery Office.

As applied to close-range anti-aircraft weapons, the word 'eye-shooting' simply means the method of aiming in which the aimer judges by eye and without any calculating instruments where to point his gun, in order to hit a moving target.

There is nothing difficult nor new in the principles of eye-shooting with A.A. weapons; the mode of operation is similar say, to throwing a boot at a cat running along the top of a wall. To allow for the movement of the target during the time of flight of the bullet, the gun has to be pointed ahead of the target at some position along its future path.

460. Foresights. Looking at the eye-shooting foresight, you will see that it consists of a number of equally spaced rings, one, two and sometimes three. In the case of all modern sights the inner ring is the 100-knot ring, the next one the 200-knot ring and the third one, if fitted, the 300-knot ring. Note. In the older type of sight there was also a very small ring around the centre of the sight. There was no special use for this ring and it is no longer fitted.

461. The object of these rings is to provide you with a scale for applying the amount of aim-off speed you have estimated. The 100-knot ring shows you the amount of aim-off to take for an aim-off speed of 100-knots, the 200-knot ring shows you how much to allow for 200 knots aim-off, and so on. In fact, the rings are aim-off speed rings. For aim-off speeds other than the exact figures of 100, 200 or 300 knots, say 30, 160, 250 or 330 knots, you have to gauge the distance between (or outside) the metal rings of the sight which simply give you a scale of aim-off speeds.

462. The method of using the sight is very simple. Look at the aircraft, note its direction of flight and estimate its aim-off speed. Point the gun so that the aircraft is flying towards the centre of the sight, with its nose the distance from the centre corresponding to your estimate of its aim-off speed. As the attack develops and the aim-off speed increases, bring the nose of the aircraft further and further out from the centre, always adjusting direction of aim-off to keep the aircraft flying towards the centre of the sight.

To assist you in applying direction of aim-off correctly, when the amount of aim-off is large, some sights have 'radial wires' pointing towards the centre from the outer rim of the sight. These are valuable because, although wrong estimation of aim-off speed is the most common cause of missing the target, misses are due quite often to incorrectly gauging the direction of aim-off, particularly when the aim-off is large.

At weapons which may have to be used against surface craft you will find 'ticks' fitted at 10- or 20-knot intervals along the horizontal and vertical crosswires inside the 100-knot ring. These are to assist you in holding the correct point of aim after you have found it by spotting.

463. Backsights. Most backsights are of the aperture type with rubber eyepiece. Having placed your eye correctly in the eyepiece, you can forget about the backsight and concentrate on pointing the foresight in the correct direction. You must, however, be quite certain first that you have centred your eye correctly in the eyepiece, otherwise you will introduce an error in your aim. In modern backsights there are crosswires or crossed cards to assist you to centre your eye. A glance at them just before you take aim will enable you to put your eye correctly on the line between centre of foresight and centre of backsight. Having got it central, keep it central.

In the heat of action, unless you guard against it, unbeknown to yourself, you will aim without putting your eye to the backsight. This is fatal, so see that it does not happen.

464. At certain weapons 'bead' backsights are fitted. The principles of eye-shooting with these sights are the same as with aperture sights, but you keep your head well to the rear, so that you can see the bead, the foresight and the target all at the same time, and instead of keeping your head in a fixed position you have to move it about as necessary to take aim.

To take the correct aim with a bead backsight, the bead must be covering the nose of the aircraft, when the nose of the aircraft is where you want it in the foresight.

In the case of the Oerlikon gun, which vibrates greatly when firing, you will find that although there is a fitting for a rubber eyepiece fitted to the backsight, you have to keep your head well to the rear and use it like a bead backsight. The sight is designed to be used in this way; the rubber eyepiece should not be on the sight.

AIRCRAFT RECOGNITION

465. There are three things you must learn about enemy aircraft, viz.:

I. To be able to recognise them.
II. To know their speeds.
III. To estimate their range.

466. Recognition. You must be able to recognise aircraft for the following reasons:

(i) So that you will know whether it is an enemy aircraft or a friendly one, since you may have to decide for yourself whether or not to fire at it.
(ii) So that you will be able to judge its approach angle, especially if the approach angle is small.
(iii) So that you can make a good guess at its speed.

You should take a pride in your ability to recognise aircraft and to judge approach angle. Get hold of any cards, models, pamphlets, newspapers or magazines that you can and study them carefully. Do not try and learn too many types at once but get to know the three or four types in general use really well; then you can start adding to your collection as other types come into use. Some credence should be given to the opinions of youths in this matter; some of them have surprisingly accurate knowledge.

467. Estimation of Speed. As you have previously read, you must know the flying speed of an aircraft before you can estimate the aim-off speed correctly. Judging the speed of an aircraft depends almost entirely on knowing the performance of the different types, and you must learn this when you are studying how to recognise aircraft.

Unless you have had very considerable experience, you will not get much assistance in judging speed from the noise of the aircraft or from looking at it, except that it obviously goes faster when diving. You can generally assume that, when attacking, your target is going at full speed, but do not forget that, if diving, it will probably be going much faster than its full level flight speed.

A good rule for judging aircraft speeds at the present time is given below, although new types coming into service may not fit into this rule.

468. Type of Attack.

Fighter	450 knots
Dive-bomber	350 knots
Low level bombing	350 knots
Torpedo attack	250 knots.

469. Estimation of Range. You should be able to estimate the range of an enemy aircraft by eye in order that you will know when to open fire. The estimation of range depends entirely on practice and experience, and you must get all you can. You must remember that varying weather conditions and differences in the sizes of aircraft may produce misleading effects. For example, if you are used to dealing with medium-sized aircraft, you will tend to under-estimate the range of a larger aircraft and open fire too early. Therefore, when studying recognition, you must note which are large machines and which are small ones. Very often recognition drawings and silhouette cards do not make this point clear, but you can spot it at once with the models.

470. To check your estimate of range when you are learning, a simple instrument called the 'A.A. Range Indicator' can be used, preferably by an instructor or another person. There are two types of this instrument but they both work on the same principle, namely, that you hold a plate at arm's length, and where the aircraft fills the aperture you read off the range. You will not be able to use this instrument in action if you are manning a gun, so you must learn to estimate the range by eye.

The 'Maximum Effective Ranges' of close-range weapons are as follows:

2-pounder multiple Pom-Pom and Bofors in local control	1,700 yards.
Oerlikon 20mm. single gun	1,000 yards.
0.5 in. machine gun.	800 yards.
0.303 in. and 0.30 in. weapons	400 yards.

Note. Against approaching targets, fire should be opened when the present range is some 200 or 300 yards greater than the above figures.

Consider a fighter aircraft approaching at 300 knots. It covers a nautical mile (2,000 yards) in 12 seconds. It is within effective range of a .303 machine gun for 400 yards coming towards, and 400 yards going away, a total of 800 yards, which it can travel in under five seconds. You haven't much time, have you?

THE POM-POM DIRECTOR MARK IV.

471. In earlier types of Pom-Pom directors, the necessary 'Aim-off' at the director and thus at the guns was done by 'eye-shooting'.

In the Pom-Pom Director Mark IV, the eye-shooting principle is abandoned and the target's vertical and lateral movement is measured by an instrument called the GYRO RATE UNIT. These movements are combined with the time of flight of the shell and produce vertical and lateral deflections.

The transmission from the director to the Pom-Pom is by remote power control, whereby the Pom-Pom mounting automatically follows the director.

472. The Pom-Pom director has a full crew of eight men, whose duties are as follows:

The Control Officer.
The Gyro Rate Unit Operator.
The Director Layer.
The Director Trainer.
The Vertical Rate Follower.
The Lateral Rate Follower and Communication Number.
The Range Follower.
The Radar Operator (in Radar Office).

THE 2-POUNDER MARK VIII GUN ON THE MARK VII MOUNTING. [See Plate 34]

473. This Multiple Pom-Pom has four barrels and is found in destroyers and cruisers.

The mounting may be fitted with or without a Pom-Pom director, and in the former case, laying and training is by remote power control. As a general rule, Pom-Pom directors are fitted in cruisers and not in destroyers.

The crew consists of eight men. The captain of the gun is in general charge and operates the firing clutch lever. The remainder of the crew are gun layer, trainer, ammunition feed numbers and loaders for right and left guns.

Ammunition is supplied in belts; eight belts per gun, each belt consisting of 14 rounds, are loaded on to the feed rails. The first and last round of each belt rests on the rails and are connected to the next belt by connecting links. The remainder of the belt hangs in a bight.

474. Mounting fitted with Remote Power Control. The motive power of mountings fitted with R.P. 50 remote power control is electric. An indicating lamp is fitted at the mounting to show that this source of supply is flowing.

When in director control, a power change-over switch at the mounting is put to DIRECTOR and the mounting will automatically follow the director and the director will fire the guns, when the firing clutch lever is put to ELECTRIC. Note. Any or all guns may be put to SAFE, by means of interrupter levers at each gun. Normally these are set to FIRE. If it is necessary to bring the mounting back to a convenient position for loading, this is done by putting the power change over switch to LOCAL from DIRECTOR and taking over the control of the mounting with a joystick, fitted at the mounting. The mounting can also be fired by means of a local firing trigger on the joystick, when being laid and trained by the joystick.

475. Mounting fitted without a director. In this case, laying and training is by hand, the gun layer and trainer using eye-shooting sights. The guns can be fired either by 'Hand' or 'Electric' depending upon the position of the firing clutch lever. In 'Hand' the guns are fired by turning the hand firing gear, in 'Electric,' pressing the local firing pistol energises a circuit, which clutches the firing motor to the firing cam and fires the guns.

The latest type of mounting fitted without a director is power-controlled by means of a joystick on the mounting.

THE 20mm. OERLIKON GUN. [See Plate 35]

476. Description of Gun and Mounting. The Oerlikon is an automatic gun designed for close-range anti-aircraft fire, with an effective range of 1,000 yards. It is mounted on a single shoulder-controlled mounting, or on a twin power-operated mounting.

477. Operation of Gun. The gun is operated by the pressure set up by the explosion of the round. The empty case is blown back against the breech, forcing it to the rear against the pressure of the barrel springs, which carry the moving parts forward again.

The breech is not locked at the time of discharge and the round is fired a fraction of an inch before it is fully home in the chamber, the neck of the case swelling to form a gas seal.

The barrel and casing do not recoil; the whole force of the explosion is utilised in propelling the projectile and operating the moving parts.

478. Loading. The gun is cocked by means of the cocking lanyard.

The gun layer presses the magazine catch lever as far forward as it will go, otherwise the interlock mechanism will not be cocked. It is essential that the magazine catch lever be pushed fully forward, either by the knuckles or finger tips, as few men have sufficient arm length to push the catch lever fully forward with the palm of the hand, when behind the shoulder piece in the firing position. If the lever is not pushed right forward, the catch will not be cocked, with the result that the magazine interlock will still render the firing gear inoperative.

The loading number places a loaded magazine in position forward end first and swings the rear part of the magazine down smartly to seat it; the lever is automatically released, locking the magazine in position. The action of shipping the magazine presses down on the ends of the catch and releases the magazine interlock from engagement with the trigger gear, and the gun can then be fired.

It is possible to remove an empty magazine and ship a fresh one although the magazine catch lever has not been pushed as far forward as it will go. In this event the magazine interlock gear will not have been released and the gun will not fire.

479. Automatic Firing. With the gun cocked and a loaded magazine in position, a full round is lying in front of the breech face ready to be driven into the gun.

With the safety catch lever to FIRE, pressing the firing lever releases the breech mass, which flies forward under the action of the barrel spring, driving the live round into the chamber.

The breech mass at the instant of firing is still travelling forward. The force of the explosion, as far as the rearward direction is concerned, is then absorbed in checking this forward movement and reversing its direction, against the action of the powerful barrel springs.

On firing, the empty case is blown back against the breech face piece, forcing the moving parts of the gun to the rear, so compressing the barrel springs. (The moving parts consist of the breech, the bolt, cotter, two breech bars, and barrel spring casing, and they, being held together by the cotter, move as one part.)

480. The force of the explosion has now been overcome and the barrel springs are fully compressed and buffering of the extreme rearward movement has taken place.

As the barrel springs, assisted by the buffer springs, exert themselves, the run out commences. If the firing lever is held to FIRE, the top of the breech face piece will pick up a fresh round from the magazine during its run-out movement and the cycle of operations will be repeated until the magazine is empty.

481. Holding back the Breech Mass after the Last Round in the Magazine has been Fired. A catch automatically holds the breech mass in its rear position after the last round in the magazine has been fired, so that when the empty magazine has been exchanged for a full one, it is not necessary to cock the gun as on the first occasion. The gun is held cocked and it is only necessary to cock the magazine catch lever and load a fresh magazine.

482. The Double Shoulder Piece on Shoulder-controlled Mountings. The double shoulder piece, which is adjustable for width and is fitted at the rear end of the casing by a bayonet joint, together with the harness fastened round the body, gives adequate control of the mounting enabling a rapidly moving target to be followed with precision. Accuracy of aiming is very largely dependent on smooth footwork which requires constant practice.

483. Balance Spring. To assist in easy elevation of the gun, a spiral counter-balance spring is provided at the left-hand side of the bracket. At the front end of the cradle the gun lies in a 'shoe' in which it is held fast by a securing bolt; this gun securing bolt takes the thrust of the gun when fired and care must be taken that the bolt engages properly with the underside of the gun and that it is kept greased and functioning correctly. The cradle can be secured in the horizontal or vertical position by the stops provided. If a gyro gunsight is fitted, it should always be left horizontal.

484. The Drum Magazine. With each gun are supplied six drum magazines, each capable of holding sixty rounds, one loading stand and two ratchet levers for tensioning the magazine spring.

Every possible care must be taken to avoid damage to the magazine, otherwise failures will almost certainly result. Before loading a magazine, it should be tested for freedom of its moving parts by first ensuring that the tension indicator is showing zero, after which the ratchet collar should be lifted and the axis shaft rotated through its full travel by means of the boss on the centre of the ratchet lever handle. If the muzzle covers provided are in use, the following precautions must be taken. The last two rounds to be loaded into magazines are to be either practice or practice tracer rounds, so that the first round to be fired will carry away the muzzle cover and the second will do so in the event of the first round missing fire. H.E. ammunition will explode on hitting the cover.

485. Grease on Ammunition. Ammunition supplied in boxes is not greased.

For the gun to function it is essential that each round should be lightly greased with Grease No. 0 before loading into the magazine. This should be done by hand and not with a brush. Oil is not to be used. A little grease applied shortly before firing to the cartridge case visible in the mouth of the magazine helps.

486. To Charge a Magazine. Place the magazine upon its side on the loading stand, pulling up the ratchet collars. By applying the ratchet lever with the boss on the centre of the ratchet lever engaged with the pin within the ratchet collar, and turning the spring axis, wind the feeder block to the opening of the magazine. Insert the rounds, pushing them in with the thumb and taking particular care that the feeder block remains in contact with the first round inserted, and that none are allowed to fall forward after being inserted.

If this should happen the magazine will require to be stripped. The feeder block should be moved inwards slowly during charging, by operating the ratchet lever; in this manner the feeder block is controlled, so that it cannot move a greater distance at one time than is required to insert one round. When the magazine has been charged, the ratchet collar is allowed to go down, permitting tension to be applied by the ratchet end of the lever.

487. Tensioning the Spring. When the magazine is fully loaded with 60 rounds it should be fully tensioned by rotating the magazine lever as far as possible. Should the magazine be partly loaded, e.g., 30 rounds, it is to be tensioned until the indicator reads 30, followed by two further clicks on the ratchet. To put tension on a magazine loaded with less than 60 rounds, it is necessary to hold the ratchet collar, while using the ratchet lever. Care must be taken that the magazine interlock plunger is free, otherwise the breech block will not remain in the rear, i.e., cocked, position when the last round is fired from the magazine. This plunger is spring loaded and is situated at the rear of the magazine cartridge feeder. If a magazine is loaded only to be stored, the spring is merely given a slight tensioning. Make sure that the magazine is fully tensioned before placing it on the gun. If this is not done stoppages will result. Should the magazine be given no tensioning at all, the rounds would be liable to fall out or become disarranged in the magazine when removing it from the loading stand.

488. To Release the Tension on the Spring. If a magazine that has been charged and tensioned is not required for ready-use purposes, the tension is to be released to that small amount which is necessary, as described above, to prevent the rounds from becoming disarranged. To do this:

(i) Ship the ratchet lever and take the weight of the spring by the lever, while lifting the ratchet collar.
(ii) Allow the lever to revolve under the action of the spring, until it approaches the lifting handle.
(iii) Engage the ratchet collar, replace the ratchet lever in the former position and continue, for as long as necessary, until the indicator shows about 15.

489. To Unload a Magazine. If it is desired to unload a charged and spring-loaded magazine, it should be placed on the loading stand and the rounds pushed out one by one, by hand. This relieves the pressure of the spring at the same time. If the magazine is charged but not tensioned, it must be tensioned before unloading, so that the spring may force the rounds forward to the opening.

490. Caution. Ammunition is greased and care must be taken to see that the grease which is in sight in a loaded magazine is not removed. This grease is necessary for the functioning of the loading arrangements.

491. Maintenance. The following are the routines which should be carried out with the Oerlikon gun: - Daily. Remove magazine. Sponge out bore, taking particular care to see that the chamber is left clean and greasy. Lubricate breech and breech block guideways in magazine opening without easing the spring. Weekly. Remove magazine. Ease the barrel springs and lubricate the top of the breech. Remove the shoulder piece, hand grips, the trigger cover plate and trigger casing, drain out any water in the gun body. Lubricate the trigger mechanism and reassemble. Cock the gun, ease springs again and re-cock the gun.

After firing carry out a daily and weekly routine. See that the gun securing bolt at the front end of the cradle is free and grease it.

EXTRACT OF CHAPTER XV - TRAINING CLOSE-RANGE GUNS CREWS

568. There are numerous methods of training close-range guns crews. At all anti-aircraft schools, non-firing practices are carried out against aircraft. These can then be analysed,immediately, so that the gun layers and trainers can at once see the mistakes that they have made in their aim.

Dome teachers are also used for exercising close-range guns crews. In these, realistic photographs of attacking aircraft are thrown on to the inside of the roof of a dome-shaped building. The gun-layer aims a sight at the aircraft and the instructor can at once tell whether he is aiming correctly or not.

Films. Various films are distributed to all ships to instruct the close-range crews in eye-shooting and tracer observation.

Portable aiming teachers. These are also distributed to ships and are very useful for elementary aiming practice.

569. Precautions During Firing Practices. In all practice firings, when director firing is in use, a safety number is to be employed at each gun to ensure the safety of the towing ship or aircraft, or in the case of a throw-off firing, of the target ship. This rating is stationed in a position where he can observe the bearing or elevation on which the gun is trained or laid. He may be at the trainer's or the layer's telescope or have a special set of open sights, according to the mounting in use. He must also have a whistle. Should the safety number observe that the gun is trained or laid so as to endanger the towing ship or aircraft he must blow his whistle immediately and order 'Half cock' and then give orders as necessary for pointing the gun in a safe direction. When the bearing or elevation is again safe, the safety number is to report either 'Target visible' or in the case of a throw-off firing 'Safe bearing'. On hearing this report the O.O.Q. or Captain of the gun is personally to inspect the director receivers and then give orders as to the method of training and laying to be employed.

RECORDS AND RECORDERS

570. In order to find out any mistakes that have been made, so that these can be put right, records are taken of all the events during the practice. These, when put together, form an analysis of the practice. Records to be of any value must be absolutely truthful and accurate. Recording, like any other art, requires constant practice. There are various forms of records that have to be taken and these may vary for each type of practice.

EXTRACT OF CHAPTER VIII - HIGH ANGLE FIRING

Principles of Deflection. [See Plate 27]

421. When calculating deflections in high angle firing, it is always assumed that the aircraft is flying at a level height and constant speed. Let us first consider that the enemy aircraft flying towards the ship is such that its future position, *i.e.*, when the shell bursts, is directly above the gun. From Plate 36, P is the present position of the aircraft. F is the future position of the aircraft, directly above the gun, G.

422. The height of the aircraft can be measured and the time of flight (t) from G to F is also known, so that we know the average speed of the shell as it travels from G to F. This is called AVERAGE PROJECTILE VELOCITY (a.p.v.) and the distance G F is this velocity multiplied by the time of flight (a.p.v. x t).

The speed of the aircraft (u) is estimated by the Control Officer and if the aircraft is to travel from P to F during the time of flight (t) of the shell, the distance P F must be u x t. The deflection or aim-off must therefore be the angle P G F, which can be calculated from the ratio (u X t)/ (a.p.v. X t) or u/(a.p.v.) and to hit the plane at F we must fire when it is at P, with the gun aimed off an amount equal to this angle.

423. So far, we have considered the case of one aircraft coming from a certain direction, and flying so that its future position when the shell burst is directly over the gun. If, however, we go further and imagine that the aircraft can come from any position, as long as its future position is at F directly over the gun, we find that P, the present position of the aircraft can be anywhere on a circle, whose centre is at F and whose radius is u t. Now let us suppose that the aircraft is such that its future position F, instead of being directly overhead is at 60° from the horizontal (See Fig. II) [Plate 36]. This aircraft is flying at a constant height towards the ship and can come in from any position on the circle with centre at F and radius u t.

424. If, however, we look at this circle from the gun G we notice that it now appears to be an ellipse and not a circle, as was the case when the future position F was directly overhead. It can also be imagined that the circle becomes a thinner and thinner ellipse as F approaches the surface of the sea. If the speed of the aircraft is greater, then the circle becomes larger because u x t, which is the radius of the circle, becomes larger. This principle, which is called the ellipse method of calculating deflection, is used in all existing long-range high angle control systems.

425. We must study the deflection screen of an H.A.C.S. IV table. An optical system inside the table throws on to the screen the image of a circle, which is engraved on a plate. This circle can be tilted by a mechanism, according to the angle of sight and will thus show on the screen as an ellipse, whose shape will vary according to the angle of sight. The optical unit inside the table is moved according to u/(a.p.v.) so that any variations in these will show on the screen as changes in the size of the ellipse. The track of an aircraft is also shown on the deflection screen by means of a wire, which is pivoted at the centre and rotated in agreement with an arrow in the Control Officer's binoculars. The Control Officer, in the H.A. director, keeps this arrow along the fuselage of the aircraft and thus the correct track is sent down to the deflection screen.

426. The deflection screen operator sits facing the screen, looking at the ellipse. He has two handwheels, one either side of the screen, marked Vertical Deflection and Lateral Deflection. These are connected to wires, which can be moved across the face of the screen. The duty of the deflection screen operator is to keep these deflection wires over the intersection of the wire marking the track of the aircraft and the ellipse. By moving the deflection wires from the centre of the ellipse to the point of intersection, the deflection screen operator measures the vertical and lateral deflection of the aircraft and sends these away to the red pointers at the elevation and training receivers at the high angle guns and so gives the guns the necessary 'aim-off,' both for elevation and training.

H.A.C.S.-FUZE PREDICTION

427. In the beginning of this chapter we saw that, besides allowing for 'aim-off,' a fuze had to be set on the shell, so that it would burst at the future position of the aircraft. In order to do this, we must have some means of finding out what the range of the aircraft is going to be when the shell arrives. In H.A.C.S. this is done by 'Prediction', that is to say that we measure the present range of the aircraft continually and by means of a range plot at the opposite end of the H.A. table to the deflection screen, we note the way in which that present range is altering and from this we forecast what the range will be in the future. This is done as follows:

428. Mounted in the H.A. director is a **High Angle Rangefinder**. This works on the same principle as the L.A. rangefinder, inasmuch as the deflecting prism inside the instrument is moved for range but the operator moves his working head for height. The reason for this is fairly obvious, because if the working head were connected directly to the prism of the rangefinder, the operator would have to move the working head continually, owing to the fact that the rate of change of range of an aircraft is extremely high, owing to its speed. The rangefinder is, therefore, designed so that the operator only has to move his working head when the aircraft changes height and as long as the height is correct, the change in the angle of sight to the aircraft, as the director layer keeps on, operates a mechanism in the table, which converts this measured height into range. This moves the prism in the rangefinder and also goes to the range plot in the H.A.C.S.

429. This observed range appears in the range plot as a series of short lines, which slope across the moving paper of the plot. The 'pricker' underneath the plot is operated when the rangetaker in the H.A. director presses the 'cut push' with his foot. The observed plot is liable to be irregular, especially when the rangetaker throws off and re-cuts on the aircraft or through any errors in aim on the part of the director layer, and this irregularity makes it difficult to predict the future range from its slope. In order, therefore, to get a plot with a smooth slope, another plot is introduced on the paper, called the generated plot. This is produced by the operators on the table keeping pointers to the 'mean' of the observed readings, for both angle of sight and height. The generated plot appears in the range plot as a series of lines about twice as long as those of the observed plot.

430. A third pricker is also operated by the Radar set. The Radar aerials are mounted on the H.A. director and are pointed at the aircraft, when the layer and trainer get on. Continual ranges are taken by Radar and these appear on the range plot as a series of small holes. The range plot operator, therefore, sees on his plot, three sloping plots.

Mounted in the H.A. director is a High Angle Rangefinder.

(i) The observed plot.
(ii) The generated plot.
(iii) The Radar plot.

He then, by means of a hand wheel at the end of the table, moves a cursor with a length of wire attached to it, until the wire is placed in such a position that the knob on the end of the cursor is a continuation of the slope of the plots.

431. The operator aligns his cursor parallel to the slope of the generated plot and over the latest readings of the observed plot; if the Radar plot is working accurately, he uses this plot rather than the other two. By moving his handwheel the plot operator sends away to the fuze setting receivers at the guns continual fuze numbers for the predicted future range of the aircraft. At the guns these fuzes are set when the 'load' lamp lights at the receiver. The load lamp is worked automatically by the H.A. table at regular intervals, as is also the fire buzzer, which tells the director layer when to fire the broadside, whose shell are fuzed for the correct future range.

Appendix G

RFD Company History

During the First World War, Reginald Foster Dagnall managed an Airships Limited factory making blimps and balloons, He was an experienced balloonist and airship pilot who launched his own business called RFD. The company manufactured flotation bags for Short Brothers aircraft in case of ditching on water. After 1918 the firm made various products for aviation, including life-rafts, aircraft flotation bags, towed targets for air-to-air/ground-to-air gunnery training, barrage balloons and gliders. Raymond Quilter and James Gregory formed the GQ Parachute Company in 1931 and merged with RFD in 1964.

During the Second World War the RFD company became responsible for making the fabric envelope for the inflatable dome trainers of Charles Bell and his CB Projections company. With Technicolor ceasing their involvement in Dome Trainers, RFD, having an association with them, stepped in and took over production of the Trainer. In time the Dome Trainer became the responsibility of RFD's engineering section.

After the Second World War, Sweden expressed an interest in the inflatable 'Portobel' Dome Trainer, and RFD undertook a sales trip to Scandinavia and the Low Countries. A 'Portobel' Dome and equipment supplied by CB Projections were used for demonstrations. The Ministry of Supply (MoS) also required Domes with more sophisticated equipment and to cater for a wider range of weapons (see plates 20 to 22). Orders from the above customers gave RFD a healthy order book for Portobel sales. They signed a manufacturing licence in 1948 with Lieutenant Commander Bell (who left the Navy in December 1945) and CB Projections. RFD eventually bought all rights to the Portobel Domes in 1956 and continued to make components for the internal equipment of the Stephens Dome Trainer. Between 1948 and 1951 RFD sold approximately 300 of the 30ft diameter Portobel Dome systems to the Royal Navy and to forces in Sweden, Finland, Iceland and America.

For naval gunnery, a rolling platform beneath a gun was developed. This platform was moved by large cams operating underneath the platform. Sky effects were added by using a system like that described for the S.F.G.T. (see Plate 8). This was superseded by a commercially available effects projector giving cloud effects. Additional sound effects were added, i.e., aircraft noise apart from that of the attacking aircraft, mixed battle noise and gunfire. Panoramic scenes were shown by slide projectors to give a ground scene or sea scene around the base of the Dome, with fluorescent lighting giving a blue tint to the screen.

Initially, RFD used Technicolor films, but during the 1950s they developed their own films and cams with a light-coloured aircraft on a dark background. The films were made using models as before and depicted Spitfire, Mosquito, Meteor and Firebrand. A second series of films, again using models, was created and was first used in the 1960s, with aircraft shapes for the Russian ILIO, MiG 15, IL 28, and LA 17.

All the developments used standard 35mm projectors, with a limited number of 16mm projector systems. The equipment incorporated new ideas and models of equipment as they became available. RFD was also involved in developing and producing simulated weapon systems for use in the Dome with graticule projectors, future spot receivers and electrical connections to the weapons trigger. The majority of these simulators were of 40mm Bofors types, although 20mm Oerlikon and other weapons were also fitted.

Post-war customers suggested to RFD that, since there was now no frantic need to train A.A. gunners, the company should consider making a Dome as a solid structure which would not be portable. RFD built a 30ft Dome constructed of wooden panels bolted together, each side covered with plywood and covered with roofing material on the exterior. An experimental Dome was constructed from aluminium, possibly to be resistant to termites and other wood-eating insects, but this was not developed.

Over the 1950s the inflatable Dome was gradually discontinued and replaced with 30ft diameter wooden Domes. These, in turn, were superseded by a wooden 40ft diameter and later a 60ft diameter option. In the early 1980s the company developed a new design of wooden dome of 17m (55ft) diameter in connection with its new ADT3 (Air Defence Tactical Training Theatre) Rapier training system for the British Army and RAF Regiment.

In 1980 the engineering side of RFD became G.Q. Defence Equipment Ltd, still part of the RFD group. This continued to manufacture Dome Trainers as well as other engineering products such as ground-to-air and air-to-air towed targets, and infantry and anti-tank weapon shooting trainers (Cine Target Training Equipment/Marksman Trainers). In the early 1980s a 17m Dome and ADT3 Trainer system was developed to replace the projector/mirror system with a computer-controlled projection system through a prism, using computer-controlled simulation techniques to provide training for ground-to-air missile operators as well as training the more conventional ground-to-air gunners.

In 1986 the RFD Group was taken over and the new owners sold the G.Q. Defence Equipment Ltd which made the Dome Trainer and other products to the Ferranti Company. In the early 1990s Ferranti went bankrupt and was bought by GEC-Marconi. This in turn was purchased by BAE Systems in 2000.

Sources and Bibliography

Published sources

Admiralty, A.M.S.I. (Guard Book) Admiralty Merchant Shipping Instructions. (B/BIBBY/7/4/10)

Admiralty (1916). C.B. 1256. Action off Jutland 31 May–1 June 1916: Narrative. (The National Archives. ADM 186/569)

Admiralty (1918). C.B. 1384. Analysis of Torpedo Firing at the Battle of Jutland. (The National Archives. ADM 186/586.)

Admiralty (1920). Cmd. 1068. Battle of Jutland 30th May to 1st June 1916: Official Despatches with Appendices. London: H.M.S.O.

Admiralty (1922). C.B. 0938. Naval Staff Appreciation of Jutland.

Admiralty (1924) Narrative of the Battle of Jutland. London: H.M.S.O.

Admiralty (1927). Cmd. 2870. Reproduction of the Record of the Battle of Jutland. London: H.M.S.O.

Anatomy Act 1832. Irish Statute Book. Government of Ireland.

Angelucci, Enzo and Paolo Matricardi. *World Aircraft: World War II*, Volume I (Sampson Low Guides). Maidenhead, UK: Sampson Low, 1978.

Army, Association of the United States. 1953. *United States Army Combat Forces Journal:* Vol 3

Arthur, Max, *Lost Voices of the Royal Navy* (1945)

Bacon, Admiral Sir Reginald Hugh, *The Jutland Scandal*. London: Hutchinson, 1933.

Bellairs, Carlyon, *The Battle of Jutland: The Sowing and the Reaping*. London: Hodder & Stoughton Limited, 1919.

Bergström, Christer, *Barbarossa: The Air Battle, July–December 1941*. London: Chevron/Ian Allan, 2007.

Bone, David W., *Merchantman Rearmed*

Brown, Maurice, *We Sailed in Convoy*

Costello, John and Hughes, Terry, *Jutland 1916*. New York: Holt, Rinehart and Winston, 1977.

de Zeng, H.L., D.G. Stanket, and E.J. Creek, *Bomber Units of the Luftwaffe 1933–1945: A Reference Source,* Volume 1. London: Ian Allan Publishing, 2007.

Die großen Luftschlachten des Zweiten Weltkriegs: Flugzeuge – Erfolge – Niederlagen, Aerospace Publishing, 1994.

Donald, David (ed.), *Warplanes of the Luftwaffe*. London: Aerospace Publishing, 1994.

Doughty, Martin, *Merchant Shipping and War*

Dressel, Joachim and Manfred Griehl, *Bombers of the Luftwaffe*. London: Arms and Armour (DAG Publications), 1994.

Elphick, Peter, *Liberty – The Ships That Won the War*

Evans, Bob, *HMS* Eaglet*: The story of the Royal Naval Reserves on Merseyside*

Gardiner, Juliet, *Wartime Britain 1939–1945*

Gordon, Andrew, *The Rules of the Game: Jutland and British Naval Command*. London: John Murray, 2005.

Howarth, Stephen & Law, Derek (eds), *50th Anniversary of the Battle of the Atlantic, 1939–1945*

Hurd, Archibald, *Britain's Merchant Navy*

Jarvis, Adrian & Smith, Kenneth, *Albert Dock, Trade and Technology*

Jones, R.V., *Most Secret War: British Scientific Intelligence 1939–1945*. Hamish Hamilton, London, 1978.

Kerr, J. Lennox (ed.), *Touching the Adventures of Merchantmen in the Second World War. 'Lanyard', Stand by to Ram!* (a graphic account of episodes in the great Battle of the Atlantic)

Patents (Google), 1951. Improvements in or relating to optical apparatus for throwing a shadow image.

Poolman, Kenneth, *Experience of War: British Sailor*.

Roskill, S.W., *Merchant Fleet at War 1939–1945*, Alfred Holt & Co.

Sadler, John, *Fourth Service, Merchantmen at War 1939–1945*

Van der Vat, Dan, *Atlantic Campaign: The Great Struggle at Sea, 1939–1945*

Websites

https://www.unithistories.com/officers/RN_officersP1a.html

https://wallyswar.wordpress.com/gunnery-course

https://tailendcharlietedchurch.wordpress.com/tail-end-charlie-ted-church/rear-gunner-sentinel-of-the-skies/gunnery-training/

http://pippaettore.com/Horrific_WWII_Statistics.html

https://www.americanairmuseum.com/mission/1514

http://www.thepeerage.com/p64715.htm

https://www.naval-history.net/WW1NavyBritishLGDecorations1919.htm

https://doi.org/10.1038/158443d0 Royal Commission on Awards to Inventors

https://www.bbc.co.uk/radio4/history/making_history/makhist10_prog11b.shtml

https://www.tandfonline.com/doi/full/10.1080/09524142.2017.1369304

https://liverpooluniversitypress.blog/2020/02/03/a-day-in-the-life-of-john-keats-medical-student-and-assistant-surgeon/
https://patents.justia.com/inventor/leonard-s-snell - Leonard Snell, Patents for Rolls-Royce. Accessed 30 May 2024
https://allthatsinteresting.com/robert-liston#:~:text=Despiteper cent20beingper cent20knownper cent20asper cent20the,aper cent20300per cent20percentper cent20mortalityper cent20rate.
https://guides.loc.gov/chronicling-america-wwi-declarations
https://weaponsandwarfare.com/2018/02/24/tale-of-the-tanks-de-moles-invention/
https://warbirdsnews.com/warbirds-news/warbird-collections/commemorative-air-force-news/12-planes-christmas-p-63f-kingcobra-pinball.html
http://p63kingcobra.com/p63_operation_pinball.html
https://en.wikipedia.org/wiki/Western_Approaches_Tactical_Unit
https://www.in70mm.com/cinerama/archive/gunnery/index.htm
https://liverpoolwarmuseum.co.uk/
https://en.wikipedia.org/wiki/Reginald_Victor_Jones
https://www.historyofsimulation.com/flexible-gunnery-simulators/
https://www.woolworthsmuseum.co.uk/1940s-remembernewcross.htm
http://www.westendatwar.org.uk/page_id__151_path__0p2p.aspx
https://mha.mun.ca/mha/research.php
https://www.londonremembers.com/subjects/v1-and-v2-rockets?memorial_id=9333
https://alondoninheritance.com/out-of-london/launch-and-landing-sites-of-the-first-v-two-on-london/
http://www.flyingbombsandrockets.com/statsbyweek.html
https://www.youtube.com/watch?v=LyDlq77GVPM
https://historyproject.org.uk/interview/bernard-happe
http://ww2talk.com/index.php?threads/raf-air-gunners-training-school.56048/
http://www.bcatp.org/978-no-8-bgs-lethbridge
https://weaponsandwarfare.com/2018/03/10/instruments-of-darkness/
https://hoyorkney.com/portfolio/the-arctic-convoys/

1. FARRINGTON, K., (2011). Handbook of World War II: An Illustrated Chronicle of The Struggle For Victory. London: Anness Publishing Ltd. Accessed via Hoy on 12.12.23
2. THE NATIONAL ARCHIVES OF THE UK (TNA), (1945). ADM 1/17563 Synthetic Training Devices of the Royal Navy – Descriptive List. Unpublished Archive Document. Accessed via Hoy on 21.12.23
3. THE NATIONAL ARCHIVES OF THE UK (TNA), (1937-1946). ADM116/5790 Main Fleet Base – Scapa Flow: Inception, Development and History. Unpublished Archive Document. Accessed via Hoy on 21.12.23

https://theairtacticalassaultgroup.com/forum/showthread.php?t=31054

https://www.liverpoolmuseums.org.uk/archivesheet71
https://en.wikipedia.org/wiki/Junkers_Ju_88
https://en.wikipedia.org/wiki/Junkers_Ju_87
https://www.britannica.com/topic/Admiralty-Landships-Committee
https://www.world-war.co.uk/actions.php
Ancestry.com. UK, Naval Officers' Service Record Cards and Files Index, 1880–1950
https://www.ancestry.co.uk/family- tree/tree/167253683/family/familyview?fpid=432265943814&usePUBJs=true
http://www.nationalarchives.gov.uk/documentsonline/navy-cards-and-files.asp
https://www.jameslindlibrary.org/articles/astley-paston-cooper-1768-1841-anatomist-radical-and-surgeon/
https://www.jameslindlibrary.org/articles/john-hunter-1728-93/
https://en.wikipedia.org/wiki/Henry_Stephens_(doctor)
https://www.fountainpennetwork.com/forum/topic/8013-what-ink-do-registrars-use/
https://www.stephenshouseandgardens.com/about/history/henry-inky-stephens
https://www.ianvisits.co.uk/blog/2016/06/08/the-tiny-london-museum-of-ink-bottles/
https://spectrum.ieee.org/tech-history/dawn-of-electronics/from-world-war-ii-radar-to-microwave-popcorn-the-cavity-magnetron-was-there
https://www.churchillarchive.com/explore/catalogue?showDetailsId=CHARper cent2023
https://dailybritain.wordpress.com/tag/stephens-ink/
https://en.wikipedia.org/wiki/Henry_Stephens_(doctor)
https://www.jameslindlibrary.org/articles/john-hunter-1728-93/
https://www.jameslindlibrary.org/articles/astley-paston-cooper-1768-1841-anatomist-radical-and-surgeon/
https://spartacus-educational.com/SPgermany.htm
https://www.npg.org.uk/whatson/national-memory-local-stories/resources/learning-resource-themes/dirt-and-danger-tragedy-and-glory-enduring-the-war/midshipman-archibald-dickson/
https://en.wikipedia.org/wiki/HMS_Indefatigable_(1909)#Battle_of_Jutland
https://en.wikipedia.org/wiki/HMS_Invincible_(1907)
https://www.gracesguide.co.uk/Bede_John_Francis_Bentley
https://www.tulliehouse.co.uk/thecollection/photograph-midshipmen-hms-queen-mary-wwi
https://www.npg.org.uk/whatson/national-memory-local-stories/resources/learning-resource-themes/dirt-and-danger-tragedy-and-glory-enduring-the-war/midshipman-archibald-dickson/
https://en.wikipedia.org/wiki/SMS_Wiesbaden

https://www.atlasobscura.com/places/old-operating-theatre
https://oldoperatingtheatre.com/
https://www.nationalarchives.gov.uk/education/resources/british-response-v1-and-v2/#:~:text=Theper cent20peopleper cent20ofper cent20Britainper cent20called,5per cent2C475per cent20deathsper cent2Cper cent20withper cent2016per cent2C000per cent20injured
https://www.youtube.com/watch?v=OslNiebkUGQ&feature=emb_logo
https://www.quora.com/In-the-ETO-are-there-any-stats-on-the-B-17-losses-on-flak-vs-fighters-vs-mechanical-failure
http://www.dreadnoughtproject.org/tfs/index.php/Battle_of_Jutland_Official_Despatches
https://battleofjutlandcrewlists.miraheze.org/wiki/HMS_Milbrook_Crew_List
https://www.jutland1916.com/ships-table/
https://vimeo.com/162655850?ref=fb-share
https://www.nmrn.org.uk/
https://www.jutland1916.com/our-goals-two/
http://www.gwpda.org/naval/s0600000.htm
https://patents.google.com/?q=(Henry+Christian+Stephens)&q=(A63J25per cent2f00)&inventor=Henry+Stephens&assignee=Mini+Of+Supply&litigation=NO
www.PeriscopeFilm.com
https://www.britishpathe.com/video/dome-trainer
https://www.youtube.com/watch?v=0OmOQs0ziSU
https://www.youtube.com/watch?v=PIYVwqHM488
https://play.google.com/books/reader?id=GyAiAQAAMAAJ&hl=en_GB&pg=GBS.RA2-PA43
http://www.mapleleafup.net/forums/showthread.php?t=2598&page=10

Video research

https://boultonandpaul.com/gun-turrets/
https://boultonandpaul.com/history/# Accessed 1 January 2024
16 Inch Gun Training Film. https://www.youtube.com/watch?v=0OmOQs0ziSU
three. 16 Inch Gun Training Film. https://www.youtube.com/watch?v=0OmOQs0ziSU.
4. Flak Training for Pilots in WW two. 1940. https://www.youtube.com/watch?v=PIYVwqHM488 (accessed 23 July 2020).
Army, Association of the United States. *United States Army Combat Forces Journal: Volume three.* January 1953. https://play.google.com/books/reader?id=GyAiAQAAMAAJ&hl=en_GB&pg=GBS.RA2-PA43 (accessed 4 August 2020).

Flak Training for Pilots in WW two. 1940. https://www.youtube.com/watch?v=PIYVwqHM488 (accessed 23 July 2020).

https://www.britishpathe.com/video/dome-trainer. *Pathe New Dome Trainer 1951.* https://www.britishpathe.com/video/dome-trainer (accessed three August 2020).

Patents, Google. *Improvements in or relating to optical apparatus for throwing a shadow image.* 17 October 1951. https://patents.google.com/?q=(Henry+Christian+Stephens)& q=(A63J25per cent2f00)&inventor=Henry+Stephens&assignee=Mini+Of+Supply&litigation=NO (accessed 4 August 2020).

RAF Gun turret drill - 7/7. 1940. https://www.youtube.com/watch?v=dIIqY81T67E (accessed 23 July 2020).

Training film for navy gunners, 1940's - Film 1186. 1940. https://www.youtube.com/watch?v=ZyDErZQZews (accessed 23 July 2020).

U.S. NAVY WWII NAVAL AVIATOR TRAINING FILM 'THIS IS IT' REEL 1-33064. 1944. https://www.youtube.com/watch?v=fNBwBHTWec4 (accessed 23 July 2020).

Index